Drawn to Greatness

Disney's Animation Renaissance

Michael Lyons

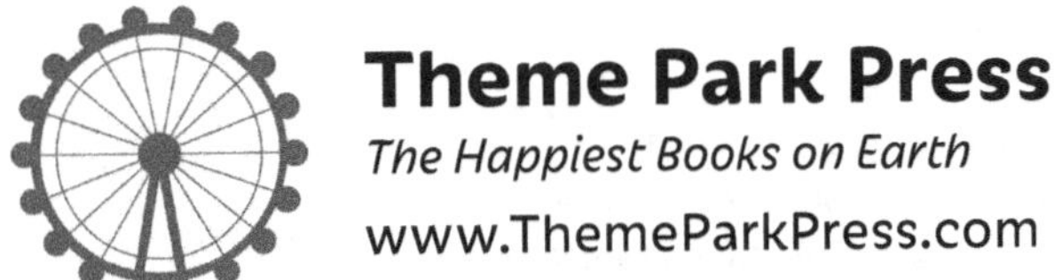

Theme Park Press
The Happiest Books on Earth
www.ThemeParkPress.com

Editor: Bob McLain
Layout: Artisanal Text
ISBN 979-8-89609-090-8
Printed in the United States of America
Theme Park Press | www.ThemeParkPress.com
Address queries to ben@themeparkpress.com

For my wife, Michelle,
who always has more faith in me than I have in myself.

Contents

Introduction

"We have worlds to conquer here."

Walt Disney once said this to an artist at his studio when discussing his thoughts on the possibilities for animation. During production on 1940's *Fantasia*, a story artist asked Walt if he felt that they were "taking full advantage of the cartoon medium."

Walt's response:

"'This is not the cartoon medium. It should not be limited to cartoons. We have worlds to conquer here....'"[1]

This book is about artists who looked to conquer those worlds over fifty years after Walt said this, during an unprecedented time at The Walt Disney Studios.

A period dubbed Disney's Animation Renaissance.

Movies like *The Little Mermaid* (1989), *Beauty and the Beast* (1991), and *The Lion King* (1994) brought Disney animation to new heights and sought to conquer worlds that may have even surprised Walt himself.

What follows is the chronological story of this time at The Walt Disney Studios when their animated features experienced a resurgence in popularity after decades of disappointments.

The majority of the book takes place in the 1990s, as the timeline for the Renaissance is 1989 through 1999. However, the first chapter begins just after Walt's death in 1966, re-counting the '70s and the majority of the 80s, to provide background to the events that preceded the Animation Renaissance at Disney.

Each subsequent chapter covers two to three of the films released during the Renaissance, with the final chapters covering the year 2000 and then briefly the years after through the present day.

---

1 Neil Gabler, *Walt Disney: The Triumph of the American Imagination* (New York, Alfred A. Knopf, 2006), p. 300.

Much of this book is told by those who were a part of Disney's Animation Renaissance: producers, directors, animators, art directors, story artists, and executives, just to name a few.

Their insight included in this book is from interviews conducted during the Renaissance while they were working on their respective films, and their thoughts and perspectives will reflect that. These interviews are gathered here for the first time.

Other quotes and viewpoints in the book are compiled from various sources: magazines, newspapers, websites, documentaries, and books. They have all been cited here in the footnotes and the bibliography.

When it comes to books, it's an understatement to say that there have been countless written about Disney, particularly the company's history, and particularly centering on the animated films.

The reason for this one is an opportunity to look back at a more recent era at Disney. Mickey Mouse debuted over ninety years ago. Snow *White and the Seven Dwarfs* was released during The Great Depression; it's been over half a century since Walt Disney left us, and dedicated historians are still chasing down information about these periods like archeologists on a dig site.

Drawn to Greatness: Disney's Animation Renaissance seeks to capture a moment in time that's still somewhat in our "collective rear-view mirrors" before it fades into the distant horizon.

The goal of any author is to write a book that, ultimately, they would like to read. That's what follows here. Whether you are a passionate Disney fan and historian, or your fandom is more casual, and whether you are a devotee of film and animation or someone who simply likes a good comeback story, there is something here for you.

This book also looks to celebrate the Disney Animation Renaissance. It was all fantastic, unprecedented work, but it didn't always come easily. At times, the challenges that many at Disney faced are also discussed here, along with how they had overcome them and the perspectives they brought.

Rafiki said it best in *The Lion King*: "The past can hurt. But the way I see it, you can either run from it or learn from it."

Let's learn from it and return to Disney's Animation Renaissance when the studio sought out "worlds to conquer."

CHAPTER ONE

"Legend has it..."

Disney's Animation Renaissance Begins

"In the old days, when we'd walk into a restaurant for lunch, we'd mention what movies we were working on, and no one had heard of them," laughed director John Musker. "We'd ask the waitress, "Didn't you see the ads?' and she'd say, 'Wasn't that movie done thirty years ago?' and we'd say, 'No, no, we just did that last year!'" [1]

These restaurant conversations were happening thirty to forty years ago, when Musker worked as an animator at the Walt Disney Studio. He and a number of his peers were feeling increasing disappointment. As Musker remembered, "The films that were being done in the late '70s and early '80s didn't reflect the sensibilities of these younger artists that were just getting into the industry."

At this time, Disney, home of such iconic masterpieces as *Snow White and the Seven Dwarfs* (1937), *Pinocchio* (1940), and *Cinderella* (1950) noticed that tarnish had appeared on what had once been the glistening realm of film fantasy.

It's so hard to grasp that concept today. Disney is now an entertainment goliath with an umbrella that includes not just their own Feature Animation Studio, but other studios such as Pixar, Marvel, Lucasfilm, and Fox, as well as T.V. networks and theme parks around the globe. The sun truly never sets on Disney, but they were once like a "washed up" Hollywood star waiting and hoping for their "comeback role."

"I was twenty years old when I started," remembered Don Hahn, who came to the studio in the mid-'70s and would go on

1 John Musker interview with Michael Lyons, January 13, 1997.

to a successful career as a producer with Disney, "and animation was kind of in this 'cartoon ghetto'. It was something that maybe you dropped your kids off to see, but it certainly wasn't for adults. They certainly weren't the successes that these films have become." [2]

"Animation was in the dumps back in the early eighties," recalled animator Andreas Deja, who joined Disney in 1980 and would emerge as a major creative talent. "We couldn't even find people out of art school who were interested in animation. It was a 'kiddie' medium." [3]

Just forty years ago, the words "Disney animation" weren't synonymous with what *is*, but, sadly, what once *was*. But this didn't stop the creative talents working at the Disney Studio from holding out hope for Disney animation.

Ron Clements, another animator at Disney during this challenging time (who would also go on to co-direct animated films) recalled with a laugh, "I remember saying, at one point, 'If wrestling can become popular again, then so can animation!'" [4]

Clements, along with Musker, Hahn, and Deja, are just some of the many creative architects of a time at the studio known as Disney's Animation Renaissance. For ten years, from 1989 to 1999, Disney animation experienced an unprecedented time of growth and expansion that many say Walt Disney himself could have never envisioned for the industry.

During this decade, there were groundbreaking films at the studio like 1991's *Beauty and the Beast*, which became the first animated feature to receive the Academy Award nomination for Best Picture; there was *The Lion King* in 1994, which shattered box-office records and made its mark solidly in our pop-culture consciousness. There was the first fully computer-animated feature in 1995 with *Toy Story*, giving the world some of the most beloved characters and popular film franchises of all time, through a partnership with the Pixar Studio.

But how did this Disney Animation Renaissance begin?

---

2 Don Hahn interview with ML, March 20, 1996.

3 Andreas Deja interview with ML, February 17, 1997.

4 Ron Clements interview with ML, January 13, 1997.

To truly understand, one needs to go back to December 15, 1966. A sad milestone day in entertainment, the day that Walt Disney passed away.

About Walt's passing, commentator Eric Sevareid said, at the time, on the *CBS Nightly News*:

> "'It would take more time than anybody has around the daily news shops to think of the right thing to say about Walt Disney.
>
> He was an original, not just an American original, but an original, period. He was a happy accident; one of the happiest this century has experienced; and judging by the way it's been behaving in spite of all Disney tried to tell it about laughter, love, children, puppies, and sunrises, the century hardly deserved him.
>
> He probably did more to heal or at least soothe troubled human spirits than all the psychiatrists in the world. There can't be many adults in the allegedly civilized parts of the globe who did not inhabit Disney's mind and imagination at least for a few hours and feel better for the visitation.
>
> It may be true, as somebody said, that while there is no highbrow in a lowbrow, there *is* some lowbrow in every highbrow.
>
> But what Walt Disney seemed to know was that while there is very little grown-up in a child, there is a lot of child in every grown-up. To a child, this weary world is brand new, gift-wrapped; Disney tried to keep it that way for adults...
>
> By the conventional wisdom, mighty mice, flying elephants, Snow White and Happy, Grumpy, Sneezy and Dopey-all these were fantasy, escapism from reality. It's a question of whether they are any less real, any more fantastic than intercontinental missiles, poisoned air, defoliated forests, and scraps from the moon. This is the age of fantasy, however you look at it, but Disney's fantasy wasn't lethal. People are saying we'll never see his like again.'"[5]

Perfect. Mr. Sevareid summed up the emotion that so many were feeling at the loss of such an impactful person. Not only did Walt have an immense influence on the pillars of the entertainment industry – film, television, and amusement parks – but he changed them, as well.

---

5 Bob Thomas, *Walt Disney: An American Original* (New York, Hyperion, 1994), p.355.

Walt did this through his innate sense of story and his ability to be so involved in all areas of his ever-growing studio and company. Walt was so close to so much that was going on. Right up until his diagnosis of and surgery for lung cancer, he continued to remain involved in everything: from live-action films, to the possibility of a Disney-themed ski resort, to acting as an on-air host for his weekly television show to new attractions at Disneyland, the Florida Project, EPCOT, and the production of a brand-new animated feature film.

Each of the projects would bear more than just his "stamp of approval"; they would also benefit and be better thanks to his creative intuition.

So, without Walt, where would this guidance come from? In his book, *Art Afterpieces*, legendary Disney animator Ward Kimball stated: "'Walt's passing was a terrible blow to the studio and its creative structure,' he wrote. 'The studio had always been a one-man operation, and without the man around to inspire and lead the way, many of us had to shoulder more responsibility than ever before.'"[6]

And shoulder is precisely what the artists at Disney did. This responsibility fell to a group of animators dubbed "Disney's Nine Old Men." This was a nickname Walt gave to his upper echelon of animators at the studio. He borrowed the term from President Franklin D. Roosevelt, who had referred to his Supreme Court Justices as "Nine Old Men."

Kimball was one of these "Men" at Disney, along with fellow animators Les Clark, Marc Davis, Ollie Johnston, Milt Kahl, Eric Larson, John Lounsbery, Wolfgang Reitherman, and Frank Thomas. All of them had worked on Disney's most classic films and are now legends in the animation industry.

After Walt's death, it was these artists who moved forward with so many of the projects that were in motion. One of these was the studio's next animated feature, *The Jungle Book*, the last feature that Walt was personally involved with. Based loosely on the work of author Rudyard Kipling, the film would tell the tale of a young boy ("a man-cub") named Mowgli, who

---

6   John Canemaker, *Walt Disney's Nine Old Men and The Art of Animation* (New York, Disney Editions, 2001) p.121.

is befriended by Baloo the bear and Bagheera the panther as they help him get back to "the man village."

Opening on October 18, 1967, *The Jungle Book* was a significant hit with both critics and audiences (and is still one of the studio's most beloved by several generations) earning $11.5 million in its domestic release alone.

From here, the artists moved on to their next animated feature film, 1970's *The Aristocats*, a story of a cat named Dutchess and her kittens, who are kidnapped by a villainous butler. Even though the animated films were continuing "after Walt," those working on them, like Frank Thomas, admitted that it just wasn't the same.

As Thomas said: "'We were very aware of the fact that we didn't have Walt anymore to guide us, to give us direction, to bounce ideas off of anymore.'" [7]

Many like Thomas believed that, because of this, the films were lacking the spark that was there when Walt would offer his creative "two cents." By the time work was underway on the next animated feature, 1973's *Robin Hood*, Thomas couldn't help but feel that the chinks in the armor were beginning to show.

The film was a re-telling of the classic tale of Sherwood Forest, this time with a cast of anthropomorphic animals. In a 1973 letter to animator Larry Ruppel, Thomas voiced his concerns about *Robin Hood* by stating: "'We obviously decided to keep it on the 'fun' side, but I have worried that the audiences would have felt that it was too flimsy-that we were not being quite serious enough with our characters.'"[8]

Robin Hood was a hit despite this, showing that audiences did indeed have an appetite for new Disney animated feature films (it even played as the Christmas Show at New York's Radio City Music Hall).

Critics, however, were, well, critical. Film critic Jay Cocks of *Time* magazine wrote: "Even at its best, *Robin Hood* is only mildly diverting. There is not a single moment of the hilarity or deep, eerie fear that the Disney people used to be able to

---

7 Ibid, p.203.
8 Ibid, p.203.

conjure up, or of the sort of visual invention that made the early features so memorable."[9]

Some of *Robin Hood*'s animated movements of the characters were also recycled from past films like *Snow White and the Seven Dwarfs* (in the "Phony King of England" song sequence), which seemed like some "visual evidence" to many of how uninspired things at the studio seemed to be.

Additionally, many artists like the Nine Old Men, who, at this point, had been working at the studio for four decades, were beginning to eye retirement.

There was talk at the studio of possibly "phasing out" animation so that the Disney company could focus on its other endeavors, like their theme parks in California and Florida. Luckily, a contingent knew that the animated films were the cornerstone of Disney and that these films gave life to so much else in the company.

During production on *Robin Hood* in 1970, Eric Larson, another member of Walt's "Nine," was put in charge of recruiting and training fresh talent who would take the reigns as a new generation of Disney animators.

Larson and his peers would become mentors to this new generation, including Musker and Clements, and several animators who would become legends in their own right. Additionally, this group of young animators would also include Henry Selick, who would direct *The Nightmare Before Christmas*, as well as two young artists named Tim Burton and Brad Bird, whose careers in live-action films would take them well beyond the halls of Disney animation.

In all, Disney hired twenty-five new artists between 1970 and 1977. The studio made the next animated feature, 1977's *The Rescuers*, a transition film, a production in which the two generations of animators would work together.

The film, which was based on the book by author Margery Sharp, had been "kicking around" the studio since 1962. *The Rescuers* told the tale of two mice, Bernard and Bianca of "The Rescue Aid Society," who help rescue a young girl named Penny from the evil Madame Medusa. It proved to be a success,

---

9   Jay Cocks, "Cinema: Quick Cuts," *Time*, December 3, 1973, Content.time.com (accessed January 11, 2021).

earning $19 million domestically at the box office (even more impressive when one realizes that the film was released about a month after *Star Wars* hit theaters).

Critics also noted how *The Rescuers* proved to be a "return to form" for the Disney Studio. *The Los Angeles Times*' critic Charles Champlin called the film "the best feature-length animated film from Disney in a decade or more...",[10] while industry periodical *Variety* declared the film to be "the best work by Disney animators in many years, restoring the craft to its former glories."[11]

With *The Rescuers*' release, the majority of The Nine Old Men retired (sadly, John Lounsbery passed away in 1976, during the film's production). The question then became: "Who would take the lead from here?"

Many turned to an animator named Don Bluth. Bluth had come to work at Disney as an in-betweener (the person who completes the drawings "in-between" the animator's initial drawings), at a time when 1959's *Sleeping Beauty* was in production. "It was such a delightful experience," Bluth recalled of this time at the studio while Walt was still at the helm. "He was a man who had honest visions and was trying to lead us very well." [12]

Bluth left Disney in 1956 for a variety of pursuits, including continuing his education, operating a theater with his brother, and working for Filmation animation studio. He returned to Disney in 1971, working on *Robin Hood*, *The Rescuers*, and even directing animation for 1977's live-action feature *Pete's Dragon* and the animated featurette *The Small One* (1979).

Although he was emerging as not just a "major player" at Disney animation, but also an heir apparent, Bluth noted dissatisfaction with the mood of the studio at this time, "It was very corporate and marketing centered, but I stayed for another nine years," said Bluth. "I watched it go into a decline in those nine years, and finally, we just kept making the same picture over and over again."[13]

---

10 Charles Champlin, "Animation: The Real Thing at Disney," *Los Angeles Times*, July 3, 1977, newspapers.com (accessed January 11, 2021).

11 Variety Staff, "Film Reviews: *The Rescuers*," *Variety*, June 15, 1977, variety.com (accessed January 12, 2021).

12 Don Bluth interview with ML, July 31, 1997.

13 Ibid.

Bluth and a group of animators were very vocal about their feelings that Disney could do better than the current productions, even sending memos to the then-President of Walt Disney Productions Ron Miller, who was also Walt's son-in-law.

This underlying dissatisfaction lurked in the shadows at Disney animation. Eventually, it came to light on September 13, 1979 (a date which "lives in infamy" at the studio), when Bluth led a walkout of fourteen animators (including himself), who all resigned. Their goal was to form their own studio and restore some of the bygone glory they felt was missing from animation.

"Leaving Disney, at that period, was much like getting off the Queen Mary into a little dingy and sailing into the fog," said Bluth. "We didn't know where we were going. We were young, naive, and ambitious enough to think that we could make a great picture, and everyone would see that and beat a path to our door."[14]

Bluth eventually would direct his own ambitious and successful animated features, but his walkout would not only cause Disney to hemorrhage talent, it also crippled production on the studio's next animated feature, *The Fox and the Hound*, which had currently been in production. That film wound up having to delay its release date to July of 1981, from its original release date of Christmas 1980.

The Fox and the Hound was a modest success. The story of a young fox and puppy who grow up together and, as they enter adulthood, learn that they should be sworn enemies and not best friends.

There was a message of prejudice within *The Fox and the Hound*'s story, but told in a kind, friendly, and very safe way. It wasn't the landmark production that the studio needed to move animation forward with this new generation of animators, as they had hoped.

As the 1980s continued, animation production, not just at Disney but at many studios throughout Hollywood, began to decline. Fewer and fewer theatrical features were made, and most animation seen by audiences was produced for Saturday morning television. These shows (produced by studios like

---

14 Ibid

Hanna-Barbera and Filmation), with their lower budgets and accelerated production schedules, were made at a factory-like pace and were a far cry from the quality seen during the "Golden Age" at Disney. They were, however, all that animation had to offer at this time.

To help pull animation out of this downward spiral, Disney looked to their next production, *The Black Cauldron*, which held great potential to be a landmark for Disney animation. The film would be based on a series of books called *The Chronicles of Prydain* by author Lloyd Alexander, an otherworldly fantasy/adventure a la J.R.R. Tolkien's *The Lord of the Rings*.

This type of story was the "rage" in Hollywood at the time, with everything from gritty "sword and sorcery" films like *Conan the Barbarian* to fantasies like *The Dark Crystal* (both 1982) emerging as audience favorites.

The darker elements inherent in such stories were also going to allow Disney animators to delve into an arena never attempted before at the studio and potentially also expand acceptance of Disney animation by an older demographic.

The production dove headfirst into its ambitions. *The Black Cauldron* was the first animated film at Disney to be filmed in widescreen 70 MM since *Sleeping Beauty*, the soundtrack would be recorded in six-track Dolby stereo, and the film would be rated PG (a first for a Disney animated feature).

There was even talk at one point during production that the studio would be able to use emerging holographic technology that would allow for a character to seemingly "step off" the screen. This, unfortunately, never came to be.

Sadly, *The Black Cauldron* didn't live up to its ambitious hopes and turned into a production mired with problems. Tim Burton, who worked on the film, discussed these challenges with author Bob Thomas:

"'I think the company was really at odds with itself. They had this feeling of moving into the future and contemporizing, but they didn't know how to do it. There was a foot in the past and a foot in the future and no firm footing in either. *The Black Cauldron* was one of the things that steered me out of animation.'"[15]

Co-directed by Richard Rich and Ted Berman (who had also directed *The Fox and the Hound*), *The Black Cauldron* centered on young Taran, who attempts to rescue his clairvoyant pig, Hen Wen, from the sinister Horned King, who wants to use the pig's abilities to unlock the secrets of an ancient, magical cauldron, that he believes can help him rule the world.

The film went through what many call a disorganized and disjointed production. Amid this tumult, there was a change in executive leadership at Disney and one that would prove to be a seismic shift with immensely positive "aftershocks" echoing in the company for years to come.

In 1984, Roy E. Disney, Walt's nephew, resigned his seat on Disney's Board of Directors. He disagreed with the direction in which the company seemed to be heading. After leaving, Roy was instrumental in engineering a series of events that resulted in Ron Miller's replacement with Frank Wells as President and Michael Eisner as Chief Executive Officer.

Wells had come from Warner Bros., while Eisner was at Paramount, where they both had a proven track record and led those studios through very successful strings of hit films. With them came Jeffrey Katzenberg, who had worked with Eisner at Paramount and would assume the role of Chairman at The Walt Disney Studios.

The new team brought with them hope as they had an eye on future possibilities. Still, as with any leadership change, it brought a sense of uncertainty as well, particularly for the future of Disney animation.

On February 1, 1985, a decision was made to move the animation studio off the Disney studio lot in Burbank, CA (where it had been for over forty years at this point). This relocation was because the new incoming team would be moving into offices in the hallowed halls of the animation building on the studio lot.

"The first thing that happened was that we were moved out of our very safe little nest there," remembered animator Glen Keane, an emerging talent at this time. "They moved into the

---

15 Bob Thomas, *Disney's Art of Animation: From Mickey Mouse to Beauty and the Beast* (New York, Hyperion, 1991), p. 113.

animation building, and we moved into some warehouses in Glendale. You had the feeling that you were like a rich kid in this sheltered environment, and finally your dad said, 'Okay, now go out and get a job!' You felt like, I guess this is it, we really have to make it work if we're going to make it work."[16]

This new, incoming team that was moving in at Disney had never worked in animation and didn't have a robust working knowledge around the production of an animated film. This was evident after an early, less-than-favorable screening of *The Black Cauldron* left many concerned.

Katzenberg decided that the film needed to be edited and that some of the film's darker aspects should be excised. Editing a finished animated film was unheard of, as productions moved from storyboards to rough-cut versions and then to finished animation. Unlike live-action movies, all scenes in an animated feature were "locked in."

Despite this, several minutes of *The Black Cauldron* were taken out of the film, leaving many animators concerned that their new leadership team didn't fully grasp the medium.

The changes to the film didn't help *The Black Cauldron*. When it was released on July 26, 1985, the film disappointed, bringing in $21.3 million at the domestic box-office. It was beaten by the much-less-expensive non-Disney feature, *The Care Bears Movie*.

Katzenberg noted that *The Black Cauldron* was, in fact, more of a misguided film that had all good intentions but ignored the core audience that is so important to Disney animated films. He said: "'These [animated] films are not made for kids; they're made for the kids that exist in all of us.'"[17]

This realization around the potential of animation gave the Disney artists a positive pause about their future. Another tremendous glimmer of hope was that shortly after Eisner took over, Roy E. Disney returned to the studio as Vice Chairman and Chairman of the Animation Department. Walt Disney's nephew guiding animation was the "white knight" many had been waiting for to save the day.

---

16 Glen Keane interview with ML, March 16, 1995.

17 Bob Thomas, *Disney's Art of Animation: From Mickey Mouse to Beauty and the Beast* (New York, Hyperion, 1991). P.115.

Additionally, Peter Schneider, who had a respected career in the theater, was brought on as the first President of Disney Animation in 1985. While continuing the legacy of revered animated Disney films may have seemed daunting, Schneider remembered having a different perspective

"The refreshing and reassuring aspect," he said, "was that no matter what we did in the future, it could be no worse than *The Black Cauldron*, in my opinion. Therefore, it was very freeing."[18]

At Disney, these "new eyes" turned to another animated film that was concurrently in production with *The Black Cauldron*.

Another group of artists had broken away from production on *The Black Cauldron* and worked on *Basil of Baker Street*. Based on a series of books by author Eve Titus, the film would tell the story of a mouse who lives in Sherlock Holmes' house and emulates the renowned detective as a sleuth himself.

In the film, Basil and his fellow mouse, Dr. Dawson, would square off against the villainous Ratigan, yup a rat (voiced by legendary horror movie icon, Vincent Price), to thwart a plot to dethrone the queen.

Basil of Baker Street would be co-directed by Disney veterans Dave Michener and Burny Mattinson (who had both been at the studio for over thirty years at this point), along with two up-and-coming young animators who were making their directorial debut with the film: Ron Clements and John Musker.

The two who had been experiencing so much frustration at Disney (as evidenced in the aforementioned story about their lunches) suddenly felt a light shining at the end of the long, dark animation tunnel.

"It was a good collaboration," remembered Clements of the film, noting that the team "shared a certain view of that movie."[19]

Eisner and Katzenberg were happy with the film's early storyboards and gave the film the "green light" to move forward. With a title change to *The Great Mouse Detective*, the film was released on July 2, 1986, and while it wasn't a box-office smash, critics were upbeat and almost surprised in their praise for the film.

---

18 Peter Schneider interview with ML, January 23, 1997.
19 Ron Clements interview with ML, January 13, 1997.

A recurring theme in reviews was how *The Great Mouse Detective* felt more aligned with what audiences were more accustomed to when it came to Disney. Roger Ebert noted: "What's fun is the carefree way the animators swing through their story, using the freedom of the cartoon form to blend 19th-century realism with images that seem borrowed from more recent special effects pictures."[20]

Some of these "borrowed images" came from a then-burgeoning technology. The climax of *The Great Mouse Detective* would feature a chase between Basil and Ratigan inside Big Ben's clockwork, which was brought to life through computer-generated imagery (CGI).

While computer animation was used in *The Black Cauldron*, *The Great Mouse Detective* was the first film from the studio to utilize this technology extensively. Computers allowed the filmmakers to realize the clock's movements by combining the CGI with the hand-drawn character animation. This allowed for what looked to be sweeping camera moves that weren't usually possible in the medium.

The two-minute Big Ben sequence was also a large part of *The Great Mouse Detective*'s marketing and publicity. With the possibilities it was opening, the sequence was also a harbinger of things to come at Disney animation and the industry itself.

In addition to using this emerging technology to fully realize the vision of an animated film, another part of Disney animation's future path over the next decade would be the arrival of competition from other studios.

Since Walt himself first embarked on creating a full-length animated feature with 1937's *Snow White and the Seven Dwarfs*, other studios threw their hats into the ring, producing full-length animated features of their own.

For almost fifty years, these animated features garnered interest and attention. Still, few ever scaled the box-office or popular heights that even the most modest Disney animated feature ever had...until November of 1986.

This was when Don Bluth, the name that had become synonymous with the unsettled nature of the Disney studio

____

20 Roger Ebert, "*The Great Mouse Detective* Movie Review," *Chicago-Sun Times*, July 2, 1986, rogerebert.com (accessed January 13, 2021).

in the '70s and '80s, re-emerged and released his latest film. Partnering with movie blockbuster magician Steven Spielberg as a producer, Bluth directed *An American Tail*.

Released by Universal, *An American Tail* took place in 1885 and told of Fievel Mousekewitz, a young mouse separated from his family as they emigrate from Russia to America.

The film would be Bluth's second feature. His first 1982's *The Secret of NIMH* had caught Spielberg's attention and led to the collaboration. "Steven provided an arena; he provided the money and plenty of ideas," said Bluth.[21]

Bluth's style and character design for both films were very "Disney-esque." Still, the tone of *An American Tail*, with its story of struggling immigrants, was very different from Disney.

Critics were mixed, but audiences went to *An American Tail* in droves. The film generated $47 million domestically at the box office, making it the highest-grossing animated film during an initial release, at its time. The movie came with a slew of marketing and a song that not only became a chart-topping hit but was also nominated for that year's Best Song Oscar. Additionally, the film outgrossed *The Great Mouse Detective*.

This success led to another collaboration between Spielberg and Bluth. Eventually, it inspired Spielberg to create his animation studio, Amblimation, which opened in 1989.

More than anything, *An American Tail* caused many in and outside the industry, for the first time, to sit-up and take notice of another major player in the animation game.

At the Disney studio, however, there was a very philosophical attitude toward competition. "Other people's successes never diminish your own success," said Schneider. "I think that's a very important thing one must learn. They don't have to fail for me to be successful, and I don't have to fail for them to be successful. Good films will always be successful, and I think we have to root for the animation industry always to produce great films."[22]

This confidence was primarily due to a vision that the new leadership team at the Disney studio had in mind: breaking new ground while remaining loyal to the hallmarks of Disney.

---

21 Don Bluth interview with ML, July 31, 1997.
22 Peter Schneider interview with ML, January 23, 1997.

"We can't look over our shoulder and say, 'What would Walt have done?'," added Schneider. "All Walt would have done is tell a great story, fill it with great characters and push the boundaries. As long as we do that, I think we'll make our own personal statement as to what animation is, respecting and honoring the tradition of what Walt did, as well as re-interpreting it."[23]

This was true in every way of the studio's next major animation project, *Who Framed Roger Rabbit*, which would, ironically, be a partnership with Steven Spielberg.

The film had been lumbering around Disney since 1981 when the studio acquired the rights to the source material, the book *Who Censored Roger Rabbit* by author Gary K. Wolf. The film's production accelerated in 1985, with Michael Eisner behind it, bringing in Spielberg and his Amblin Entertainment production company to co-produce.

With director Robert Zemeckis at the helm, fresh off of his blockbuster, *Back to the Future* (1985), *Who Framed Roger Rabbit* would take place in a 1940's film noir Hollywood where cartoon stars ("Toons") exist in the real world. One of these Toons, Roger Rabbit (the voice of Charles Fleischer), would enlist human detective Eddie Valiant (Bob Hoskins) to clear his name after Roger is framed for the murder of Marvin Acme (Stubby Kaye).

The film would combine animation and live action to make it one of the most ambitious undertakings in filmmaking. Director Zemeckis, along with Richard Williams, a prominent and Academy Award-winning figure in the industry who would direct all of the film's animation, shared a similar vision.

In past live action/animation collaborations, the two would exist on a flat plane (as in the "penguin dance" sequence from Disney's 1964 hit *Mary Poppins*) but never truly looked as if they existed in the same space. *Who Framed Roger Rabbit* sought to change that.

Williams said: "'I told Bob I was convinced every single rule about the use of animation and live-action was baloney, and if we made the film, I'd throw them all out and let him move the camera.'"[24] He added, "'We agreed that the key to making the combination effective would be the interaction. We thought

23 Ibid.

24 Charles Solomon, *Enchanted Drawings: The History of Animation* (New York, Random House, 1994), p.282.

the cartoon characters should always be affecting their environment or getting tangled up with the live actors.'"[25]

In *Who Framed Roger Rabbit*, the animated characters would move in and out of frame, be a part of tracking camera shots, cast shadows, hold live-action props and, essentially, exist alongside their human co-stars.

As computer technology hadn't come of age just yet, the task of accomplishing this fell to the animator's hand drawings, a partnership with George Lucas' special effects house, Industrial Light and Magic, and post-production that lasted for over a year.

In addition to *how* the Toons were incorporated in *Who Framed Roger Rabbit*, was the landmark feat of *who* was incorporated. To add a touch of "time and place" to the proceedings, animated stars of the Disney canon such as Mickey and Minnie Mouse, Donald Duck, Goofy and Dumbo would appear in cameos.

Additionally, Disney and Amblin were able to partner with other studios to have some of their stars like Bugs Bunny, Daffy Duck, Betty Boop, Droopy Dog, and Woody Woodpecker "crossover" to cameo in the film. Icons like Mickey sharing a scene with Bugs and two of animation's most famous Ducks, Donald and Daffy, trading barbs in their own way was, and still is, astonishing to see in its once-in-a-lifetime significance.

Ahead of its release on June 22, 1988, (by Disney's Touchstone Pictures, the banner used for films geared more toward an adult audience) as trailers and marketing began, *Who Framed Roger Rabbit* generated early "buzz" that movies had not seen in years. Roger Ebert captured this in his review of the film, when he wrote:

"I stopped off at a hot dog stand before the screening of *Who Framed Roger Rabbit* and ran into some other movie critics. They said they were going to the same screening. I asked them what they'd heard about the film. They said they were going to see it for the second time in two days. That's the kind of word of mouth that money can't buy."[26]

Ebert's feelings were echoed by so many critics who

---

25 Ibid, p.282.

26 Roger Ebert, "Runaway Hit From A Rabbit," The *New York Post*, June 22, 1988, p.23.

marveled at the film. *Who Framed Roger Rabbit*, released at the height of the summer movie season, generated the same unique "magic" that had been seen in theaters by Spielberg's other summer-blockbusters-of-a-generation, such as *Raiders of the Lost Ark* (1981) and *E.T.- The Extra-Terrestrial* (1982).

Audiences responded, and by the end of *Who Framed Roger Rabbit*'s run, the movie had generated over $156 million domestically, making it not just the second highest-grossing film of the year (behind *Rain Man*) but also, at the time, the 20th highest-grossing film of all-time.

Additionally, the film won four Academy Awards, including a Special Achievement Oscar for Williams' work on the animation.

In addition to the box-office, the critical accolades, and the awards, the significance of *Who Framed Roger Rabbit* is the spark it re-ignited for animation. "*Roger Rabbit* reminded us how much we loved cartoons," summed up Don Hahn, who served as associate producer on the film [27]

Part of the film's success, with appearances by so many iconic cartoon stars, resulted in a renewed interest in animation history, which had been a part of ongoing research and documentation by many for some time, but now indeed came to the forefront.

Who Framed Roger Rabbit also demonstrated audiences' appetite for new animation, significantly beyond the family demographic that seemed to have a hold on the industry for so long.

The new Eisner and Katzenberg team, now several years into their tenure at the studio, also began to fall in love with animation. They knew that there was an unchartered future for Disney animation that had been a dry and barren wasteland for too long.

Thanks to the dedication and devotion that Disney was about to give to animation, a rainstorm was coming to this drought. As a result, the staff at Walt Disney Feature Animation, as it was renamed in 1986, grew from one hundred and sixty to six hundred.

---

27 Don Hahn interview with ML, March 20, 1996.

Most notably, while *Who Framed Roger Rabbit* was in production, the new leadership at the studio set a new, ambitious schedule: Disney would begin releasing one new animated feature film each year, something even Walt himself had been unable to accomplish.

For the artists at Disney, the excitement of what was yet to come was palpable. "I knew that there was all this talent that was just building up, and I just felt like something had to happen," said Chris Buck, an animator at the time who would go on to direct some of Disney's biggest hits.[28]

Katzenberg quickly learned just how powerful the medium was to Disney, saying, "'...animation is the foundation on which the entire company was built. So, if there was any single thing that the new management of Disney had an absolute obligation to do, it was to reaffirm its commitment to animation.'"[29]

The future was, quite literally, like a blank sheet of animation paper. Disney's Animation Renaissance was about to begin.

---

28 Chris Buck interview with ML, January 21, 1999.
29 Hank Gallo, "A Twist on Disney's Future," *The New York Daily News*, November 17, 1988, p. 43.

CHAPTER TWO

"Up Where They Walk, Up Where They Run…"

Oliver & Company & The Little Mermaid

"Once Upon a Time in New York City," the song that opens Disney's 27th animated feature *Oliver & Company,* has lyrics that are fitting and prophetic:

> "...beginnings are contagious there
> They're always setting stages there
> They're always turning pages there for you."

The lyrics refer to the innocent young kitten who is the star of the film and the setting in New York City. They could also apply to the artists who created what could best be called a foundation for a groundbreaking decade to come and the Disney studio itself.

Oliver & Company was the first fully animated feature produced under Michael Eisner and Jeffrey Katzenberg's supervision and the first film in their "one-new-animated-film-a-year" promise.

The movie was a merging of two worlds: more traditional, Disney animation aspects, such as talking animals, speaking with all-star voices, but this time, there would be a contemporary setting, feel and tone with New York City, in all of its '80s grittiness.

The concept for *Oliver & Company* came from one of the Disney studio's infamous "Gong Show" meetings. The name and concept for these meetings came from a popular '70s TV talent show of the same name, in which amateur acts would perform for celebrity guest judges, who would sound a nearby gong for those they didn't like.

The same idea applied to the Disney "Gong Show" meetings, except here, artists could pitch ideas for future animated features to Eisner, Katzenberg, and Roy E. Disney. Those that weren't approved received their version of the "gong."

It was here that Pete Young, a story artist with the studio, pitched an idea: "*Oliver Twist* with Dogs," a re-telling of Charles Dickens' literary masterpiece, a la *Robin Hood*, this time with a kitten, who is befriended by a cast of canines. The film was given the green light, under the original title *Oliver & Dodger*.

In line with so many films produced at Disney in the 1980s, early drafts of the film were much more somber in tone. Story artists removed some of these bleaker elements through several revisions, and the story stuck to Dickens' original work's basic structure. George Scribner, who had been an animator at Disney for many years at this point, directed *Oliver & Company*, which opens with an aesthetically pleasing postcard shot of Manhattan as Huey Lewis sings "Once Upon a Time in New York City." We are then with the titular character, the orphaned kitten, left behind after his fellow kittens are all adopted.

Alone on the city's rainy, scary streets, Oliver is befriended by street-smart mutt Dodger, who allows the kitten to join his gang of fellow strays: Tito the chihuahua, Rita the Saluki, Francis the bulldog, and Einstein the Great Dane. The gang's owner/leader is a sad-looking pickpocket named Fagin, who works for the imposing, mobster-like Sykes and his Doberman sidekicks.

While out with the dogs, Oliver is separated from them and adopted by a kind-hearted young girl named Jenny, who just happens to be rich and lives in her luxurious apartment with her spoiled poodle, Georgette.

When Dodger and the gang "rescue" Oliver from Jenny's and bring him back home, Fagan notices Oliver's Park Ave address on his collar and decides to hold the kitten for ransom to help pay back his debt to Sykes.

However, Sykes gets involved and kidnaps Jenny, which results in an impressively choreographed car chase scene that culminates on the elevated tracks of the subway.

As the studio did with films like *The Jungle Book* and *The Aristocats*, Disney enlisted some marquee names for the voice cast in *Oliver & Company*. Among them, singer Billy Joel as Dodger, Bette Midler (who, at this point had made several popular live-action films for Disney's Touchstone Pictures) as Georgette, Cheech Marin as Tito, Dom DeLuise (ironically a stalwart voice in many Don Bluth films) as Fagin, Robert Loggia as Sykes, Sheryl Lee Ralph as Rita, Roscoe Lee Browne as Francis and (then) child star Joey Lawrence as Oliver.

The characters were brought to the screen by that same generation of animators trained and mentored by the Nine Old Men. They were now not only on their own, but they were also under new guidance and direction while drawing inspiration from the past. Mike Gabriel, who served as supervising animator for Oliver, said: "'By studying some of the classic Disney characters, like Thumper in *Bambi*, we learned that young characters didn't have to be cloying or just a cute ball of fur. They worked because they were sincere and genuine. That's what we wanted for Oliver.'"[30]

Andreas Deja, serving as supervising animator for Dodger, knew that immediate parallels would be drawn to Tramp's character from Disney's 1955 classic, *Lady and the Tramp*. Andreas noted: "'...we wanted Dodger to have a unique look, so we gave him a rougher and scroungier appearance that seemed to fit in with the city setting.'"[31]

With a mindset of ensuring that the "Disney DNA" was still evident in the film, *Oliver & Company* also had a new creative perspective, especially in the design of the villain, Sykes.

Early in the film's production, the filmmakers sought to create a more ambiguous villain, quietly chilling and imposing. As Frank Thomas and Ollie Johnston detail in their book, *The Disney Villain*, this approach eventually had to be changed, to the chagrin of Sykes' supervising animator, Glen Keane:

"The story development called for more and more action for Sykes, however, and the concept of keeping him in the shadows had to be abandoned. Glen Keane was disappointed in

---

30 John Grant, *Encyclopedia of Walt Disney's Animated Characters*, (New York, Hyperion, 1993), p.328.

31 Ibid, p.329.

how this massive man looked when he had to move about like an ordinary person. 'There was some stuff in the warehouse where he walks down the hallway; you wished you hadn't seen him walk around when he did.'"[32]

Sykes is an example of the filmmakers looking to make *their* mark with this film, as *Oliver & Company* wanted to expand the growing acceptance of animation that had started that same year with *Who Framed Roger Rabbit*.

The use of contemporary music in *Oliver & Company* was a way to bridge traditional Disney expectations with pop music sensibilities. The movie would be the studio's first, full-fledged musical in some time (in the conventional sense) where characters would burst into song instead of songs playing on the soundtrack.

The differentiator with *Oliver & Company* would be that most of the songs would be performed by a Top 40 pop artist of the moment, such as Huey Lewis singing "Once Upon a Time in New York City" at the film's opening. It was convenient that Billy Joel provided Dodger's voice as he could sing that character's big showstopper, "Why Should I Worry?" Rita's song "Streets of Gold" was performed by Ruth Pointer of the Pointer Sisters, and, of course, you couldn't have Bette Midler voicing Georgette without the character having a song, which she had with "Perfect Isn't Easy," with lyrics by her former collaborator, singer Barry Manilow.

Films featuring a song that could easily translate to the *Billboard* music charts were inherent in many '80s-era films. While none of the songs in *Oliver & Company* were major hits on the radio, using these contemporary artists was another marketing method to help promote the movie.

This music would also help the story *feel* more contemporary, as would the vision to bring all of the elements of New York City – such as traffic and billboards – as never before. For this, the filmmakers turned, once again, to the ever-emerging technology of computer animation.

The computer animation would realize aspects such as gridlocked traffic and rattling subway trains, with the

---

32 Ollie Johnston & Frank Thomas, *The Disney Villain*, (New York, Hyperion, 1993). P.184.

hand-drawn characters interacting with these elements. Director Scribner noted that computers "'do the inanimate objects, freeing the animators to spend more time on the flesh-and-blood creations. And because New York City itself is in some respects another character in the picture, we wanted it to be realistic, not just static backgrounds. We wanted lots of movement and traffic.'"[33]

Looking back now with our more discerning eye, it's easy to spot the computer-generated elements in *Oliver & Company*, as the technology was still in its nascent stages. That said, the computer animation adds an element of more freeing cinematic possibilities, much like the Big Ben sequence in *The Great Mouse Detective*.

Dodger's bouncing from car to car and across a moving cement mixer during his musical number gave a choreographed feel to the sequence. Also, the climactic car chase between Sykes' limousine and Fagin's dilapidated scooter, during which both wind up on the subway tracks, is as exciting as those in many of the big '80s action movies at the time.

This ending scene is also one of the darker aspects of *Oliver & Company*. There are genuine, dangerous stakes for the characters, and Sykes' resulting (and surprisingly violent) comeuppance is more akin to *Lethal Weapon* than a Disney animated feature.

This tone is felt throughout the film, particularly early on, when Sykes threatens Fagin by trapping his head in the automatic window of his limousine and gives him a time frame to pay his debt, and if he doesn't, there is the not-so-subtle threat of death.

This shift in tone from previous Disney films was a large part of what Eisner and Katzenberg had been focused on, to begin moving animation from one era and mindset to another, most notably from a storytelling perspective. Unlike previous animated films at the studio, *Oliver & Company* used both storyboards and a screenplay during production. Adding a script to the process helped provide a guidepost for the film.

When *Oliver & Company* debuted on November 18, 1988 (Mickey Mouse's 60th birthday!), critics noted how the film was

---

33 John Culhane, "'Oliver & Company' Gives Dickens a Disney Twist," *The New York Times*, November 13, 1988, p.44.

more current than traditional Disney offerings. The results were a collection of mixed reviews.

Like *Newsday's* Lynn Darling, some were supportive of the film, writing: "Happily, *Oliver & Company* is a contemporary cartoon that pulls off a tricky balancing act. It can take an occasionally sly eye to the crazy city in which it's set without losing sight of the innocence at the core of the movie's charm."[34]

Others like *New York Daily News* critic Kathleen Carroll called *Oliver & Company* a "Grim Disney Tale," in the headline for her review, in which she stated that the film "adopts the same dark, sinister view of the world as *Who Framed Roger Rabbit*. The musical numbers are not worth barking about. Most offensive of all, the movie is riddled with commercial plugs – neon signs and billboards promoting not only Coca-Cola but *USA Today*."[35]

What particularly stung about these reviews were other, consistently glowing reviews for another studio's animated film, *The Land Before Time*, that opened the same weekend as *Oliver & Company*. Not only was this film going head-to-head with Disney, but it was directed by none other than Don Bluth.

With *The Land Before Time*, Bluth had Spielberg on-board as executive producer as well as fellow blockbuster wizard and *Star Wars* creator George Lucas.

The story of a young group of dinosaurs making their way to a hallowed place called "the Great Valley" surprised many when it came in at number one at the box-office opening weekend, grossing $7.5 million. With this, *The Land Before Time* beat *Oliver & Company*, which came in at a disappointing number four over its opening weekend, not only behind the animated dinosaur epic but *Child's Play* and Disney's live-action *Ernest Saves Christmas*, as well.

However, as the holiday season of 1988 continued, *Oliver & Company* held firm in the top ten films. It eventually surpassed *The Land Before Time* at the box-office, with *Oliver* taking in $53 million and *Land* at $48 million, domestically.

---

34 Lynn Darling, "An Animated Twist on Dickens," *Newsday*, November 18, 1988, p.13.

35 Kathleen Carroll, "'Oliver' is a Grim Disney Tale," *New York Daily News*, November 18, 1988, p.57.

Could it be that the Disney name held more sway for audiences? Was there a thirst out there for new animated films from the studio with its distinctive voice?

Signs were pointing in that direction, and ultimately, *Oliver & Company,* as author and animation historian Jerry Beck noted, "represented the final dress rehearsal for the great successes of the 1990s."[36]

The first of these that would signal a triumphant return to form for Disney debuted one year after *Oliver & Company* in November of 1989. However, it had been an idea that had been "swimming" around the studio for almost fifty years.

The Little Mermaid surfaced at Disney as far back as the late thirties, when Walt considered doing a "package film" that would combine several of Danish author Hans Christian Andersen's most famous fairy tales. The film had initially been slated to combine live action and animation. Biographical-like segments of Andersen's life would be intercut with animated vignette's depicting his most famous stories, *The Emperor's New Clothes*, *The Steadfast Tin Soldier,* and *The Little Mermaid.*

Eventually Walt decided not to move forward with the Hans Christian Andersen film.

In the '80s, Disney artists were challenged by Eisner and Katzenberg with finding ideas for future animated features. In looking for inspiration, Ron Clements came across Andersen's *The Little Mermaid* while browsing through a collection of fairy tales at a bookstore.

Clements pitched the idea to adapt the story at a "Gong Show" meeting, was given the go-ahead, and turned to his *Great Mouse Detective* co-director John Musker to collaborate. "I knew John was a good writer, and I asked him if he would be interested in working together. From that, we've been working together since," said Clements.[37]

Both directors would emerge as two of the Animation Renaissance's principal engineers at Disney (where they would go on to be simply referred to as "Ron n' John"). Clements

---

36 Jerry Beck, *The Animated Movie Guide*, (Chicago, Chicago Press Review, 2005) p.182.
37 Ron Clements interview with ML, January 13, 1997.

moved out to California from his native Iowa after graduating high school and worked at the Hanna-Barbera Studios. He eventually came to Disney in the mid-'70s, after the studio artists were impressed by his self-taught talents. At Disney, Clements worked on *The Rescuers* and *Pete's Dragon*, apprenticing under Frank Thomas.

It was around this time that John Musker also joined Disney. After graduating high school in 1974, Musker, a native of Chicago, took his portfolio to California and won a partial scholarship to the California Institute of the Arts (CalArts), which helped him land an internship at the Disney studio.

Musker worked as an animator on such films as *The Fox and the Hound* and *The Black Cauldron* before transitioning to co-director of *The Great Mouse Detective*, where he first collaborated with Clements.

As the two began their second collaboration on *The Little Mermaid*, Musker remembered excitement starting to build around the production, "There was a feeling of enthusiasm to be doing a fairy tale because one hadn't been done in so long."[38]

Coupled with this eagerness was a sense of weight that many began to feel settling on their shoulders. "It was the first time that a whole new generation was going back to the roots of where things began, such as with *Snow White*," added Clements. "We felt a certain intimidation because we knew that this film might be compared with those, more so, because there would be similarities. At the same time, we wanted to put a new spin on it so that it would reflect the new generation."[39]

Added to this was the fact that the studio's moderate successes with their newer animated films didn't solidify Disney's comeback just yet. "We still didn't know where animation was going," said Clements, adding, "There was a sense with each film that this could be the last one. Things had been looking up with *Great Mouse Detective* and *Oliver & Company*, but I think there was a sense that there was a lot riding on *Mermaid*."

"Jeffrey Katzenberg was very demanding on the film," remembered John Musker. "He was always challenging us.

---

38   John Musker interview with ML, January 13, 1997.
39   Ron Clements interview with ML, January 13, 1997.

There was a feeling of trying to exceed what you had done before."[40]

The story of *The Little Mermaid* became the focus. While doing pre-production work for the film, Clements and Musker spent time at the Disney Studio Animation Research Library (ARL), which was designed to house and care for artwork created for the shorts and features produced at the studio, dating back to the 1920s.

Here, the team came across artwork done for Walt's initial version *The Little Mermaid* from the 1930s. This included conceptual drawings by illustrator Kay Nielsen, who had provided similar, evocative artwork for the *Night on Bald Mountain* sequence of *Fantasia* (1940).

The Little Mermaid team struggled with effectively adapting the story, as, like much of Andersen's work, it was downbeat. While researching how to solve this, the film's artists found that Nielsen's work, provided initial, creative sparks. His art offered such seminal inspiration that Nielsen was given posthumous credit on the 1989 film.

When reviewing other production artwork and notes in the ARL, *The Little Mermaid* team saw that Walt's artists had the same struggles with the story, which was a significant reason behind why the Hans Christian Andersen project was shelved.

What helped unlock the possibilities of *The Little Mermaid* this time at Disney was to make the film even more of a musical than *Oliver & Company* had been, and they turned to Broadway for inspiration.

Howard Ashman, a talented, veteran Broadway lyricist, had been recruited by Peter Schneider to write "Once Upon a Time in New York City" for *Oliver & Company*. Ashman, along with his songwriting partner, composer Alan Menken, had brought the hit musical *Little Shop of Horrors* to Broadway in 1982.

Soon after writing the opening song for *Oliver & Company*, Ashman and Menken came up in a conversation between Jeffrey Katzenberg and producer David Geffen, who, at the time, was in the middle of production on the film version of *Little Shop of Horrors*.

---

40 John Musker interview with ML, January 13, 1997.

Katzenberg said that when Geffen "'...heard we were using an Ashman song in *Oliver & Company*, he said to me 'Howard and Alan are geniuses. They love Disney animation, and I think you should meet them.'"[41]

Bringing the duo on was a real catalyst for the production of *The Little Mermaid*. "The idea of having a musical team right in the next room, so as you were storyboarding something, you could go next door and talk with Howard and Alan," noted Musker. "Then, they could come over and see the artwork and say, 'There's something there that I can use.' In a way, that was a throwback to a system that was around in the '30s but had gone away."[42]

Ashman's experience in and knowledge of storytelling and effectively utilizing songs from his years working in the theater was incredibly impactful. He had an innate sense of what would "work" and what wouldn't. Ashman became co-producer on *The Little Mermaid*, contributing and refining the music and taking part in story sessions and early screenings to contribute to the story (sometimes in a very passionate way).

"He brought a new sensibility, in terms of how he saw music weaving into the story, that did set all this off," said Musker. "Howard's involvement was a watershed and a turning point. We had never done anything like that before. It was a big learning experience for all of us. Working with Howard made us feel as if this was something special."[43]

This partnership with the songwriting duo helped realize a strong story for *The Little Mermaid*. As the film opens, we are introduced to King Triton's undersea world and the "Merpeople." We meet 16-year-old mermaid Ariel, who is fascinated with the "human world" up above. One night, despite Sebastian the crab's Jiminy-Cricket-like warnings, she travels to the surface with her sidekicks Flounder and Scuttle the seagull. While eavesdropping on a ship, she spies human Prince Eric and is soon smitten.

When a storm blows through, Ariel winds up rescuing the Prince and bringing him to shore. Here, she realizes that she

---

41 Christopher Finch, *The Art of Walt Disney: From Mickey Mouse to the Magic Kingdoms* (New York, Harry N. Abrams, 1995) p.286.

42 John Musker interview with ML, January 13, 1997.

43 Ibid.

wants to be part of his world. Ursula, the villainous sea-witch, prays upon Ariel's desire and offers a deal: swapping Ariel's beautiful voice for a transformation to human form.

This allows Ariel to go ashore and finally meet Prince Eric, but Ursula has built-in a catch: Ariel must make the Prince fall in love with her. If she can't, Ariel will remain human, unable to return to the "Mer-world," and Ursula will keep Ariel's voice.

The Disney artists made some alterations to Andersen's original version of *The Little Mermaid*. Despite such stakes for Ariel, Disney's version features the studio's trademark "happy ending," as one would expect.

What's unexpected about Disney's take on *The Little Mermaid* is how much it differs and breaks away from past animated features. In place of more familiar voices is a cast of Broadway veterans and character actors: Jodi Benson, who voiced Ariel, had starred in several Broadway musicals but had never worked in film; another Great White Way performer Samuel E. Wright had only made two films before being cast as Sebastian the Crab; Pat Carroll, who portrayed Ursula had been starring in movies and television for thirty years as had comedian Buddy Hackett, who lent his voice to Scuttle the Seagull. Rounding out the cast were seasoned character actors Kenneth Mars as King Triton, Rene Auberjonois as Chef Louis, and young actor Christopher Daniel Barnes (star of *Day By Day*, a popular sitcom at the time) as Prince Eric.

An extremely talented cast, but among them, there was not a "marquee name" whose appearance above the film's title guaranteed a specific audience. Instead, with *The Little Mermaid*, the filmmakers didn't utilize "stunt casting." They went back to a process that Walt and his artists had used during the '30s and '40s, in which the correct vocal performance was paired with the right character, even if that meant forgoing the choice of a popular actor.

The result was spot-on casting in *The Little Mermaid*, mainly when it came to each of Ashman and Menken's songs. Jodi Benson's performance of "Part of Your World," in which she sings of her longing to be closer to Prince Eric, is, in a word, breathtaking, while "Under the Sea" and "Kiss the Girl" sung by Samuel E. Wright are incredibly infectious. During production, Ashman suggested that Sebastian change from the pompous, pretentious, proper English persona he was in early story drafts to Rastafarian, which only helped open up the musical possibilities.

Pat Carroll's performance of Ursula's significant number "Poor Unfortunate Souls" is gleeful. Carroll's throaty performance is coupled with supervising animator Ruben Aquino's work on the character that includes hip thrusts at just the right moment and inventive use of Ursula's undulating octopus-like tentacles.

It was Roy E. Disney who suggested that, for inspiration, Aquino should watch footage of an octopus from the 1959 Disney documentary *Mysteries of the Deep*. The result is a scene-stealing showcase from both the actress and the animator, coming together in one performance.

Ursula is also another example of how with *The Little Mermaid*, animators were finally able to sink their teeth into their craft, as never before. With the film, audiences could see them bringing to the screen the secrets that Walt's Nine Old Men had shared with them.

Glen Keane, who served as supervising animator for Ariel, remembered what Ollie Johnston, one of the "Nine," had taught him: "Ollie used to say, 'Glen when a character is thinking - stop! Don't move. Don't do anything. Just let them stop.' Because you're showing that there's something going on inside the character when they're not doing anything else, it's when they're moving and talking that they've made a decision. But, when a character is working in their mind, and you want the audience to crawl into their head and feel how they're feeling and thinking, just hold the character still."[44]

This idea of "personality animation" is the concept that animation is more than just a series of drawings; but instead, is about bringing forth a performance through drawings. It's why, for years, animators were dubbed "actors with a pencil."

"The misconceptions that I had about animation at the beginning were things like, 'Well, you draw funny faces and

---

44 Glen Keane interview with ML, March 16, 1995.

cartoons,'" says Keane. "I found that animation is so far removed from that. We went into serious figure drawing classes; you learned anatomy, you learned about design, we did sculptures. It was like learning from the masters."[45]

Glen came to the Disney studio in 1974. He had grown up with artistry right at home, as his father was Bil Keane, the cartoonist who created the famous comic strip, *The Family Circus*. At Disney, Glen Keane learned the art form firsthand, not just from Ollie, but other Nine Old Men members, who taught Keane daily lessons on imbuing his drawings with heart and sincerity.

"You have to really believe in the character that you are animating, which is not as easy as it might sound," said Keane. "I think that there's a tendency sometimes for people to be cynical about the character - 'Ah, that's just a cartoon. It's not real.' But, to really crawl into that character and make it live, you've got to become emotionally involved with the character."[46]

With this philosophy, Keane brought some of the richest animated personalities to the screen during the Renaissance. The first of these was his work on Ariel in *The Little Mermaid*.

Throughout the film, we, as an audience, can feel the young mermaid's longing and see this in several key sequences. One, most notably, is toward the end of the song "Part of Your World": floating through the "treasure trove" of souvenirs from the "Human World," Ariel drifts up toward the surface and toward the camera, seemingly singing directly to the audience.

The subtlety of Ariel's movements - her hair billowing around her, and the longing we can see in her face - coupled with the bold decision to frame the shot with such a unique perspective, showcased a depth to the art of Disney animation that audiences hadn't seen in several decades. It's just one of many examples like this in *The Little Mermaid*.

Critics were bowled over by this artistry when the film opened on November 17, 1989. Film critic Jami Bernard gave

---

45 Ibid.

46 Glen Keane interview with ML, February 1, 1999.

the film four stars and declared of The *Little Mermaid*: "It's funny, romantic and – OK – scary, just as it should be. This kind of terror is enthralling, stimulating. Just as yesterday's kids cowered at *Bambi* and *Pinocchio*, films that they remember now with great affection, let today's kids see how powerful animation can be."[47]

Bernard was not alone among her critic peers. *The Little Mermaid* was unanimously praised; the film wound up on many top ten film lists for 1989.

Eisner, Katzenberg, and Roy E. Disney's focus to begin widening the circle of animation's acceptance was starting.

By the end of its theatrical run, *The Little Mermaid* grossed $84 million at the North American box office, a 64% increase from *Oliver & Company*, making it, at the time, the animated film with the highest gross during its initial run.

In an interesting turn of events, *The Little Mermaid* also bested *All Dogs Go to Heaven*, the latest animated feature film from Don Bluth, which happened to open in theaters the same day as *The Little Mermaid*.

In the spring of 1990, *The Little Mermaid* found itself nominated for three Academy Awards, winning two: Best Song ("Under the Sea") and Best Score. Not counting Touchstone Pictures, this would be the first time a Disney studio film would win an Oscar since 1971's *Bedknobs and Broomsticks* took home Best Visual Effects.

Ariel quickly took her place alongside other famous Disney princesses and heroines. With the mindset of animation as the foundation for all else within the company, *The Little Mermaid* began a very targeted marketing campaign.

The film "fed" other areas of the company. Consumers could find *The Little Mermaid* products at The Disney Store, an attraction based on the film soon opened at the, then, Disney-MGM Studios theme park and a "making of" special aired on The Disney Channel.

This concept of Disney's realms working together in "marketing synergy" would become a standard that is still firmly in place today.

---

47 Jami Bernard, "Disney Scores with a Fanta-Sea of Love," *New York Post*, November 15, 1989, Section 2.

As a new decade, the 1990s, started, it was evident that Disney had a successful film that looked to have legs (not fins) that would carry it forward to future generations. It had been some time since the studio had an animated hit that had such an impact (one would have to go back to 1967's *The Jungle Book*).

Through the years, the film's music has continued to play on ("Under the Sea" is always used as an upbeat "party atmosphere song" in Disney's parks and shows). *The Little Mermaid* has also given way to direct-to-video sequels, an animated TV series, multiple theme park attractions, and even (in an ironic turn of events) a Broadway musical. Today, the young children who saw the film during its initial run now share it with their children in a time-honored Disney tradition.

During production on *The Little Mermaid*, co-director Musker admits that he didn't foresee this popularity at all. "For me, personally, as far as any sense of, 'Will the public like this?' or 'Will this be a big hit?' I honestly had no sense of that. We were very innocently trying to just make the best film that we could. In hindsight, you can see how things have worked out, but I had no idea that it would reach the audience that it has and move into some of the pop cultural things, the way it did."[48]

With *The Little Mermaid*, the Disney Animation Renaissance was underway. For their follow-up, the studio would dare to attempt something that Walt himself never wanted to try: an animated sequel.

---

48 John Musker interview with ML, January 13, 1997.

CHAPTER THREE

"Tale as Old as Time"

The Rescuers Down Under &
Beauty and the Beast

During the Holiday Season of 1990, Hollywood was run by a ten-year-old. On November 16th, John Hughes' comedy *Home Alone*, the now-classic Christmas movie, in which a young boy (played by Macaulay Culkin) defends his house from two burglars after his family mistakenly leaves him at home, opened in theaters everywhere.

The film generated tremendous buzz before its opening weekend and, after its first three days in theaters, had made $17 million at the box-office. But, as there always is at the box-office, there can only be one film in the number one spot

Home Alone was on its way to becoming one of the biggest films of all time and blindsided any other movies competing against it at the box-office. One of these was Disney's newest animated feature, *The Rescuers Down Under*, a sequel to the 1977 animated feature, which had the unforeseen misfortune of opening on November 16th, 1990, the same day as *Home Alone*.

When the box-office results came in after the opening weekend, *Home Alone* had taken the top spot, while *The Rescuers Down Under* was fourth with $3.5 million. The family audience had spoken with their wallets, which prompted Jeffrey Katzenberg to pull all marketing and advertisements for the film. With this move, sadly, *The Rescuers Down Under* quietly withered away.

The years that followed the film's release at Disney would see tremendous successes that have been remembered for ages. In contrast, animation history has seemingly placed *The Rescuers Down Under* as a glossed-over forgotten stepchild of this era.

This is a shame, and the film deserved so much better. It was, in many ways, a groundbreaking effort for Disney and helped pave the way for blockbusters that would follow.

When the original *Rescuers* was in various production stages, several iterations of the story, including a version set in Antarctica and another involving circus animals, showed plenty of possibilities for the characters.

As the original film had proven to be popular and well-remembered by a generation who would be old enough to now take their children to the theater, plans for a sequel surfaced in the late '80s as Eisner and Katzenberg continued to focus on ramping up the studio's animated output.

With the film *Crocodile Dundee* being such a tremendous hit and the action genre so popular, the inspiration for sending Bernard and Bianca on an epic adventure in Australia surfaced. Mike Gabriel and Hendel Butoy, both animators at the studio since the early eighties, were tapped to co-direct.

Peter Schneider recruited Thomas Schumacher to serve as producer on the project. Schneider had previously collaborated with Schumacher before the two joined Disney when Schumacher worked on the Mark Taper Forum staff at the Los Angeles Music Center. Additionally, Schumacher had extensive experience in the performing arts, most notably as the Director of the 1987 Los Angeles Festival of the Arts and as General Assistant Manager of the Los Angeles Ballet.

This theatrical mindset of bringing divergent teams together was a spirit that Schumacher brought with him to Disney. "No one has a journey alone in the animation business," said Schumacher. "You are always traveling with many other people, in lock-step, arm-in-arm. The power of collaboration and the joy of seeing people at their best is what this is about."[49]

The first step in this for *The Rescuers Down Under* team was to craft a story that was the epic adventure that the artists envisioned and deliver on the quiet, emotional impact that the first *Rescuers* had.

---

49 Thomas Schumacher interview with ML, August 21, 2000.

Story artist Joe Ranft, who had been at the studio since 1980, was brought on board to guide the story team on the film. Schumacher said," 'Joe was the very center of *The Rescuers Down Under.'"*[50]

Brenda Chapman, who would go on to become the first female co-director of an animated film with DreamWorks' *Prince of Egypt* in 1998, as well as the first female director to win an Oscar for Best Animated Feature with Pixar's *Brave* (2012), was a story artist on Joe's team for *The Rescuers Down Under.* She recalled of Ranft, "'He created a great working atmosphere, even when we were frustrated with some of the creative decisions.'"[51] One of these frustrations surfaced when the story artists wanted the young boy, who was to be the lead character in the film, to be Aboriginal, but were forced to go with a white-blond boy, who wound up as the character of Cody in the movie.

This authenticity that all wanted on *The Rescuers Down Under* would be found in the setting and in the indigenous animals who would serve as supporting characters in the film. The artists traveled to Australia for a twelve-day research trip. They studied several locations throughout the country, including the Australian Outback, the Uluru/Ayers Rock, and Kakadu National Park.

In addition to finding inspiration in such vistas, the artists also observed Australia's indigenous creatures and even traveled to the San Diego Zoo back home to do the same.

As the film went into production, the Disney studio in Burbank, California, turned to their "satellite studio" in Lake Buena Vista, Florida, at the (then) Disney-MGM Studios theme park for assistance. The smaller studio had initially been planned to produce short subjects but were asked to support and expedite production.

The artists on both coasts came together to create a film that squarely grabs the audience from its opening sequence. *The Rescuers Down Under* opens with a dizzyingly impressive tracking shot across the Outback, after which we meet

---

50 John Canemaker, *Two Guys Named Joe*, (New York, Disney Editions, 2010), p.51.
51 Ibid, p.52.

young Cody, a friend to the animals in the area. He answers a "distress call" from the animals and learns that Marahute, the giant golden eagle, has been captured and is stuck in a poacher's net.

After Cody frees Marahute and is about to fall, the eagle rescues Cody and takes the boy on a soaring ride through the Outback, in a sequence that ranks among the studio's best and truly captures the sensation of flight like none other.

This exhilarating sequence is followed by a quieter, heartfelt moment at Marahute's nest. An emotional bond is formed, as Cody, who lost his father, learns that Marahute's mate (and the father of the eggs in her nest) is not around anymore, either.

This scene was the brainchild of Brenda Chapman. Initially, Marahute was to have a voice, but Chapman decided it would work better if the character acted through pantomime. She also studied the movements of hawks and incorporated that. As the two hug and then Maruhute takes flight to an accompanying soaring score by Bruce Broughton, we as an audience can feel the heart in the moment. As animation historian and author John Canemaker states: "It is, in fact, the emotional glue that binds the entire film."[52]

After, Cody is discovered by Percival C. McLeach, a notorious poacher who had set a trap for Marahute. McLeach discovers one of the eagle's feathers in Cody's pack and kidnaps the boy to get him to reveal the location of Marahute's nest.

From here, we go to snowy New York City and are reacquainted with our heroes from the first *Rescuers*, the two mice, Bernard and Bianca. During a romantic dinner, Bernard is about to propose to Bianca when they are called away by the Rescue Aid Society, who informs them that they have received a distress call from Australia and a young boy is in trouble.

Bernard and Bianca board a flight atop Wilbur the albatross, and they are off to Australia There are two more stunning flight sequences, one that takes us through the snow-blown streets of New York and another that soars right above the Sydney Opera House.

---

52   John Canemaker, *Paper Dreams: The Art and Artists of Disney Storyboards*, (New York, Hyperion,1999) p. 245.

Once at the Outback, the two enlist the help of kangaroo mouse Jake, and they are all off to rescue Cody (and Marahute) from McLeach.

Bob Newhart and Eva Gabor returned to voice Bernard and Bianca, respectively, with John Candy voicing Wilbur, brother of Orville, the albatross from the original (comedian Jim Jordan who had voiced Orville, had passed away before production).

George C. Scott provided the villainous McLeach's voice with soap opera actor Tristan Rogers as Jake.

The Disney tradition of recognizable voices was back with *The Rescuers Down Under*, but there would be much about the production that would be new for the studio.

The biggest of these was the Computer Animation Production System (CAPS). Author Christopher Finch explains this advancement in animation filmmaking by describing the system this way:

"...CAPS takes existing animation drawings and effects and backgrounds and combines them so that they can be seen in video form. It also provides the means to color the images electronically (only the backgrounds are colored with brush and paint). The CAPS system, therefore, replaces the old ink and paint department and is operated by former members of that department who were retrained to work at computer workstations, bringing their years of expertise with them."[53]

While this leap forward assisted with expediting the film's production, it did signal the end of hand-painted cels, a hallmark of the animation industry. It was also the first significant signal of the ever-encroaching advancement of computer technology in animation.

In addition to CAPS, *The Rescuers Down Under* utilized computer-generated imagery (CGI) for several film elements. The impressive opening tracking shot across the Outback and Wilbur's flight into Sydney were realized using this technology, as was McLeach's hulk of a poaching truck. It helped make these scenes white-knuckle rides and Bernard's attempt

---

53 Christopher Finch, *The Art of Walt Disney: From Mickey Mouse to the Magic Kingdom*, (New York, Hyperion, 1995), p.296.

to escape the treads of McLeach's tank-like vehicle rival sequences in any *Indiana Jones* film.

Computers also helped co-directors Butoy and Gabriel realize their vision for the film. They looked to director David Lean's work (such as epics like *Lawrence of Arabia*) for inspiration. This is evident in many of the film's key sequences. *The Rescuers Down Under* emerged as the first of several animated movies from Disney that sought to borrow from the studio's past and emulate live-action filmmaking in its camerawork, staging, lighting, and other elements.

Additionally, as they had with *The Little Mermaid*, the film's supervising animators continued to amplify the concept of personality animation. In *The Rescuers Down Under*, this was true of animation in its purest form with several of the characters who didn't speak and instead expressed themselves through pantomime and their actions.

Joanna, McLeach's sidekick, the pet monitor lizard is a perfect example of this. Animated by David Cutler, she is as strong as any villain's sidekicks, but even more so as author John Grant notes:

"Joanna manages to be every bit as satisfying a sidekick as, say, Sir Hiss, without the benefit of any dialogue at all; the only sounds that she can make are snarls, whimpers, yelps, and the like."[54]

Then, there was Marahute, not only a fully realized character in the quiet moments with Cody earlier in the film, but also animated in such a way that audiences immediately have a sense of the character's power and majesty.

The giant eagle was animated by Glen Keane, fresh off his success with Ariel. In *The Rescuers Down Under*, he once again brought his thoughtful artistry to this character, as he discussed: "'The more I can relate to the eagle and understand the way it moves, the more I can feel like it's me flying in the air. And once I can feel like it's me flying and I'm not just doing a drawing, then it takes the animation to the next level up, and the audience believes it because the artist believed it.'"[55]

---

54 John Grant, *The Encyclopedia of Walt Disney's Animated Characters* (New York, Hyperion, 1993), p.353.

55 Ibid, p.354.

It's, far and away, the most exhilarating sequence in *The Rescuers Down Under*. With Cody atop Marahute, soaring through clouds and over waterfalls, the feeling of flight is palpable. Without a doubt, it ranks as one of Disney's most stunning examples of animation.

This striking artistry came together with a plot that weaves in many characters, stories, and adventurous vignettes. Unfortunately, none of these strengths could buoy *The Rescuers Down Under* at the box-office when it opened on "Home Alone Day," November 16th, 1990.

The film had tremendous advance publicity and even opened as a "double feature" of sorts (something Disney hadn't done for many years). It was paired with a brand-new Mickey Mouse featurette, *The Prince and the Pauper*, a 25-minute short film adaptation of the Mark Twain novel starring Mickey, Donald, and Goofy in the lead roles.

Critics praised both this short and *The Rescuers Down Under*. Joseph Gelmis raved of both the film and *The Prince and the Pauper*: "This double bill is the one movie show in town you can take kids to this holiday season with confidence that you won't be embarrassed or bored."[56]

Ironic that *The Rescuers Down Under* wasn't the "one movie show" in town that Holiday season that families went to. *Home Alone* made $476 million worldwide and secured its place as one of the most popular films of all time. Meanwhile, *The Rescuers Down Under* generated only $27.9 million in the United States.

After only one weekend, pulling advertisements and marketing certainly didn't help, and the film slowly slipped into a realm of "Oh yeah," as animation fans would shake loose the cobwebs of their memory when the film was mentioned in the years that followed.

It has since gone on to be remembered fondly, notably by both the generation who first grew up with *The Rescuers Down Under* and film enthusiasts who constantly seek to assist the underrated gem by singing its praises.

However, at the time, the film's discouraging performance didn't do much for Disney to continue to secure its foothold

---

56 Joseph Gelmis, "Snappy Mice, Zippy Mickey," *New York Newsday*, November 16, 1990, Section II.

in animation. After *The Little Mermaid* and before *The Rescuers Down Under*, the studio had been supporting itself with re-issues of their classic animated films, as well as an animated feature, *Duck Tales the Movie: Treasure of the Lost Lamp*, which had come out in the summer of 1990 in response to the popularity of Disney's animated television series, *Duck Tales*. At the time, Disney had jumped into television animation with success, producing other popular shows *Chip 'n Dale: Rescue Rangers* and *Adventures of the Gummi Bears*. Television animation had been a realm that Disney steered clear of for many years, but these shows proved popular enough that they became a window into the Disney world for an entire generation. While released by Walt Disney Pictures, *Duck Tales the Movie: Treasure of the Lost Lamp* was produced by the Walt Disney Television Animation Studio and was not a tremendous hit, grossing only $18.1 million at the box-office.

If Disney genuinely wanted to make their next animated feature successful, it would involve catering to audiences beyond just the family market that veered away from *The Rescuers Down Under*. The studio was going to have to make sure that moviegoers knew that what was coming next from Disney wasn't going to be a great *animated* film; it would be a great *film*.

This would involve one of the most demanding audiences in the world: New York audiences. In September of 1991, the Disney studio decided to screen their latest animated feature at the New York Film Festival, held each fall in Manhattan. One of the longest-running and most prestigious film festivals in the United States, the New York Film Festival is a non-competitive festival hosted by the Film Society of Lincoln Center.

The festival started in 1963 and has featured screenings of films by such directors as Bernardo Bertolucci, Ingmar Bergman, Robert Altman, and Martin Scorcese. Not exactly what one would immediately consider as a backdrop for the latest offering from the studio who gave us talking mice and singing dwarfs.

As an added level of difficulty, at the time of the festival, the film that Disney was looking to screen wouldn't be complete for another two months. Therefore, it would be shown in a "work-in-progress" form. All dialogue and music had been recorded, but not all of the animation was complete. The film would be a patchwork of completed scenes, rough drawings, and even still, storyboard images. This can make for a very schizophrenic movie-watching experience for a casual audience, let alone the discerning crowd that would be watching at the New York Film Festival.

Despite all of these waves pushing against their decision, this is how Disney decided to introduce their 30th animated feature, *Beauty and the Beast,* to the world. Many New York journalists sharpened their already critical pens. Jack Matthews of *New York Newsday* wrote:

"Of all the eccentric decisions made by this year's New York Film Festival committee, the most eccentric may have been the acceptance of Walt Disney Studios' offer to let the festival screen an unfinished print of *Beauty and the Beast*. Eccentric because films are rarely shown as work-in-progress at festivals, doubly eccentric because festivals tend to avoid movies that 6-year-olds can understand and which figure to outgross Canada in the same fiscal year."[57]

However, the wringing of many hands at Disney and forecasting where animation was headed was quickly put to rest on that early autumn night in New York City. The still-not-complete screening of *Beauty and the Beast* was met with enthusiasm by the customarily reserved audience, who rose to their feet for a standing ovation at the film's conclusion.

This early success provided promise for Disney's latest animated feature.

The story of *Beauty and the Beast* dates back to a 1756 French fairy tale by an author named Jeanne-Marie Leprince de Beaumont. At Disney, *Beauty and the Beast* had come up for consideration as a feature as far back as the 1930s, after Walt and his artists had completed *Snow White and the Seven Dwarfs*. While it never came to be at Disney during this time, other studios did adapt their versions, most notably French director Jean Cocteau in 1946, a 1976 made for TV movie with George C. Scott as the Beast and a popular TV series that aired from 1987-1990.

---

57 Jack Mathews, "From Disney's Animators, A Beauty of a Beast," *New York Newsday,* October 2, 1991, Section II.

It was around this time at Disney that writer Jim Cox submitted a treatment that set the film in the French countryside, which would carry over to the finished film. Glen LeRoy created a re-write that involved such bizarre elements as "body-swapping" and wizards that were quickly abandoned.

Disney approached Richard Williams of *Who Framed Roger Rabbit* to direct *Beauty and the Beast*. He declined but recommended Jill and Richard Purdum, who owned a commercial animation studio in London, to direct. The "Purdum version" (as it came to be known) was a non-musical and a much somber drama.

When a rough cut of this version was screened for Peter Schneider, the results weren't favorable, and the decision was made to completely re-work *Beauty and the Beast* and take it in another direction.

Joining the project at this tumultuous time was screenwriter Linda Woolverton, a novelist and writer for television animation before joining the film. She was asked to re-write a script for *Beauty and the Beast*, which had already been re-worked over several years at the studio.

Since joining the studio, both Eisner and Katzenberg had been adamant that if the story was to be a primary focus, Disney needed to shift away from only using storyboards and begin incorporating screenplays for their animated features.

Beauty and the Beast would rely heavily on the screenplay, incorporating scenes into a storyboard instead of solely relying on the storyboard process.

Woolverton would become the first woman to write an animated feature at the studio, and her work on *Beauty and the Beast* would prove to be a turning point for the film.

Wolverton infused her love of reading and independence into Belle, a character who could go "toe-to-toe" with the imposing Beast. She said of the character, "'Belle is a strong, smart, courageous woman. She sacrifices herself for her father. There are great themes of passionate love in the story, almost operatic themes. She's a Disney heroine who reads books. We've never seen that before.'"[58]

---

58 Bob Thomas, *Disney's Art of Animation: From Mickey Mouse to Beauty and the Beast* (New York, Hyperion, 1991) p.143.

Assisting with this rising tide of change for *Beauty and the Beast* were Howard Ashman and Alan Menken, coming off of their success with *The Little Mermaid*. With this film, not only did the duo contribute their Broadway-caliber songs, but Ashman once again brought his talents for not just story-telling but story problem solving to the process.

With the story heading in a new direction, the Purdams, who had a different perspective, eventually left the project; *Beauty and the Beast* was given to first-time directors Kirk Wise and Gary Trousdale.

Wise and Trousdale, like many of their peers, had come to Disney in the mid-eighties, both graduates of the California Institute of the Arts. Wise had started in character animation, while Trousdale was in effects. Before *Beauty and the Beast*, the two had worked on the story for *The Rescuers Down Under*.

They had formed a synergistic working relationship that proved to be perfect for co-directing a film like *Beauty and the Beast*. Wise said: "'A lot of directors are more comfortable with just splitting the movie into sequences and saying, 'Okay, you do this, and I'll do that.'" He also added: "'Gary and I do better when we collaborate; we like splitting up the areas of production more than splitting up the movie.'"[59]

Together, both Wise and Trousdale would helm two other Disney animated films over the next ten years, after *Beauty and the Beast*. Along with them on all of these films was producer Don Hahn.

Hahn came to the studio in 1976 and worked as an assistant director under Disney Legend Wolfgang Reitherman, a member of the Nine Old Men, who directed a number of the studio's animated features in the '60s and '70s. Hahn had served in several roles from production manager and associate producer on the Disney's animated films in the '80s and had a front-row seat for the launch and successful flight of the Animation Renaissance at Disney.

As producer, Hahn stated that he is the "film's advocate." He added that he goes "'...to bat for it in all areas with management, with marketing, with consumer products, to be the

---

59 Ibid p.158.

spokesperson, the host, the representative of the movie, to all areas of the Company. There has to be a single person who can look out for the interests of the movie.'"[60]

Beauty and the Beast was going to need this champion, as Disney was telling a very familiar story, in what seemed like a standard way, but with the traditional fairy tale filtered through the lens of an increasingly new perspective at the studio.

The film opens, creatively and grippingly, using stained glass windows to inform us of the "back story" of how the Beast was, in fact, a prince who an enchantress cursed after he was cruel to her. She transformed him into a hideous creature with a spell that can only be broken if he can love someone and find someone who returns his love.

This opening was a new spin on the Disney tradition of storybooks opening (such as in *Pinocchio* and *Cinderella*) to begin a story.

From here, we meet the film's heroine, Belle (voiced by noted Broadway star Paige O' Hara), and we learn about her perspective and intelligence through the charging opening song, "Belle." We also learn that Gaston (Richard White, another Broadway veteran), the most popular and most selfish man in town, longs for Belle. His affections are unrequited, and we meet Belle's father, Maurice (character actor Rex Everheart), the village's eccentric inventor.

When Maurice leaves the village to take his latest invention to a fair, he becomes lost in the woods and makes his way to the Beast's castle for refuge. Here, he is befriended by enchanted objects – Lumiere the candlestick (Jerry Orbach in full Maurice Chevalier voice), Cogsworth the clock (David Odgen Stiers of *M*A*S*H* fame), Mrs. Potts the Teapot (the perfect casting of Angela Lansbury) and Chip (child actor Bradley Pierce) the teacup, just to name a few.

As author Bob Thomas noted, these enchanted residents were the brainchild of Howard Ashman. The lyricist saw them as an antidote for a slower paced second act and added extra magic to the story.: "Ashman's solution was to make important

---

60 Ibid, p.157.

characters out of the servants who have been reduced to inanimate objects by the sorceress's spell...They would provide comedy and music while helping to advance the plot."[61]

The Beast eventually imprisons Maurice. Belle discovers this and takes his place, so her father can be free. The enchanted objects look to make Belle feel welcome and provide *Beauty and the Beast* with its tentpole moment: "Be Our Guest." The infectious showstopper of a musical number is performed for Belle by Lumiere and the other objects. An early version of the story had them performing the song for Maurice when he comes to the castle. The filmmakers discovered that the song worked better later in the film with Belle. Their instincts were correct, and "Be Our Guest" would elicit Broadway-style applause in movie theaters and set the bar high for similar scenes in future Disney animated features.

As Belle spends more time at the castle, she begins to see more than the imposing Beast and instead considers the kind, caring heart within. But, as this happens, jealous Gaston leads a group of torch-wielding villagers, who descend upon the castle to "Kill the Beast!" in the film's climactic battle.

But, as the lyrics to the title song and beautiful ballad, "Beauty and the Beast" state:

> "Bittersweet and strange
> Finding you can change
> Learning you were wrong..."

Belle and the Beast learn more about themselves and each other. They reflect the film's messages: looking beyond what you can initially see, the power of kindness, and, in all of its sincerity, the fact that love conquers all.

Adding to the two characters' emotions coming together for this first dance was an unlikely ally: computer animation. With *Beauty and the Beast*, the filmmakers once again used CGI to help tell their story, but this time it wasn't utilized for an action scene; this time, the technology was used as never before.

The film used computer animation in various ways, but most notably to create a three-dimensional ballroom for the

---

61 Ibid, p.146.

"Beauty and the Beast" song sequence. Combining the hand-drawn character elements with this allowed the filmmakers to mimic the movements usually only possible in a live-action film. In the scene, the camera seems to "swoop" down from the chandelier to the floor below, where the camera then "moves toward" a dancing Belle and Beast. Seamlessly blended, the technology adds not only a *visual* element of depth but an emotional one, as well.

The use of CGI this way in *Beauty and the Beast* was another "game-changer." The technology wasn't used simply as a "showcase," but instead as another tool to assist with telling an animated story and another way to allow animation filmmakers to tell their story using similar tools available to live-action directors.

Scenes like this also underline another element at work in the film. The Beast and Gaston mirror each other: one, a monster with a human heart and the other, a human with a monstrous soul. Gaston would be brought to the screen by supervising animator Andreas Deja.

The character would be the first of three iconic villainous performances in a row that Deja crafted during the Animation Renaissance. A native of Germany, Andreas first applied for a job as a Disney animator at ten years old after seeing *The Jungle Book*. He kept focused on this dream and years later, after high school and artistic training, joined the studio in 1980.

Since then, Deja has concentrated on not copying the Nine Old Men but instead building on all they accomplished. "It's not a question of doing what the old guys did and moving a dog exactly like they did in *Lady and the Tramp*. It's just the degree of excellence that you're always after. Some animators are less bothered by that..." he laughed, adding, "...and others, like me, are driven crazy by it!"[62]

For Gaston's inspiration and all his work, Deja consistently would turn to the legendary Disney artists who came before him, including Art Babbit, a genius of the medium, who had worked on several films during the studio's Golden Age in the '30s and '40s. "He said that an animator has to be interested

---

62 Andreas Deja interview with ML, February 14, 1994.

in so many things," remembered Deja of Babbit. "You have to be able to do a dinosaur doing the Charleston one day, and the next, you do a beautiful, realistic princess."[63]

For the vain Gaston, Deja found the character's roots in the blustery villain Brom Bones, from *The Legend of Sleepy Hollow* section of Disney's 1949 feature *The Adventures of Ichabod and Mr. Toad*. The animator added another layer, a touch of realism that he found in Hollywood.

Deja noted, "'It's not the eighteenth century, it's really NOW...You see these guys in clubs and restaurants and at the gym, of course. And then it starts to get a bit interesting...How modern? And Belle is too, in a way, being a girl who knows what she wants.'"[64]

Belle emerges with confidence right from her opening scene. At the ripe-young age of twenty-three, James Baxter supervised the animation of Belle. Baxter began working at Disney during his summer vacation after dropping out of art school, securing a job as an in-betweener on *Who Framed Roger Rabbit* and quickly ascended from there.

Baxter noted that Belle was a vibrant character to animate in that her strength and independence were so groundbreaking. Baxter said: "'It seems to be very difficult in a lot of stories to have the female lead be the motivator of the action, instead of just sitting there and having things happen to them...'"[65]

Belle, indeed, takes action, riding off to the Beast's castle to face him, courageously taking her father's place, and refuses to back down to the Beast's loud and threatening actions. In turn, she gradually changes the Beast as the character transforms perspective. This can be seen in the subtle acting that the character's supervising animator, Glen Keane brought to the Beast.

For the Beast's look, Keane used an amalgam of several animals from a buffalo, a lion, and a boar, and he observed a gorilla at the Los Angeles Zoo to incorporate animal movements into the character.

---

63 Ibid.

64 Ollie Johnston and Frank Thomas, *The Disney Villain*, (New York, Hyperion, 1994) pp.208-209.

65 Bob Thomas, *Disney's Art of Animation: From Mickey Mouse to Beauty and the Beast* (New York, Hyperion, 1991) p.182.

It all came together to form a distinct animal-like look that one couldn't pinpoint to one species. With this, Keane brought his talents for imbuing his work with emotion and depth to the Beast, a challenge for the animator, as the character's conflict for most of the film comes not from without but within.

As Keane noted, "'Usually in our pictures, the characters have an outside obstacle to overcome: the witch in *Snow White*, the stepmother in *Cinderella*. In *Beauty and the Beast*, his enemy is himself. It's that selfishness of the Beast inside him that he has to conquer and overcome.'"[66]

This is most evident for both the Beast and Belle, in the song "Something There," where each character confronts the feelings that are developing for the other, as they grapple with their internal struggle.

The song is one of the many now memorable and classic, created for the film by Alan Menken and Howard Ashman. As he did with *The Little Mermaid*, Ashman's creative fingerprints are all over *Beauty and the Beast* and he guided the film to its finale. *Beauty and the Beast*'s production would be different for him and the entire team.

Ashman had been diagnosed with AIDS in 1988, during the production of *The Little Mermaid*. As his health declined during the making of *Beauty and the Beast* and Ashman grew weaker, he could not travel to the Disney studio in California. The film's creative team flew to his home in Fishkill, New York (a suburb about 50 miles North of New York City) to work on the movie with him.

In March of 1991, Ashman's condition had worsened, and he was hospitalized. Even here, when he could barely speak, he still stayed in touch with the team and provided notes and comments on the story and songs.

Sadly, on March 14th, 1991, Howard Ashman passed away at the age of 40 due to complications from AIDS. As part of his indelible legacy, the music he provided for Disney stands as a mighty pillar for the studio's Animation Renaissance.

When *Beauty and the Beast* was released to theaters on November 22nd, 1991, the film's dedication read: "To our

---

66 Ibid p.174.

friend Howard, who gave a mermaid her voice and a beast his soul, we will be forever grateful."

This appreciation for what Ashman and the other artists did on the film was shared by all. Critical reviews unanimously praised the film, placing it on almost every top ten list for the year, as *Beauty and the Beast* went on to become the third highest-grossing film of 1991, with $145 million domestically.

On February 19th, 1992, the film's expectations were continually exceeded when *Beauty and the Beast* became the first animated feature film to receive the Academy Award nomination for Best Picture, a landmark feat that Walt himself was unable to accomplish with his classic films.

In all, *Beauty and the Beast* received six Oscar nominations, with three of the songs ("Beauty and the Beast," "Belle," and "Be Our Guest") taking up a large portion of the five songs nominated that year. The film would wind up taking home two Oscars, one for Best Original Score and one for Best Song, "Beauty and the Beast," an incredible, posthumous affirmation of Ashman's work.

Additionally, the song had proven to be a Top 10 hit on radio, performed by Celine Dion and Peabo Bryson.

As they did with *The Little Mermaid*, Disney wisely used all their ever-growing realms to provide the film with an immortal existence. In addition to a flood of merchandise, the characters appeared at the theme parks in shows, parades, and eventually attractions.

However, several years after the film opened, new, continued life was infused into *Beauty and the Beast*. With the film and *The Little Mermaid* creating a conversation around the fact that animation was the new home for Broadway musicals, Disney decided to step up to that rally cry.

On April 18th, 1994, Disney debuted a Broadway musical adaptation of *Beauty and the Beast* at the Palace Theater in New York City. The production expanded the story, adding additional songs and brought so much of that hard-to-define "Disney magic" to life on stage. The film won a Tony Award and allowed Disney to initiate a new entity of the Company, Disney Theatrical Productions, which would focus on future Broadway shows.

As years passed, love for the film has only increased. In 1997, Disney produced the popular direct-to-video sequel, *Beauty and the Beast: The Enchanted Christmas*; in 2002, the film was re-issued to IMAX theaters with a deleted song, "Human Again," added back into the film, and in 2017, Disney released a successful, all-star, live-action re-make. This was so successful, it began a new trend at Disney, where a number of their popular animated films have been re-imagined in live action.

Beauty and the Beast has continued to endear itself to audiences, animation enthusiasts, and Disney fans, making it evident that the standing ovation for that work-in-progress screening all those years ago in New York was a small harbinger of the praise to come.

Like *The Little Mermaid*, *Beauty and the Beast* has become a movie not only for a new generation of artists but a new generation of audiences, who quickly and continually embraced the film the same way a generation five decades earlier had done with *Snow White* and *Pinocchio*.

Even with this success, resting on their laurels wasn't going to happen any time soon at the studio. Disney animation had more to come, and it was waiting inside a magic lamp, ready to be released.

CHAPTER FOUR

"A Dazzling Place
I Never Knew"

Aladdin & The Nightmare Before Christmas

Could they do it again? This was the question on many lips as November of 1992 neared, and Disney readied their newest animated feature to make its debut.

The twelve months that had just passed were like one giant party, thanks to the success and shower of accolades that befell *Beauty and the Beast*. In October 1992, the film was released on home video, causing a resurgence in popularity. There seemed to be no slowing down this juggernaut of success. What "poor, unfortunate soul" of a film would be chosen as the follow-up to *Beauty and the Beast* in the Eisner-Katzenberg "one new animated film a year" plan?

In 1988, Howard Ashman submitted a 40-page treatment of a musical adaptation of *Aladdin*, based on the famous Arabic folk tale from the book *One Thousand and One Nights*. Disney chose this story, dating back to the 8th century, about a young man who finds a magic lamp that unleashes a wish-granting Genie as their follow-up to *Beauty and the Beast*.

And although *Aladdin* would be rooted in this story's traditions, the film itself would be anything but traditional. *Aladdin* uprooted what many considered Disney tradition to be.

Andreas Deja, who would animate the villain in the film, remembered a day as he finished up work on Gaston in *Beauty and the Beast* when his assistant, who had just seen some early artwork from *Aladdin*, came into his office.

"'Do you know what they're doing over there?' she said, agitated. 'Do you know what they're doing to the Genie? They're going to have him turn into Arnold Schwarzenegger.'"[67]

Deja didn't believe it, so he went over to have a look for himself and, sure enough, there was early animation of this comical Genie transforming into a litany of familiar celebrity caricatures: not only Schwarzenegger but Groucho Marx, Jack Nicholson, and Ethel Merman, just to name a few.

Deja realized just how different Disney's take on *Aladdin* would be, "'That's when it dawned on me...' We're not going to be doing this one by the book.'"[68]

John Musker and Ron Clements were once again co-directing for *Aladdin*, fresh off their success with *The Little Mermaid* and veering off in a new direction. The directors started with the treatment that Ashman had penned.

In this version, Ashman was somewhat faithful to the source material but gave the Genie a Cab Calloway-like flavor. In the story, Aladdin had a mother and three friends, Babkak, Omar, and Kassim. Additionally, Princess Jasmine, Aladdin's love interest, was fashioned as a spoiled-rotten princess.

Ashman and Menken had also penned six songs, including "Proud of Your Boy," a ballad Aladdin sings about how he longs to make something of himself and please his mother; "Babkak, Omar, Aladdin, Kassim," a fast-paced song of friendship and Jasmine's "Call Me A Princess," in which she sings about how she loves the finer things in life.

Musker and Clements re-worked this story slightly, adding a more comical Genie. In April of 1991, the entire film was laid out on story reels and presented to Katzenberg. It didn't go well.

Katzenberg noted, "'It just wasn't compelling.'"[69] Something that emerged from the screening was that Aladdin was not

---

67   Joe Rhodes, "What Would Walt Say?," *The Los Angeles Times*, November 8, 1992, latimes.com (accessed March 4, 2021).

68   Ibid.

69   Richard Corliss, "Aladdin's Magic," *Time*, November 9, 1992, content.time.com (accessed March 1, 2021).

a captivating character. "'We would look at the story reels,' Katzenberg said, 'and even Jasmine was blowing him away.'"[70]

In a painful move for all involved, what resulted from that meeting was that *Aladdin*'s story needed a complete overhaul, and the team would have to start over again (even more challenging: the film was now one year into production).

The characters of Aladdin's mother and best friends were excised. The persona of Jasmine shifted to that of a more confident character, who resents her father attempting to arrange her marriage to a suitor.

These changes, unfortunately, meant that a number of the songs that the late Ashman had created for *Aladdin* would need to go, as well. Several of the original songs would remain, but with this change, onboard the production came another Broadway veteran, lyricist Tim Rice (of *Evita* fame), who would be partnered with Alan Menken to fashion new songs for this refurbished version of the story.

As the film went through these changes, Musker and Clements held firm to their initial thoughts for *Aladdin*. They wanted the film to be faster paced, infused with contemporary sensibilities, and a shift from what one expected from Disney.

The first animator hired on to *Aladdin* was Eric Goldberg. Goldberg had been animating since he was a teenager and, at this point, was a seasoned veteran of the industry, who had gained the respect of his peers by having a talent for being a "chameleon" in animation, as he could adapt to a variety of styles.

When Musker and Clements asked Goldberg to come onboard the film in 1990, he owned his own, London-based animation studio, "Pizzaz Pictures," for six years, where he produced animation for several award-winning commercials. The directors knew that Goldberg's sensibilities would be perfect for *Aladdin*.

Goldberg would be the supervising animator for the Genie but began to create designs for all of the characters. For inspiration, Goldberg turned to one of his artistic heroes, artist Al Hirschfeld, most famous for his caricatures of Broadway

---

70 Ibid.

actors and singers that appeared in *The New York Times*. His work was featured there for over seven decades. He also contributed celebrity caricatures to other publications, such as *TV Guide* and *Rolling Stone*, becoming one of the most recognizable artists in magazines and newspapers.

"His work is eminently animatable," said Goldberg of Hirshfeld. "What he gets into a still drawing are the things that we strive for in animation. His work has elegance, simplicity, and suppleness of line."[71]

Hirschfeld's style was highly linear, with his caricatures looking as if they were created with one continuous, swooping line. *Aladdin*'s production designer Richard Vander Wende was partially basing the look and the backgrounds of the film on Arabic calligraphy, which had shapes like those in Hirschfeld's designs. In a fortuitous move, this would help merge the backgrounds and characters in a unified, creative vision.

This would also give *Aladdin* a look that was uniquely its own, particularly compared to any other Disney animated feature. But the look of the film wasn't going to be the only differentiator with *Aladdin*. There would be a casting coup with the film that would set many in the industry back on their heels, as Disney would land one of the biggest names in comedy for a critical role.

"'We always thought of Robin Williams as the Genie,'" Ron Clements admitted.[72] He and Musker wrote their story of *Aladdin* with Williams in mind, a considerable risk, as the comic genius hadn't been anywhere near close to being cast in the role.

Eric Goldberg took audio of one of Williams' stand-up routines about schizophrenia and animated the Genie in a sequence around it. Goldberg remembered, "'In the animation, I had him grow another head so that he could argue with himself about it.'"[73]

When Katzenberg showed Williams this footage and introduced him to Goldberg, the comedian signed on.

---

71 Eric Goldberg interview with ML, January 25, 1999.

72 Joe Rhodes, "What Would Walt Say?," *The Los Angeles Times*, November 8, 1992, latimes.com (accessed March 4, 2021).

73 Ibid.

Having Robin Williams a part of *Aladdin* meant that the movie was not going to go as planned, thanks to the comedian's well-loved brilliance when it came to improvisation. This was the reason he was brought on to the film, and he didn't disappoint.

Although Clements and Musker had written the Genie with Williams in mind, he quickly veered off in the first recording session, launching into his trademark stream-of-consciousness impressions and voices. In fact, during his first twenty-five recording sessions, he gave the artists twenty-five different takes.

As Goldberg recalled, "'What we got from him, though, was his entire bag of celebrity (impressions). We got everything. And, aside from the fact that you had to pick all of us up from the recording room floor, we just thought, 'We're going to have to use this stuff. It's too good not to. '"[74]

This is where Goldberg took his embarrassment of riches of Williams' overflowing performances and began to craft the shape-shifting Genie. Initially, Goldberg had envisioned the character "'...as a swirl of smoke with a nose and eyes. '"[75]

But, once Williams began his recording sessions, Goldberg knew what the character had to become, admitting, "'I felt I had a responsibility to the audience.'"[76] Goldberg had the task (and was up to it in so many creative ways) of realizing Williams's performance in the character. The animator said, "'The Genie had to deliver, both visually and in terms of humor. We had to go as far as we could go in the animation so that the audience would walk out knowing they had gotten their money's worth. '"[77]

With the combining of Williams and Goldberg's performances, not only did audiences get this money's worth, but they also probably owed the artists a payment. As Williams would slip quickly into an imitation, the Genie would morph into a caricature of the celebrity being imitated.

---

74 Ibid.

75 John Culhane, *Disney's Aladdin: The Making of the Animated Film,*" (New York, Hyperion, 1992), p.27.

76 Bob Thomas, *Disney's Art of Animation: From Mickey Mouse to Hercules* (New York, Hyperion, 1997), p.134.

77 Ibid, p.134.

In addition to these imitations, such as Schwarzenegger and Nicholson, the Genie also freely made or morphed into several contemporary references at a dizzying, almost subliminal pace. Among them were an airline flight attendant announcing the "exits" on the magic carpet before takeoff, a game show host, and a ventriloquist. Additionally, there were many "Disney in-jokes," such as a jab at a popular television campaign for Walt Disney World.

Even though the setting of *Aladdin* was purported to be the fictional, middle eastern city of Agrabah in the 8th century, the Genie seemingly was straight out of America in 1992. This type of contemporary injection was a first for Disney animation. It seemed to fly in the face of the more traditional standard that the studio's animated films should be timeless.

As it did with Deja's assistant during production, this took audiences and critics by surprise when the film opened. However, it was a *delightful surprise*, as noted by *New York Times* film critic Janet Maslin: "What will come through clearly to audiences of any age is the breathless euphoria of Mr. Williams' free associations, in which no subject is off-limits, even Disney itself."[78]

Before we even meet the Genie (which is almost the halfway point of the film), audiences are pulled in smoothly to *Aladdin*, thanks, once again, to compelling storytelling.

As the film opens, we meet an ordinary street Peddler (also voiced by Williams) who, with a mixture of comedy and mystery, breaks the fourth wall and introduces us to the story and the mysterious, seemingly, commonplace lamp.

We are then taken to the desert in the middle of the night. Here, we meet the scheming Royal Vizier Jafar (voiced by Johnathan Freeman, in a dramatic, throaty performance) and his parrot Iago (comedian Gilbert Gottfried). The two suffer a failed attempt to enter the mystical Cave of Wonders (brought to life through CGI, with its entrance in the shape of a tiger head).

They discover that they need "the diamond in the rough," who is the one-person worthy to enter.

---

78   Janet Maslin, "Disney Puts its Magic Touch on Aladdin," *The New York Times*, November 11, 1992, p.c15.

From here, we are on the streets of Agrabah, in the midst of a chase, and we meet the street urchin Aladdin (Scott Weinger with the singing voice of Brad Kane) and his pet monkey Abu (Frank Welker). The two attempt to outrun the palace guards as they look to steal food from the marketplace to eat.

Glen Keane, now one of the studio's master artists, supervised the animation of the character of Aladdin. He based the character's lean look on that of volleyball players he had seen playing at the beach and incorporated their triangular torso shape and narrow waist. He called upon what he termed the "intensity" that Tom Cruise would bring to his roles as an influence for the character's performance.

Keane added, "'I wanted to steer away from the Wimp Prince. What Ariel in *The Little Mermaid* did for the spunky Disney heroine is what we want Aladdin to do for the male leads.'"[79]

In Agrabah, The Sultan (Douglas Seale) is attempting to find a suitor for his daughter, Princess Jasmine (Linda Larkin, singing voice of Lea Salonga). The Princess, however, resents her father choosing who she should marry and is determined to make her own choices in life.

Like Ariel and Belle before her, Jasmine was a Disney Princess for a new generation. She was brought to the screen by supervising animator Mark Henn, who focused on the performance and the craftsmanship in his work.

"A lot of people can be an animator and move things around convincingly," said Henn. "The thing that I constantly struggle with is going beyond that and creating a performance. A person has to have a certain desire, approach it and ask themselves, 'What do I bring to this craft, this art form, that will, especially here at Disney, not only continue the high level that we have but also might advance it somewhere along the line?'"[80]

Henn, who joined Disney in 1980, had dreamed of becoming an animator since he was a young boy and got his dream in one of his first assignments, animating none other than Mickey Mouse in the 1983 featurette *Mickey's Christmas Carol*.

---

79 John Culhane, *Disney's Aladdin: The Making of An Animated Film*, (New York, Hyperion, 1992), p.63.

80 Mark Henn interview with ML, January 20, 1998.

Whether it's the company icon or a headstrong princess, Henn would join many of his peers as that new generation of animators who were re-defining the medium through their thoughtful artistry.

"The first thing that I usually do is put myself in whatever the character's situation is," said Henn of crafting believable personality animation. "I'm just trying to figure out how I might feel or react in a particular situation."[81]

To assist with this on Jasmine, Henn took some of his inspiration from his sister Beth and kept her high school photograph on his desk during the film's production.

Henn remembered, "'It was faded – I have carried it in my wallet for thirteen years – but I looked at my dark-haired sister and thought, 'Gosh, Jasmine is about high school age and has dark hair.'"[82]

Jasmine sneaks out of the Sultan's palace, where she meets Aladdin, who doesn't realize she is a princess. There is an almost immediate attraction between the two, abruptly ending when the guards capture Aladdin upon Jafar's orders. It's here that Aladdin discovers that Jasmine is the princess.

Jafar now knows that Aladdin is indeed the "diamond in the rough" and, disguised as an old man imprisoned with Aladdin, sneaks them both out of jail and back to the Cave of Wonders.

Deja, who animated Jafar, loved the work that Jonathan Freeman provided but said that the actor's disparate appearance from that of the character threw him off at first. "He looks nothing like the character," said Deja. "I got the voice recording first and had no idea who he was or what he looked like and based my design strictly on his voice. I saw this very linear, skinny skeleton-like creature with this big turban. Then, he [Freeman] came by and visited, and he looked nothing like that. I couldn't put his voice and body together!"[83]

As he always does, Deja then looked inward at the villain's motivations to round out the personality. "'What drives Jafar,' he asked himself. 'Hunger for power drives him. He answered.

---

81 Ibid.

82 John Culhane, Disney's Aladdin: The Making of An Animated Film, (New York, Hyperion, 1992), p.41.

83 Andreas Deja interview with ML, February 17, 1997.

'it starts with ambition – and greed. Familiarize yourself with the story.' He told himself, 'and with people driven by greed and the lust for power.'"[84]

In the story's early drafts, Jafar had a much different relationship with his "villainous other half." Originally, Jafar's temper was volatile, with Iago being the calming force, whispering in his ear, to cool him. Katzenberg saw an opportunity to swap these personalities – Jafar as quietly calculating with Iago as more explosive – and provide the film with a new dynamic.

Will Finn was the animator who brought Iago to the screen and remembered that the choice to "swap" the two character's personas had an instant, positive impact.

"'Jafar immediately became a more sinister and threatening villain, and Iago immediately became a funnier parrot. And John and Ron were the ones who pitched Gilbert Gottfried for the voice. And the day they said to me, 'You're going to do the parrot, and it's going to be Gilbert Gottfried,' I went home and said to Cindy, my wife: 'It's days like this that make it all worthwhile.'"[85]

Finn came to the studio at the age of twenty and immediately worked on *The Fox and the Hound*. He left after only nine months, pursuing other opportunities (with the Filmation studio and Don Bluth), returning to Disney in 1987, where he would eventually animate Cogsworth in *Beauty and the Beast*.

The comic sidekicks became Finn's niche and one that he excelled at and loved. He gave Iago Gottfried's toothy grimace and habit of hunching his shoulders during his comic routines. The result is a funny "release valve" to all of Jafar's evil calculating.

Jafar thinks he has obtained the lamp and leaves Aladdin and Abu trapped in the Cave of Wonders. It turns out that Abu has the lamp and when Aladdin rubs it, out comes the one and only Genie. Aladdin discovers that now that he has freed the Genie, the young "street rat" will be granted three wishes and is the Genie's "master."

---

84 John Culhane, Disney's Aladdin: The Making of An Animated Film, (New York, Hyperion, 1992), p.83.

85 Ibid, p.83.

After the two escape the Cave, Aladdin immediately wishes to be a Prince ("Prince Ali") so that he can impress Jasmine and the Sultan, marry Jasmine and live "happily ever after,"...or so he thinks. Jafar has other plans. He looks to marry Jasmine, take over the kingdom and expose Prince Ali as Aladdin.

One of the unique aspects of the "three wishes" that the filmmakers put into Aladdin is that the first one isn't just a simple "poof' wish, but instead is a grand moment in the film. The Genie doesn't just make Aladdin into a Prince but includes with it a royal caravan that parades into town in a big musical number, "Prince Ali."

This is one of the songs in *Aladdin* from the early versions of the story with lyrics by Howard Ashman. The other two were the Genie's big "show stopper, " "Friend Like Me," and the opening "Arabian Nights." The latter song caused controversy once the film was released. The American-Arab-Anti-Discrimination Committee (ADC) raised concerns over the song's lyrics, which were:

> "Oh, I come from a land, from a faraway place
> Where the caravan camels roam
> Where they cut off your ear
> If they don't like your face
> It's barbaric, but hey, it's home..."

Disney acted and changed the lyrics for *Aladdin*'s 1993 release on videocassette. The lyrics about "ear cutting" became: "Where it's flat and immense, and the heat is intense..."

The film's other songs were from lyricist Rice (who partnered with Menken). As the story evolved, Rice added "One Jump Ahead," as Aladdin outruns the guards at the beginning of the film. Rice also penned the film's ballad "A Whole New World," which Aladdin and Jasmine sing during their magic carpet ride (the song was another Top 40 hit and another Oscar winner for Best Original Song).

Aladdin continued to breathe new life into Broadway-style movie musicals and expanded into new technical realms with its use of CGI. Here, the Cave of Wonders was not only an awe-inspiring marvel of computer animation (that included a dizzying sequence that still plays like a theme park thrill ride), but the technology also helped shape one of the characters.

Supervising animator Randy Cartwright brought to life the Magic Carpet's excellent pantomime performance by hand. His pencil drawings were then scanned into the computer, where the pattern and design on the carpet were rendered. The character emerged as the first example of the two technologies merging as never before.

All of the creative forces behind *Aladdin* helped secure another success, this time with a film that slowly found its way into blockbuster status. When it opened on November 25, 1992, *Aladdin* grossed $19.2 million at the box office, coming in behind *Home Alone 2: Lost in New York*.

However, this time Macaulay Culkin wouldn't win again. Eight weeks after its initial release, a point when a film's box-office usually declines, the opposite happened with *Aladdin*. During the week between Christmas and New Year's Eve, the film became the number one movie in America and became the most successful film of 1992. By the end of its theatrical run, *Aladdin* would gross over $217 million domestically.

Aladdin had tremendous word-of-mouth power, most of which was driven by parents who found themselves in surprising fits of laughter thanks to Williams' Genie. This helped invite an older demographic to theaters to see *Aladdin*, a rarity for Disney films up to this point.

The Genie's success essentially changed animated vocal performances, characters, and animated storytelling going forward. Nathan Rabin, a writer with the film site *Rotten Tomatoes*, noted this:

"It's not too much of a stretch to say that the history of American animation can roughly be divided into pre-*Aladdin* and post-*Aladdin* eras. Though the film rode the wave of late 1980s/early1990s Disney hits like *The Little Mermaid* and *Beauty and the Beast*, it also represented a brash new beginning. After *Aladdin*, animated movies became increasingly star-driven."[86]

Additionally, animated features at Disney and other studios sought out some top comic talent. They began incorporating

---

86 Nathan Rabin, "How Robin Williams' Genie in Aladdin changed Animated Comedy Forever," RottenTomatoes.com, June 6, 2017, (accessed March 2, 2021).

contemporary references to recreate the lightning in a bottle (or magic in a lamp) that was the Genie.

The character was also embraced fully by the Disney company, his image appearing on any merchandise possible. His personality, a hyperactively hysterical host, made him perfect for theme park parades and shows.

At Disney theme parks, *Aladdin* was the subject of a parade, when the film opened and the characters from the film would be part of attractions, such as "The Enchanted Tiki Room," "The Magic Carpets of Aladdin" and the (now defunct) indoor, interactive theme park, DisneyQuest.

There was also a wildly popular stage show, "*Aladdin*: A Musical Spectacular," that ran at Disney's California Adventure from 2003-2016.

Not all was so magical when it came to the success and legacy of the Genie, however. Robin Williams had agreed to voice the character for Screen Actors Guild scale pay, under the condition that his name or image not be used in any marketing efforts. While Disney did honor this, they did use Williams voice in commercials and other marketing campaigns, which Williams was not happy with and felt violated their agreement.

Williams did not return to voice the Genie in the 1994 sequel, *The Return of Jafar*. At the time, the sequel was a rarity for Disney and more proof of just how popular *Aladdin* was. *The Return of Jafar* was released "direct to video" on VHS and went on to become one of the best-selling home videos of all time. With this success, "direct-to-video" sequels would become part of the Disney "model" for many of their animated films in the future.

After a change in leadership at the studio, the relationship with Williams and Disney improved. The comedian returned as the Genie in *Aladdin and the King of Thieves*, another "direct-to-video" sequel released in 1996.

With these successes, *Aladdin*, like *The Little Mermaid* and *Beauty and the Beast*, had a life well beyond its initial screen version. With the prevalence of home video, there was now an opportunity to enjoy these films whenever one wanted, and as much as one wanted (to some parents' chagrin).

Like many animated films of this period, *Aladdin* also became an animated TV series, a Broadway musical, and, most recently, was remade as a live-action film in 2019, with Will Smith placing his distinctive stamp on the character of the Genie.

All the success that came from *Aladdin* once again proved to audiences in 1992 that Disney animation wasn't just back, it was like the Genie itself, able to transform into something new for a new audience.

Could they do it again? Thanks to *Aladdin*, the answer was "Yes." But, for their next animated feature, the studio wouldn't "keep moving forward," but instead would take a step back.

In fact, Disney went back to the early 1980s, taking out of mothballs some conceptual artwork that a young artist, at the time, had created for a potential holiday television special.

The special was *The Nightmare Before Christmas*, and the young artist was Tim Burton.

Burton struggled as an animator at Disney, working on films like *The Fox and the Hound* and *The Black Cauldron*, which in no way represented his sensibilities. The studio did allow him to make two short subjects, *Vincent* (1982), a black-and-white stop-motion short subject about a young boy (with a striking resemblance to Burton) who dreams of being Vincent Price. Additionally, Burton directed a live-action version of *Hansel and Gretel* in 1983 for The Disney Channel and a live-action short film *Frankenweenie* (1984).

The latter film, also shot in black-and-white, told the story of a young boy who "rebuilds" his dog as a Frankenstein-like monster after it is run over by a car.

And, while his unique, creative style would feel stifled at Disney, these films would prove to be springboards for Burton. He eventually left Disney and launched an immensely successful career as a live-action film director with movies such as *Pee-Wee's Big Adventure* (1985), *Beetlejuice* (1988), and *Batman,* which broke almost every box-office record imaginable when it opened in 1989.

Around this time, Burton's agent contacted Disney to let them know that their client was interested in the artwork and story of *The Nightmare Before Christmas*. Burton wanted to revive the project, and Disney owned the content, as the artist had created it while working there.

Disney, meanwhile, wasn't even aware that the artwork was still languishing at the studio. Still, when discovered, they soon became interested, not just in returning the art but in partnering with Burton.

The director's attorney Melanie Cook remembered that the studio was eager to work with Burton, saying, "'This was post-*Batman*. And having already lost Tim when he was an animator there, no way they were going to let him get off the lot twice.'"[87]

Knowing his views clashed with what Disney was known for, Burton had reservations about re-joining the studio for the venture. At the time, Burton said: "'We were worried they were going to try to fit us into the type of cartoon movies they've been having so much success with.'"[88]

The director didn't want *Nightmare* transformed into an upbeat fairy-tale; he wanted a darker story, in look, in tone... in every way. And, he didn't want the film made through traditional 2D animation. Burton wanted to utilize an even more traditional art form: stop-motion animation.

With stop-motion, small, puppet-like figures are painstakingly posed and photographed one frame at a time. At this point, the technique had been around since the silent era and had been used in a number of films through the years, such as 1933's *King Kong* and 1963's *Jason and the Argonauts* (brought to life by legendary stop-motion artist Ray Harryhausen).

While directors like George Pal and studios like Rankin/Bass made careers out of stop-motion, Disney had only dabbled in this unique three-dimensional form of filmmaking. In 1959, the studio used stop-motion for their short subject *Noah's Ark*, and the medium was also used for two 1961 live-action films: the opening credits sequence of *The Parent Trap* and for effects in *Babes in Toyland*.

The Nightmare Before Christmas would use this technology for a full-length feature. To direct the film, Burton chose Henry Selick, who had built a successful career in stop-motion and, like Burton, had started his career as an animator at Disney during *The Fox and the Hound*.

After leaving Disney, Selick had worked at several studios and eventually gained notoriety for his short subjects and

---

87 Steve Daly, "Ghost in the Machine," *Entertainment Weekly*, October 29, 1993, p.31.
88 Ibid, p.31.

stop-motion animation work for MTV. As computer animation encroached on the traditions of animation in the 1990s, Selick was undeterred in his passion for the craft of stop-motion.

"Even in this day of super-impressive computer effects, which are only going to get more impressive over time, stop-motion still has this hold on my imagination," he said, adding, "I feel like I'm further and further out on a limb in the land of stop-motion, but the last thing I'm going to do is throw in the towel and try to compete, head-to-head, with everyone else in computers."[89]

Burton also enlisted another of his creative partners, musician Danny Elfman, who had written the score for all of the director's live-action efforts. With *Nightmare,* a musical, he would be writing the music and lyrics for the film's songs and providing the singing voice of the film's protagonist.

As Elfman and Burton began to collaborate on the film, they created a rough storyline, and songs began to be crafted, but a screenplay had yet to be penned. Michael McDowell, the writer of *Beetlejuice*, was brought in, but after "creative differences," he left the project.

Burton then turned to his collaborator on *Edward Scissorhands* (1990), writer Caroline Thompson, to come aboard to craft the script. However, when Thompson joined the project, Elfman had not only written several songs for the film, but sets had been created, and puppets had been built. Thompson traveled to the studios in San Francisco and found that the animators were already working and shooting scenes. Observing them at work and observing the scenes, she then crafted the screenplay. "It was like being an architect and being called in to build a house people were already living in," remembered Thompson.[90]

This circuitous production came together to tell the story of Jack Skellington (speaking voice of Chris Sarandon with Elfman singing), the hero of *The Nightmare Before Christmas.* We learn as the film opens that each holiday has its own "town" with doors leading to them on trees in a forest.

---

89 Henry Selick interview with ML, February 23, 1996.
90 Caroline Thompson interview with ML, March 11, 1996.

Jack is the Pumpkin King of Halloweentown and, as the story begins, it is Halloween night, another successful year, and the bizarre citizens of Halloweentown must go to work planning for next year.

Jack, however, feels that something is missing, a longing for something more, and he wanders out of Halloweentown.

The idea of the main character struggling with their place in the world, trying desperately to fit in, had been a recurring theme in several of Burton's films up to this point, and the director has noted how he had felt like this throughout his life.

Elfman related to this, as well. He called *Nightmare* "'one of the easiest jobs I've ever had. I had a lot in common with Jack Skellington.'"[91]

Jack leaves to the dismay of Sally (voice of Catherine O'Hara). Sally is a stitched-together rag doll and the creation of Dr. Finklestein (William Hickey). She also carries a torch for Jack.

"I grew my part of the story out of the Sally character," said Thompson of the female lead, who was much more of an Elvira-like persona in early versions. "I wanted her to be much frailer, more like a little match-stick girl version of a Frankenstein monster." [92]

Sally also has premonitions of a dangerous future, as Jack wanders into the forest, finding doors to other holidays on nearby trees. After curiously opening one, he stumbles into Christmastown.

Jack, who has never seen another holiday other than his own, is so taken aback he can't help but wonder "What's This?" singing the song of the same name, one the songs that Elfman crafted. *Nightmare*'s songs stand in stark contrast to the upbeat, "Broadway-ready" tunes that had been part of the previous Disney films. If there was a stage analogy, Elfman's were more akin to a somber operetta like *Sweeney Todd* (which Burton would adapt as a film in 2007) than anything else, which certainly fit with the film.

The whole concept of Christmas so enraptures Jack that he concocts a plan to take over the holiday, putting his own, Halloween-esque spin on it. The result is disastrous, almost

---

91 Mimi Avins, "Ghoul World," *Premiere*, September 26, 1993, pp.24-30, (quote accessed through Wikipedia.com on March 2, 2021).

92 Caroline Thompson interview with ML, March 11, 1996.

bringing an end to both holidays (there *is* a happy ending, it's not *that* dark).

As *The Nightmare Before Christmas* neared its release date, an early screening elicited some concern from many at the studio, namely Jeffrey Katzenberg. At the time, Selick observed, "'They've never had a film like this before, and they're terrified.'"[93]

Indeed they were. The film's gruesome characters and bleak, almost shocking moments (Santa Claus *does* get kidnapped after all) caused Disney to change some of their release decisions.

Nightmare was originally to be released by Walt Disney Pictures but then shifted over to the Touchstone banner, as there was a thought that it had more "adult" concepts. Additionally, its original release date of Thanksgiving was bumped up to October to align the film more with Halloween than Christmas. Finally, the official title was changed to *Tim Burton's The Nightmare Before Christmas* to affiliate the film with what audiences had expected from the director.

Disney returned to The New York Film Festival to premiere *The Nightmare Before Christmas* on October 9, 1993. From here, *Nightmare* was given a limited release on October 13, 1993, and then opened wide on October 29, 1993.

While some critics praised the movie's artistry and originality, others were less favorable. Owen Gleiberman in *Entertainment Weekly* dubbed it "Holloween." *Nightmare* went on to gross $50 million in the U.S., which was nowhere near *Beauty and the Beast* or *Aladdin*.

By Christmas season, the film was barely showing in theaters, and the *Nightmare* toys that had been created as part of the film's release were now relegated to toy store bargain bins.

The thought was that the movie was a valiant effort at something decidedly different, and it was time to move on to other projects. But, over time, many at Disney would find themselves like Jack, saying, "What's This?"

In the decade that followed *Nightmare*'s release, a cult following continually grew into something bigger. During this time, the film's small fan base grew outside of Disney's usual base to include Burton's regular fans, as well as many in the "Goth community."

---

93 Steve Daly, "Ghost in the Machine," *Entertainment Weekly*, October 29, 1993, p.31.

Additionally, collectors began to rabidly seek out all things *Nightmare*. Richard Kraft, a California-based talent agent, was one of them. By 1995, he had seen the film 300 times and was seeking out one of every piece of merchandise that had been produced when the film was released, as well as original puppets and sets used in the film's production.

"'*Nightmare* works on so many levels,' said Kraft. "'Visually, it's so overwhelming that you can sit through the movie just to marvel at the technical side of it and everything in it is so 'Tim Burtony' and so delightful.'"[94]

Many shared Kraft's passion for the movie, and by 2006, the groundswell of support for *Nightmare* was something that Disney couldn't ignore any longer. That October, the film returned to theaters in 3D (ironically, now being released under the Walt Disney Pictures banner). Additionally, *Nightmare* product was no longer a rare, hard-to-find collectible, but instead, Jack and Sally began to appear as regularly in Disney merchandise as Mickey and Minnie.

In 2012, Burton directed a feature length, stop-motion re-make of his live-action short *Frankenweenie* for Disney. The film debuted in theaters its opening weekend, as part of a late-night double feature with *The Nightmare Before Christmas*.

Selick, reflecting on the immense popularity for his film that continues to grow with each year, has said, "'It just sort of had this life beyond its first release, growing from a cult-size audience to a very large cult audience of people dressed up in the costumes, and with tattoos, and with songs inspired by it...So, no, we never could have foreseen this.'"[95]

Just as the future success of *Tim Burton's The Nightmare Before Christmas* was unexpected at the time, no one at Disney was ready for the record-breaking blockbuster that was waiting for them the following summer.

---

94 Michael Lyons, "Every Collector's Nightmare," *Collectors' Showcase Magazine*, December/January 1995/1996, p.11.

95 Scott Collura, "The Nightmare Before Christmas 3-D: 13 Years and Three Dimensions Later," ign.com, October 20, 2006 (accessed on web.archive.org on March 3, 2021).

CHAPTER FIVE

"I'm Gonna Be a Mighty King"

The Lion King, A Goofy Movie & Pocahontas

There are wild animals on the stage at Radio City Music Hall. A lion, an elephant, and other beasts entirely out of their elements, yet well cared for, stare out of their cages and pens at reporters sitting on bleachers.

It's winter of 1994, and Disney is holding their annual "press event" at New York City's hallowed and palatial Radio City Music Hall to announce and discuss their upcoming animated feature. Jeffrey Katzenberg, artists, and filmmakers, sit on stools ready to talk, show scenes from the film, and answer questions. Plastic plants line the stage's side to set the mood, and large stills from the film hang on the wall behind them.

Disney is making a big deal out of talking about a movie called *The Lion King*, but what they're about to see in around another four months is that it will all be worth it.

The Lion King would sweep across the movie and animation industry in June of '94 like the wind across the African savanna. After restoring audiences' faith in Disney animation with *Beauty and the Beast* and *Aladdin*, *The Lion King* would be a grand promise of what was possible and now fulfilled.

The film would be a success, the likes of which the studio had never seen. It would also secure a place in our pop-culture consciousness with scenes, songs, and dialogue that have become part of our film and Disney lexicon.

But, before just the mere mention of the title, *The Lion King* conjured up instant memories for a generation; the film began as a conversation between Roy E. Disney, Jeffrey Katzenberg, and Peter Schneider in the late '80s.

Originally entitled *King of the Jungle*, *The Lion King* would incorporate story elements from *The Bible*, *Hamlet*, *Bambi*, and *Star Wars*.

Don Hahn, returning to his role of producer on *The Lion King*, noted, "'It has very much the hero's-journey structure to it: whereby a character is catapulted into growing up by some catastrophic incident in his life. Then, he has to conquer many things, get over many hurdles, seek the wisdom of a wise man, and return triumphant to his kingdom.'"[96]

While this story structure has been around for as long as storytelling itself, what was new for Disney with *The Lion King* was that it would be the first original animated story developed "in-house" and not generated from another source (such as a fairy-tale or book).

What was also unique about *The Lion King* was that the studio was having trouble attracting their animators to work on it. With its "talking animals," there was a feeling of "been there done that" for many artists. *The Lion King* became dubbed the "B" project at Disney, and many at the studio wanted to work on what was considered the "A" project, which was the next animated feature in the pipeline at the time.

With this, *The Lion King* resulted in many newer, younger artists at the studio getting promotions, as co-director Roger Allers noted: "'I think it gave an opportunity for a lot of young animators who hadn't had a chance to lead a character. So, they were fired up to do a good job – it was a quiet and inclusive, and creative circle. Everyone was listened to.'"[97]

Allers came to Disney in 1985, working on the storyboards for *Oliver & Company*, *The Little Mermaid*, and *Beauty and the Beast*, just to name a few. His strong sense of story led him to co-director on *The Lion King*, with *Oliver & Company* director George Scribner.

96 Bob Thomas, *Disney's Art of Animation: From Mickey Mouse to Hercules*, (New York, Hyperion, 1997), p.138.

97 Susan King, "A 'Lion's' Tale," *Los Angeles Times*, September 15, 2011, latimes.com (accessed March 9, 2021).

During production, Scribner left the project due to artistic differences, and Rob Minkoff came on board to co-direct *The Lion King* with Allers.

Minkoff, who joined Disney in 1983 as an in-betweener and worked his way up to director on the Roger Rabbit short subjects *Tummy Trouble* (1989) and *Roller Coaster Rabbit* (1990), came on-board as co-director of *The Lion King* at a time when the artists had done a tremendous amount of research.

The team had traveled to Kenya, coming back so inspired that Africa became another character in the film. Additionally, experts from zoos in San Diego and Miami brought animals, including lions, into the studio for artists to study anatomy and movements close up.

"There's a certain feline quality about the way they move, which is sort of graceful and very loose," said Ruben Aquino, supervising animator for the film's lead character, Adult Simba. "You can see this in your typical house cat, but because lions are so much larger and so much heavier, there's a difference in the way they carry their weight."[98]

Of these earlier days of the film's production, Minkoff said, "'The film was very much a drama. We kind of started over and said, let's look at this movie in a different way and try to make it a bit more, not only mythical but add a bit of magic to it.'"[99]

There were revisions to the story and the title changed from *King of the Jungle* to *The Lion King*. Through research, the team learned that a lion's natural habitat is the savanna and not a jungle.

Another idea centered on bringing more magic to the film was to make it a musical. For *The Lion King*, Disney once again turned to *Aladdin* lyricist Tim Rice, but for the music, instead of the Broadway community, the studio would look to popular music and one of the biggest names in that realm.

Rice approached Elton John to join him in crafting the songs for *The Lion King*. The legendary, award-winning musician agreed as he saw this as an opportunity to do something new with the Disney animated musical, as he told *Billboard* magazine: "'...I

---

98   Ruben Aquino interview with ML, February 14, 1994.

99   Susan King, "A 'Lion's' Tale," *Los Angeles Times*, September 15, 2011, latimes.com (accessed March 9, 2021).

said, 'Let's do it for kids because it's just a great story.' But most of Disney's animated movies have a kind of Broadway score, and I said, 'Let's not go for that, let's go for a completely different feel and just write ultra-pop songs kids would like; then adults can go and see those movies and just get as much pleasure out of them.' I mean, adults buy a lot of pop records.'"[100]

The music legend's intuitions were, of course, correct; not only did the songs that John and Rice create for *The Lion King* work for the story, but several of them went on to become inescapable Top 40 hits, playing on radio stations well into 1995.

One of these was "The Circle of Life," which opens *The Lion King*. It is performed beautifully by singer Carmen Twillie in one of the studio's most stunning and compelling animated sequences that immediately pulls us into the film. A pitch-black screen gives way to a jolting shot of a blood-red sunrise that's accompanied by the chanting Zulu lyrics that lead into the song.

Animals from all over the Pride Lands are descending on Pride Rock for the presentation of baby Simba, the lion cub who has just been born to Mufasa (the lion-like voice of James Earl Jones), King of the Pride Lands, and his wife Sarabi (Madge Sinclair). Rafiki, the wise shaman baboon (Robert Guillaume), presents Simba to all of the animals, as "The Circle of Life" builds to its crescendo and the screen "slams to black" with the title card: *The Lion King*.

An opening for a Disney animated film, unlike any other. Once it's over and the film has begun, we meet the villain, Scar. Brother to Mufasa, he is a sharp-angled scrawny lion who is now brooding in his jealousy of never being able to ascend the throne, thanks to the birth of Simba.

Scar was brought to the screen by Andreas Deja and the animator was careful with his inspirations for the third character in his triumvirate of Disney villains. The last "big cat" to be in a similar villainous role was Shere Khan in *The Jungle Book*, created by one of Deja's idols, legendary animator Milt Kahl.

"There was a big danger for me to take what Milt had done and just build everything around that," Deja said. "I had

---

100   Jim Bessman, "Elton John: 30 Years of Music with Bernie Taupin," *Billboard*, October 4, 1997, p.95, books.google.com (accessed March 9, 2021).

studied Milt's work and the tiger my whole life and knew a lot about what he put into it and how he would move this large cat around. But I thought I cannot do that. It would look like someone put a wig on Shere Khan and called it a lion." Deja also added, "There were certain elements for this particular character that is not Shere Khan. Scar is much scrawnier. He wants to be the King, but he isn't, and he wants to take on his brother, but he's physically weaker."[101]

A significant influence on the character was Jeremy Irons, the actor, who brought the same venom-dripping malevolence to his vocal performance with Scar, as he did in his Academy Award-winning role as Claus von Bulow in 1990's *Reversal of Fortune*.

"He surprises you with almost every sentence," said Deja of the actor. "The way he would shape those words, it's unexpected and very imaginative, and you close your eyes, and you just want to animate right now!"[102]

Irons was the perfect choice for Scar, as he connives to ascend the throne and allies himself with the hyenas Shenzi, Banzai, and Ed (Whoopi Goldberg, Cheech Marin, and Jim Cummings, respectively).

Meanwhile, Young Simba (Jonathan Taylor Thomas, with the singing voice of Jason Weaver) bonds with his father, Mufasa learning how we are all connected in the great Circle of Life and how our ancestors are always watching over us and unite us to our past.

But this father and son bond is shattered when Scar's plan becomes a reality. He lures his nephew to a gorge and uses the hyenas to start a stampede of a large herd of wildebeests in a terrifying action sequence that was brought to the screen, thanks again to CGI.

With *The Lion King*, the filmmakers looked to blend the computer animation into the scene seamlessly. A prototype wildebeest was hand-drawn and then replicated by the computer to be animated in larger numbers, but still not look out of place in the world with Simba and the other characters.

---

101 Andrea Deja interview with ML, February 14, 1994
102 Ibid.

As co-director Minkoff remembered, this was not without its challenges: "'The animals looked great in profile, but when the computer made them turn, they wouldn't look so good anymore.'"[103]

The CGI wizards finessed this, finding a way to make this emerging technology work for the scene. Minkoff noted, "'The technician animators had to create a herding and avoiding program, wherein the wildebeests could run and turn in random patterns without smashing into each other or passing through each other.'"[104]

The riveting sequence would end with an emotionally painful scene: the death of Mufasa.

Scar had tricked Mufasa into coming to the gorge and then engineered the death of his brother. At the end of this gut-wrenching moment comes the second one-two punch, when Simba comes across the body of his dead father.

Reflecting on this moment, Minkoff noted: "'We were trying to test the boundaries of what was possible in an animated movie, a family movie, a *Disney* movie.'"[105]

The scene in *The Lion King* became a flashpoint. Film critics immediately placed warnings to all parents in almost every review ("Richard Corliss, in *Time* magazine, said, 'Get ready to explain to the kids why a good father should die violently and why a child should have to witness the death.'")[106]

And the first generation of Disney animators spoke up, as Andreas Deja remembered in his blog in 2011: "'We wouldn't have done that,' I remember Ollie saying. 'Remember *Bambi*? We never showed the dead body of his mother.'"[107]

The sequences featuring the death of Bambi's mother and the death of Mufasa were equally extremely emotional for both the generations who first saw them in theaters, as well as generations to follow.

---

103   Jami Bernard, "Disney's 'Lion King' Roars Out of Africa," *The New York Daily News*, June 12, 1994, p.17

104   Ibid.

105   Priscilla Frank, "It Took a Disney Kingdom to Kill Cartoon Mufasa," July 19, 2019, Vulture.com (accessed March 10, 2021).

106   Perri Klass, "A 'Bambi' for the '90's, Via Shakespeare," *The New York Times*, June 19, 1994, "Arts & Leisure" Section.

107   Andreas Deja, "Ollie Johnston," *Deja View*, June 24, 2011, andreasdeja.blogspot.com, (accessed March 10, 2021).

From this painful scene, *The Lion King* mercifully switches gears quickly. Simba, banished from the Pride Lands by Scar, grows into adulthood (now voiced by Matthew Broderick, with the singing voice of Joseph Williams) and is befriended by Timon the meerkat and Pumbaa the warthog (the hysterical teaming of Nathan Lane and Ernie Sabella, respectively).

They teach Simba their "problem-free philosophy," "Hakuna Matata." Simba is then paid a surprising visit by lioness Nala (Moira Kelly, the singing voice of Sally Dworsky), his childhood friend and soon-to-be love interest. She tells Simba that Scar is now ruling and that the situation in the Pride Lands is dire.

Thanks to a thoughtful lesson from Rafiki, Simba knows that he must head back to reclaim Pride Rock from his Uncle Scar and take his rightful place in the "Circle of Life."

What made the story of *The Lion King* most compelling to all involved (and eventually audiences) is that it was utilizing an all-animal cast to tell this very human story. "There's a total absence of humans," said Deja. "They're not even referred to; they simply don't exist, and yet, it is about human problems."[108]

Word of just how special the movie is began to spread well in advance of *The Lion King's* release. In an ingenious move, Disney released the entire opening "Circle of Life" sequence as a "teaser trailer," months before opening, which generated tremendous attention.

The film was building incredible positive momentum...and then tragedy befell The Walt Disney Studios. Sadly, on April 3, 1994, Frank Wells died in a helicopter crash while skiing in Nevada.

Wells, the President of The Walt Disney Company, alongside Michael Eisner, had been instrumental in Disney's ascension in the ten years since he had joined the company. Not just a business partner, Wells was a confident and friend to Eisner and was beloved by the Disney team. His absence left a tremendous gap for the company.

When *The Lion King* bowed in theaters on June 24, 1994, the film was dedicated to Frank Wells with a title card that appeared just before The Walt Disney Pictures logo.

---

108 Andreas Deja interview with ML, February 14, 1994.

As movement toward the film's release date continued, *The Lion King* became less of a movie and more of an event (a "mane event," if you will).

Before opening at neighborhood theaters, Disney debuted the film on June 15th at different venues on each coast: Radio City Music Hall in New York and The El Capitan Theatre in Los Angeles. At these theaters, the film played with a stage show featuring the Disney characters, songs, and musical numbers, under the banner "*The Lion King* Summer Spectacular."

By the time the film came to theaters everywhere, there had been an almost non-stop parade of Disney marketing. There were commercials and "making of" specials on TV, as well as *The Lion King* toys on shelves and a fast-food promotional partnership with Burger King.

The release of the soundtrack about a month prior, soared to number one on the *Billboard* charts, a first for the soundtrack of an animated film. *The Lion King* was the first recipient of the Recording Industry Association of America's Diamond Award, for albums that sell 10 million copies.[109]

In the summer of 1994, you couldn't escape *The Lion King*, to the point that, if you did miss it, you felt left out. The concept of turning their films into much more significant events was a model Disney (and many other studios) would use throughout the '90s, with each year's promotions seemingly topping the one prior.

But *The Lion King* was so much more than marketing showmanship. It was well-crafted storytelling, artistry, and filmmaking that Disney animation had been building toward for almost a decade.

"At the screening, I attended," wrote film critic Michael Medved when *The Lion King* opened, "the crowd greeted the conclusion of the movie by rising from their seats for a two-minute ovation: in 14 years of reviewing films, I've never seen a comparable reaction."[110]

The Lion King grossed $40.9 million in its opening weekend and passed the coveted $100 million mark by July 4th.

---

109 Tim Hollis and Greg Ehrbar, *Mouse Tracks: The Story of Walt Disney Records*, (Mississippi, University Press of Mississippi, 2006), p.185.

110 Michael Medved, "Disney's Pride & Joy," *New York Post*, June 15, 1994, p.29.

With *The Lion King*, Disney indeed had something special. Not just another successful film that would endure for generations, but a story that connected with audiences in a personal and emotional way.

This success was not without its controversies. Shortly after its release, many criticized the film's scarier scenes and violence. Others seriously claimed that the hyenas' characters were racist, and that Scar was effeminate (and the film homophobic). Additionally, there were claims that the story plagiarized a popular Japanese animated TV show, *Kimba the White Lion*.

Despite this, *The Lion King* went on to generate $763 million in its initial run. The film was so successful that by the end of that summer of '94, Disney made the unprecedented decision to pull the movie from theaters and re-issue it several months later for Thanksgiving.

Within all of this massive success for Disney, this was a time of great tension at the studio, particularly between Jeffrey Katzenberg and Michael Eisner.

Katzenberg had been lobbying for a promotion at Disney. When that didn't happen after Frank Wells' death, it resulted in Katzenberg leaving Disney in the fall of 1994.

Partnering with Steven Spielberg and David Geffen, they would form their own studio, DreamWorks SKG, producing animated films and becoming a significant competitor in the industry. Katzenberg's leaving was another major change at The Walt Disney Studio in less than the span of a year.

He had been one of the instrumental leadership forces that helped shepherd Disney animation back to a rightful place of prominence.

The Lion King was a prime example of this and had quite the impact, fueling so many other areas of the company, most notably products, music, and playing a significant role in 1998 when the company opened Disney's Animal Kingdom theme park at Walt Disney World in Florida.

Additionally, the film's unique staying power created a resurgence three years after its release, when *The Lion King: The Broadway Musical* opened in 1997. The play shattered Broadway records, going on to be the highest-grossing Broadway production in history and winning the Tony Award that year for Best Musical.

In 2019, twenty-five years after its release, Disney produced a computer-animated remake of *The Lion King*, featuring photorealistic animals and settings. A testament to the story's enduring power, the remake shattered several previous box-office records, becoming the highest-grossing animated film of all time to date.

Reflecting upon the immense legacy that the original *Lion King* had, producer Don Hahn, speaking on a documentary for the film's release on DVD, summed it up perfectly, saying:

"'No one, I don't care who they are or what they say, sets out to make a worldwide event or something that influences culture. In fact, if you set out to do those things, you'd probably fail. All we have, as one of the great Disney animators Eric Larson once said, is sincerity. It's our gift to the audience. So, when you try to put that across, people feel that. '"[111]

Sincere and successful. Not bad for a film that was considered the "B" project at the studio. *The Lion King* had been the film that many artists had passed on being a part of, in favor of the other animated feature that was in production at the time, the "A" project.

However, before that "A" project came to theaters, Disney would release *A Goofy Movie*, starring one of the most well-known and beloved members of their cartoon canon.

A truly "under the radar" production, Don Hahn recalled of *A Goofy Movie,* "'It wasn't even a B movie. It was a C movie.'"[112]

Despite not being as high profile as other Disney projects, *A Goofy Movie* came about thanks to the Disney TV series *Goof Troop's* success. While still at the studio, Katzenberg greenlit the film after he bonded with his daughter on a road trip. That idea of a parent and their estranged child growing closer became the basis for the film.

Kevin Lima was chosen to direct this father-son adventure. Lima had attempted to work at Disney after graduating college in the mid-'80s but could not join the studio. "When I was

<hr>

111 *The Lion King: Platinum Edition* DVD, 2003, Disc 2.

112 Drew Taylor, "Underdogs: How *A Goofy Movie* Became Disney's Unlikely Sleeper Hit," *Vanity Fair,* April 8, 2020, vanityfair.com (accessed March 11, 2021).

in school, Disney suddenly said, 'We're not taking any more people.' Here you were, at school, wanting to work at Disney your whole life, and you're told, 'Sorry the inn is closed.'"[113]

After working on several non-Disney animated films, Lima finally came to the studio, where he worked on *Oliver & Company* and *The Rescuers Down Under*. Here, he brought his unique, outgoing sense of story and character. "I stand up on the table and act things out," admitted Lima. "I'm notorious for that."[114]

This perspective was perfect for directing *A Goofy Movie*. As the film opens, we learn (through a hysterical, nightmare dream sequence) that Goofy's teenage son Max (voice of James Marsden, singing voice of Aaron Lohr) is terrified of turning into his father (literally).

Goofy (Bill Farmer, who, at this point, had been voicing the character since 1987) is terrified that Max is falling in with the wrong crowd at his high school and the two are growing apart. So, he concocts an idea for the two of them to take a summer road trip to "Lake Destiny," a family-favorite fishing hole.

Max, however, has other ideas on the last day of the school year. He has a crush on Roxanne (Kellie Martin), a girl at school who will be going to a big party, where all the kids will be watching a Pay-Per-View concert of singer Powerline (a "mash-up" of Bobby Brown and Michael Jackson, voiced by singer Tevin Campbell).

Embarrassed at the thought of spending summer vacation with his father, Max lies, telling Roxanne that he can't make the party because he and his dad are driving cross-country to see the Powerline concert.

Goofy is oblivious to this, as he and Max set off "On the Open Road," one of the film's catchy songs by Tom Snow and Jack Feldman, with Patrick DeReemer and Roy Freeland crafting the Powerline songs.

"We wanted to create this feeling that you're about to go on this musical adventure," said Bambi Moé, who served as associate producer for the music in *A Goofy Movie*. She also added,

---

113   Kevin Lima interview with ML, January 22, 1999.
114   Ibid.

"What Tom Snow and Jack Feldman did so well provided that heart through the character's songs. They know that the best songs and musicals are the ones where it moves the story along and adds emotional subtext."[115]

In this story, Goofy and Max wind up on several road-trip adventures. Among the highlights are a stop at "Lester's Possum Park," a self-deprecating jab at Disney's theme park attraction, "The Country Bear Jamboree," and a run-in with Bigfoot that brings some well-choreographed slapstick animation and sight gags.

A Goofy Movie was produced through Disney Toon Studios, (created not at the studio in California, but at Disney's studios in Paris and Australia, as well as "outside studios" in Canada and Spain). The film was released on April 7, 1995, after a technical glitch delayed its debut from Thanksgiving 1994. "'In those days, you'd set up a camera looking at a large monitor, and you would film that monitor,' Lima explained. 'One of the pixels was blown out, and every single scene in the movie had a black dot on it. So, we had to go back and reshoot three-quarters of the film. '"[116]

When it was released, *A Goofy Movie* was not Disney's usual "event movie." It had minimal publicity and other than a fast-food promotion at Burger King, there were no toys or products. The film quickly came and left theatres, generating only $35.3 million (less than *The Lion King* made in just its opening weekend).

All of this weighed against *A Goofy Movie,* and it began to slip into obscurity. Then, three magical letters – VHS- brought it back to life. A generation now growing up with the Disney films at home began to watch the movie, over and over.

An obsessive cult following for *A Goofy Movie* continued to grow into the mainstream. In 2009, a fan-made YouTube video featuring a live-action recreation of one of the film's songs, "After Today," became a viral hit. "I would argue with anyone that "After Today" is one of the best opening numbers," said Moé. "I would love to see it performed on stage."[117]

---

115   Bambi Moé interview with ML, June 25, 2021.
116   Drew Taylor, "Underdogs: How *A Goofy Movie* Became Disney's Unlikely Sleeper Hit," *Vanity Fair,* April 8, 2020, vanityfair.com (accessed March 11, 2021).
117   Bambi Moé interview with ML, June 25, 2021.

Clothing and other merchandise from the film also began to appear. *Vanity Fair* magazine reported of a milestone celebration for *A Goofy Movie*: "A 20th-anniversary cast reunion at the 2015 D23 Expo, Disney's official biannual fan convention, felt more like a rock concert than a celebration of a seemingly obscure animated favorite."[118]

Moé said that, to this day, if the film comes up in conversation, it still elicits an amazing response: "I was out with a group of people and was talking with this young man and mentioned that I had worked on the music for *A Goofy Movie*. I thought he was going to pass out! He was so excited because he was a writer and a recording artist, and he had recorded a couple of songs from *A Goofy Movie*!"[119]

Whether it was reveling in '90s nostalgia or the universal theme of bridging the generation gap, audiences love the film. "It's so rewarding," said Moé of the film's newfound popularity. "But I have to be honest, at the time we were making it, I felt it was brilliant."[120]

A Goofy Movie is now something it wasn't when it was released: a hit. Instead, when it opened in 1995, what many audiences remembered about going to see *A Goofy Movie* was seeing a trailer just before it, which was for that eagerly awaited "A" project film, *Pocahontas*.

The idea to bring history to Disney animation started in the early '90s. Artist Mike Gabriel, co-director of *The Rescuers Down Under*, came to a "Gong Show" pitch meeting at the studio carrying a mock movie poster, a "one-sheet" he had created. The poster featured the character Tiger Lily, from *Peter Pan* with the title *Pocahontas* splashed across it. "Basically, I just didn't want to bore them," joked Gabriel. "Some people get up there and do a ten-minute story outline that's just boring as hell. So, I figured I had faith in the title, and if the title hooks them, they'll ask questions, and they'll get information that way. So, it seemed to work, even with that Tiger Lily 'rip-off.'"[121]

---

118 Drew Taylor, "Underdogs: How *A Goofy Movie* Became Disney's Unlikely Sleeper Hit," *Vanity Fair*, April 8, 2020, vanityfair.com (accessed March 11, 2021).
119 Bambi Moé interview with ML, June 25, 2021.
120 Ibid.
121 Mike Gabriel Interview with ML, March 20, 1995.

Gabriel was right and *Pocahontas* was put into production. It turns out that Peter Schneider had been interested in an animated version of *Romeo and Juliet* and saw similar sensibilities in *Pocahontas* and an opportunity for Disney to breakthrough into an entirely different subject matter.

Since starting at Disney in 1979, Gabriel, who came aboard during the training program initiated by Eric Larson in the '70s, worked as an animator on films such as *The Black Cauldron* and *Oliver & Company* before transitioning to co-director of *The Rescuers Down Under*.

With *Pocahontas*, however, Gabriel and the other Disney artists were in uncharted territory. "These films really have to find their own tone and their own style," noted Gabriel. "Early on, the more we got into the storytelling, it just became obvious that we had some very deep issues and intense themes to get across. We weren't going to be going real far in the 'yuks' direction."[122]

Although the film would be loosely based on the actual events in the life of the real Pocahontas herself, the artists made tremendous efforts during the early production of the film to do extensive research. This included numerous trips to Jamestown, Virginia, where the film and the events took place, and meetings with many within the Native American community and immersion into that culture.

"We really wanted to present certain things in this film as interesting to our audience," said Eric Goldberg, who would co-direct *Pocahontas* with Gabriel. "It would have been very easy for us to make a film about American Indians that included teepees, totem poles, and big, long feathery headdresses, the way most people are used to seeing those images from Southwest American Indians. But we didn't want to do that."[123]

Goldberg also noted that conversations with many Native Americans helped highlight just how important it was for the film to represent that community correctly. "We met with Native Americans and surviving members of the Powhatan nation," he said. "We spoke to them, and kind of got a flavor of

---

122 Ibid.

123 Eric Goldberg interview with ML, March 20, 1995.

what they were like, what they found important. They found a sense of community very important, and they wanted to see that portrayed in the film."[124]

Layered into historical realism, this would still be an animated film and would need to reflect those artistic sensibilities that differentiate it from a live-action production. Ironically, a significant influence in crafting the more realistic, historical story of *Pocahontas* would be one of Disney's most famous fairy tales, *Sleeping Beauty*.

Artist Eyvind Earle had created a very distinctive, clean, vertical style for that Disney classic that is wholly unique. The filmmakers looked to Earle's work as the primary influence for *Pocahontas*.

"The design of the film, the design of the characters, the design of the backgrounds, and the general tone of the movie is completely unforgiving," said Goldberg. "The design itself is very crisp; there aren't a lot of round edges and circles and things that are 'squashy and stretchy,' that you have a lot of cartoon liberty with. So, it means that every little nick and pop in the animation, that's a mistake, will show. It really is a daunting thing, this task we set for everybody."[125]

With the backdrop of this distinct artistry, *Pocahontas* tells a story that opens in London in 1607. Governor Ratcliffe's greed leads Captain John Smith and a group of British settlers to the "New World."

Ratcliffe (animated by Duncan Marjoribanks) emerged as a unique Disney villain, large in stature and appearance and blinded by his lust for the gold he hopes to find in the "New World," but also by more. "He reveals his Achilles heel or his weak side. He's almost sympathetic in a way," said Gabriel. "He's been laughed at in court; he's sort of been the black sheep in King James' court, so he has to prove himself; he wants to have one last chance to prove he's as good as anybody." Gabriel also noted, "Although his lust for gold is completely black and white, his real desire is to show them all back home that he's a great future king."[126]

---

124 Ibid.
125 Ibid
126 Mike Gabriel interview with ML, March 20, 1995.

When Ratcliffe, Smith, and the settlers reach the "New World" (Virginia), they are shocked to find not gold but untouched land and the indigenous residents, the Powhatan tribe led by Pocahontas' father, Chief Powhatan.

Supervising animator Ruben Aquino discovered tremendous depth in Chief Powhatan as he brought him to the screen. "When I was animating him, I wanted to emphasize the two sides of him. One side being the chief side of him, the strong leader that everyone looked up to. He was kind to his people but also perfectly willing to resort to warfare if he had to. Then, there is the other side of him that is the fatherly, warm, kind, gentle side of him that we see more of when he's with Pocahontas."[127]

The film provides the audience with the Powhatan tribe's perspectives, beliefs, and world. We learn that Pocahontas is thoughtful and free-spirited, as she explores with her "sidekicks," Meeko the raccoon and Flit the hummingbird. She fears being trapped in an arranged marriage to the warrior Kocoum and confides to Grandmother Willow (the mystical, mentoring tree that she talks with) that she wants to chart her own course.

Glen Keane, who served as the supervising animator for Pocahontas, said that the character was a true challenge in that so much of her performance was internal. "It seems that in so many of the scenes of Pocahontas that I animated, she's really not doing a whole heck of a lot. She's not running around, she's not talking a lot, she's not making faces, she's standing there, and she's looking, but she's not just looking, she sees." Keane also added, "So much of it is this invisible calling, this thing that's inside of her that's making her follow this course throughout the whole film."[128]

Keane then went back to his training with Ollie Johnston and the other Nine Old Men, focusing on what Pocahontas thought when she first sees John Smith. "We were trying to communicate our acting in much more subtle ways, which usually you don't do, except in live-action," Keane said, adding,

<hr>

127   Ruben Aquino interview with ML, March 17, 1995.
128   Glen Keane interview with ML, March 16, 1995.

"This has really moved us to ground that was forbidden before for animators."[129]

This is evident in one of the most dramatic and pivotal moments in the film when John Smith and Pocahontas meet for the first time in front of a mist-covered waterfall. With its quiet personality animation, it's easily one of Disney's most groundbreaking moments.

Goldberg notes that Keane knew precisely how this scene should play out, "The sequence where Pocahontas and John Smith first meet under the waterfall is actually Glen's story-boarding, and we veered very little from it."[130]

Keane then brought a personal perspective to it. "The more I thought about it, I said, 'Well, how did it work out for me when I met my wife?'," he recalled. "It was kind of a love at first sight thing. I met her at a movie in 1972, on line, to see *The Godfather*. We were both seniors in high school, this girl was standing behind me, and I turned around, and she was there, and I don't remember anything that she said. But I remember that whole time; I remember the orange blossoms in the air, I remember the temperature, the feelings that were there. I thought this is what this moment [in *Pocahontas*] has to be. It has to be something bigger than life, beyond just these two people standing there." Glen also added, "The place where they met was very important. To have it in front of this waterfall, with just the roar of the waterfall behind them, the mist slowly revealing Pocahontas, kind of like clouds swirling around, made it very ethereal."[131]

Keane also added, "She knows that she wants to run, but she also knows that she wants to stay. She's been tracking and following him. There's this very subtle little thing, where her tension is just to lean off to screen right and run away, but, if you watch the scene, she slowly, very slowly, inches over to the left and her head drops down slightly, which says, 'I'm going to stay here for a moment.' Then, he moves a little bit; then she looks at his gun, he drops the gun. Everything is very, very subtle."[132]

---

129 Ibid.
130 Eric Goldberg interview with ML, March 20, 1995.
131 Glen Keane interview with ML, March 16, 1995.
132 Ibid

The two characters' meeting leads into Pocahontas expressing to John Smith how she and her people respect the land in the film's Oscar-winning centerpiece song, "The Colors of the Wind."

"It's interesting because they put 'Colors of the Wind' out as a trailer prior to the movie's release," said Goldberg. "I think when you see the movie, you'll realize how it fits very well within its context. It works fine as a trailer, but it works much better not in isolation. It's better in the context of the movie, as you see how their relationship is developing." [133]

Alan Menken was back for the songs in *Pocahontas*, this time paired with lyricist Stephen Schwartz, who had written the songs for the Broadway hits *Godspell* and *Pippin* and would go on to pen the songs for *Wicked*.

"Stephen puts a great deal of heart and soul into his lyrics," Goldberg said of the songwriter. "He's got a lot of passion for what he does, and he feels very strongly that the songs should help propel the plot and get you to the next level of where the story has to be, rather than just being an isolated showstopper."[134]

Schwartz noted that the Broadway musical model finding a new home in animation during this Animation Renaissance made perfect sense. "In a stage musical, one of the most effective moments you can have is having a really fine singer standing in the center of stage by his or herself singing for three or four minutes," he said. "That can be one of the best things in the show. You can't get away with that in film. My stock line is, 'If you're going to write a ballad for a feature, the singer better be going over a waterfall in a canoe!'" laughed Schwartz, in reference to a scene in *Pocahontas*.[135]

"Just Around the Riverbend" is the song that plays during that daring canoe scene; in it, Pocahontas decides which path her life should take. "Colors of the Wind," is the musical number that opens John Smith's eyes to the world around him. "The Virginia Company" is a lively sea chanty that kicks off the film, setting the mood and historical time and place.

---

133   Eric Goldberg interview with ML, March 20, 1995.

134   Ibid.

135   Stephen Schwartz interview with ML, July 30, 1998.

In the rousing "Mine, Mine, Mine, " Ratcliffe sings about the glory gold will bring him, and John Smith wonders at the New World. Then, there's "Savages," in which both the British settlers and the Powhatan tribe prepare for battle, in a musical allegory about mistrust and ignorance toward other cultures.

There was also a song, "If I Never Knew You," which was cut from the film very late in the production process. The duet was to feature into a scene in which Pocahontas visits John Smith, imprisoned by the Powhatan tribe. The song had been recorded and almost fully animated, but the filmmakers felt that it slowed the film's pacing (a pop version, sung by Shanice and Jon Secada, played over the ending credits).

In 2005, the animation of the sequence was completed and placed back in the film for the tenth anniversary DVD release of *Pocahontas*.

The songs in the film are all brought to life through a cast that includes several Native American actors. Among them, Irene Bedard as Pocahontas (with the singing voice of Judy Kuhn), Russell Means as Chief Powhatan (Jim Cummings provided the singing voice), Michelle St. John as Pocahontas' best friend Nakoma, James Apaumut Fall as Kocoum, and Gordon Tootoosis as the shaman Kekata.

Rounding out the rest of the cast was Cogsworth himself, David Odgen Stiers performing double duty as Ratcliffe and his manservant Wiggins, Linda Hunt as Grandmother Willow, and as British settlers, Ben, Lon and Thomas, Billy Connolly, Joe Baker, and Christian Bale, respectively.

The biggest casting coup in *Pocahontas*, however, was that of Mel Gibson, as John Smith. One of the biggest box-office stars at the time, known for popular action films like 1987's *Lethal Weapon*, Gibson even did his own singing for the film and brought depth and understanding to his performance.

Smith understands the New World and the Powhatan people, as tensions run high and both sides prepare for battle in the film's climax. Pocahontas herself stops the fighting in an act of bravery, allowing both sides to see that an act of war accomplishes nothing.

Intensely dramatic scenes like this were most definitely new for Disney animation, and, as Gabriel noted, they help underline the powerful message of *Pocahontas*. "To me, it's as simple as our similarities are much greater than our differences," he said. "Even though we like to rant and rave that we're all completely different and each nation and each culture has its own idiosyncrasies and separate ideas, I think what we show in the movie is that we're not all that different."[136]

Despite such thoughtful storytelling, *Pocahontas* was criticized by several groups during its release. Even with extensive efforts to research and work closely with Native Americans while making the film, many in that community were still unhappy with how some of the characters were depicted.

Additionally, scholars didn't like how *Pocahontas* played "fast and loose" with historical facts.

Despite this, there was tremendous attention around *Pocahontas* as its release date neared. Disney's "movie marketing machine" worked overtime promoting the film. *Pocahontas* not only *felt* like an event, it *was* an event.

In addition to the usual array of toys, products, and other pre-release hype, Disney turned the premiere of *Pocahontas* into a concert and a mammoth one at that.

Partnering with New York City, in early 1995, Disney announced "*Pocahontas*: The Premiere in the Park," which would take place at the Great Lawn of Central Park on June 10, 1995.

The press immediately dubbed it "Family Woodstock"[137] as attendees would need to bring blankets and beach chairs to watch the film on four 80-foot screens set up on the Lawn. Best of all, it would be free. Tickets were secured through a lottery system. Interested fans had to write in months in advance to place their names and addresses on a list to be considered for 100,000 tickets that were going to be mailed out.

And, on June 10, all 100,000 ticket holders showed up, packing the Great Lawn five and a half hours before the evening's showtime. Live entertainment performed throughout the day and, at the end of the night, in true Disney fashion, fireworks were accompanied by Vanessa Williams's

---

136 Mike Gabriel interview with ML, March 20, 1995.

137 Elizabeth Sanger, "Disney Debuts *Pocahontas* in the Park," *New York Newsday*, June 7, 1995, Section I.

performance of "Colors of the Wind" (she sang the Top 40 radio version of the song).

It had drizzled that night, just as *Pocahontas* was projected on the giant screens, but it dampened no one's excitement for the film and the event itself. The headline on the cover of *The New York Daily News* the next day was "'Poca' Party," accompanied by an aerial view of the throngs in Central Park. It was touted as the world's largest movie premiere ever and, despite grumblings from some native New Yorkers, it was a hit.

The media coverage of the "Premiere in the Park" was inescapable, like much of *Pocahontas'* promotion that summer. The film opened on June 23, 1995 and went on to gross $141.5 million domestically.

Following in the shadow of the groundbreaking *Lion King* was not an easy thing, and because *Pocahontas* fell short of that film's box office success, many were discouraged by its performance.

Disney and the animation industry felt otherwise, noting that *Pocahontas* was a differentiator in its style, artistry, storytelling, and subject matter.

"I think we've scared the hell out of a lot of the animators," laughed Mike Gabriel, as *Pocahontas* neared the end of its production. "They all think that we're going to have to make these films every time, and they're very tough to pull off."[138]

As game changing as *Pocahontas* was, waiting "just around the river bend," five months away was another animated feature from Disney that would not only, once again, change the audience's perspectives of animation but begin to point the industry toward its future.

---

138 Mike Gabriel interview with ML, March 20, 1995.

CHAPTER SIX

"Out There"

Toy Story, James and the Giant Peach & The Hunchback of Notre Dame

Director John Lasseter didn't have a sense of just how popular his first film *Toy Story* was, until, shortly after the film opened, he was waiting at an airport.

"Disney had opened a *Toy Story* parade at Disney World," he remembered. "I went down to Disney World, with my wife and four sons, to see the parade. Flying home, from Orlando to San Francisco, we stopped at Dallas to change planes. So, I get off the plane and there, at the gate, is a little boy, who was about three or four. He was standing there with his mom, clearly waiting for his dad, and he was holding a Woody doll. This was not even a week after the movie had opened, and he was clutching this Woody doll as if it was his prized possession. That was the first time I had seen one of the toys 'in use'"[139]

This brief observation is just a snapshot (and a pretty perfect one) of just how beloved the film *Toy Story*, its characters, and its sequels would become. The first all-computer animated feature film was so passionately embraced by audiences that, even over a quarter of a century after its debut, the *Toy Story* characters remain some of the studio's most popular. Today, Woody the Cowboy and Buzz Lightyear, the Space Ranger, find themselves alongside Mickey Mouse and Donald Duck in terms of iconic popularity.

Toy Story was a flashpoint in film in so many ways. After years as a "supporting player," assisting both live-action and

---

139 John Lasseter interview with ML, January 18, 1997.

animated films, CGI would now be in the starring role. But, for years, many in Hollywood wondered if the "cold, sterile" world of computers could support a full-length feature. John Lasseter knew that it could.

He knew what Walt knew: audiences come to movies to see a good story; filmmaking technology is simply the framework for that.

"Movies are unique combinations of story, characters, and personality," he said. "Those things come together, and you have a memorable, entertaining movie." [140]

It was one of these emerging technologies and its possibilities for storytelling that first intrigued Lasseter, a native Californian and lifelong animation enthusiast who came to work at Disney in 1979, right after graduating from CalArts.

It was during these early years as a young animator that Lasseter's world changed in 1982. That year, Disney's live-action film, *Tron*, a fantasy adventure about life inside a video game, directed by Steven Lisberger, debuted. The film was significant for its extensive use of burgeoning CGI, particularly the now-famous "light cycle" scene.

Lasseter recalled his reaction to first seeing this sequence: "It blew me away! A little door in my mind opened up. I looked at it and said, 'This is it! This is the future!'"[141] The young artist was so enthusiastic; he convinced leadership at Disney to do a test film using computer animation.

Partnering with fellow animator Glen Keane, the two created a thirty-second test film of a sequence of author Maurice Sendak's popular children's book, *Where the Wild Things Are*.

The Disney Studio showed little interest at the time, which led Lasseter to leave Disney and work at Lucasfilm. Here, Lasseter worked on special effects for other films as well as a computer-animated short, *The Adventures of Andre and Wally B.*, in 1984.

Two years later, Steve Jobs (co-founder and chairman of Apple Computer, Inc.) purchased Lucasfilm's computer division and incorporated it as an independent company. This

---

140   John Lasseter interview with ML, August 27, 1999.

141   John Lasseter interview with ML, August 27, 1999.

new company would be Pixar (the name was the brainchild of co-founders Alvy Ray Smith and Loren Carpenter, who combined the words "radar" and "pixer"). It was here, at Pixar, where Lasseter would be one of the founding employees.

The new studio produced several computer-animated short subjects, with Lasseter directing them. One of these, 1988's *Tin Toy*, involved a wind-up toy, who attempts to escape the clutches of an overly playful infant.

"*Tin Toy* came directly from my love of toys," said Lasseter. "I based the little tin toy on a lot of the toys that I had."[142] In addition to impressive and startlingly tactile animation, the short, along with Pixar's others, demonstrated that computer animation could create compelling personalities and stories (albeit short ones, in this case).

Tin Toy went on to win the Academy Award for Best Animated Short Subject and caught the attention of The Walt Disney Studios. "Disney had talked to us, and based on our short films, they were interested in having us possibly doing a feature film for them," recalled Lasseter. "They said, come back and talk to us when you have an idea and I always thought that there was a lot more potential with toys alive, and I thought there were more stories to be told."[143]

Lasseter, a lifelong toy collector, knew that this was a subject that was near and dear to not only his heart but those of his peers, as well. "I believe there is a connection between a love of toys and animation," said Lasseter. "I found, at many animation studios, there are toys all over animator's desks. To be an animator, a good character animator, I believe there is a quality that can best be described as a child who's never grown up. Because I think to be a good animator, you need a good child-like take on things. So much of animation is through observation and capturing the certain essences of things that people find familiar and showing it to them in ways that they've never seen before. There's sort of this wide-eyed wonderment to things. I think, along with that, we all have this love of toys."[144]

---

142 John Lasseter interview with ML, January 18, 1997.
143 Ibid.
144 Ibid.

From this love, Lasseter pitched what he called "a buddy picture with toys"[145] Jeffrey Katzenberg had been interested in having Lasseter come back and work for Disney, but when the director's allegiance was to Pixar, the studio instead initiated an agreement with the computer animation studio. Three animated features would be developed and produced at Pixar Animation Studios in Emeryville, California with The Walt Disney Studios marketing and releasing them

The first of these would be *Toy Story*.

Andrew Stanton, the second animator hired at Pixar, who co-wrote *Toy Story*, recalled how different the initial story was: "'This little, tiny toy gets left on the side of the road at a rest stop and goes on a road trip to find his owners, and he bumps into this hand-me-down ventriloquist doll who tries to help him. It was very convoluted, but we thought it was great at the time.'"[146]

The characters eventually changed to those of Woody and Buzz. Still, the original versions were much different from the beloved characters we know and love, as noted by Pixar Archivist Christine Freeman: "'There are so many different iterations of what Buzz and Woody might have looked like. In the archive, we have boxes of 'Pointy Nose Woody,' 'Big Hair Buzz,' 'Scary Woody'…We have lots of artists' good taste to thank for the film we saw.'"[147]

We also have several writers and script revisions to thank for the story that *Toy Story* became. In the original versions, Woody was a very unsympathetic character, almost the villain of the film. After several meetings and conversations with Katzenberg (as well as a disastrous screening of the film), the *Toy Story* team returned to the initial "buddy movie" concept and the idea that a toy's purpose in life is to be played with.

This helped craft the world we see in the finished film, *Toy Story*, where toys exist but are lifeless when humans are around, and we are unaware of their existence. The movie opens with a birthday party for a young boy named Andy.

---

145 Ibid.

146 Olly Richards, "'Best Idea Wins': How Pixar Grew Up," *The Telegraph*, November 21, 2015, telegraph.co.uk (accessed March 19, 2021).

147 Ibid.

The young boy's toys are in his bedroom, listening to the party downstairs to determine which new toys will be joining them. Among them is Woody the Cowboy (Tom Hanks), Andy's favorite toy. There's also Bo Peep (Annie Potts), a porcelain doll, who also functions as a lamp, Rex (Wallace Shawn), a nervous and sheepish T-rex, Hamm the piggy bank (John Ratzenberger), Slinky Dog (voiced by Jim "Hey Vern, it's Ernest" Varney) and Mr. Potato Head (legendary acerbic comedian Don Rickles).

"A lot of what was read and how they read it helped the characters to evolve," said *Toy Story* producer Bonnie Arnold of the voice cast. "Jim Varney, for instance, who's doing the role of Slinky. Initially, the character of Slinky was a little bit different, but as soon as we decided on Jim and we had Jim do a recording, Slinky became more of a hound dog, which of course fits Jim's voice."[148]

Into the comfortable world of these toys comes Andy's latest birthday gift, a Buzz Lightyear action figure (voice of Tim Allen). A bright, shiny new plaything that seemingly has all the latest technology but has just one flaw: he doesn't realize he is a toy; he believes that he is an actual "Space Ranger" who has landed on a strange planet.

Andy loves playing with Buzz and begins leaving Woody behind. A rivalry starts, and jealousy surfaces within Woody. The two inadvertently find themselves lost from Andy and in the next-door home of the villain, Sid, the toy torturing kid, whose favorite pastime is blowing up toys with firecrackers.

Woody and Buzz must now bond and work together to escape and return to Andy's house. As an added element of difficulty, it turns out that Andy and his family are moving, so the cowboy and Space Ranger must catch up with the moving truck in the film's uber-exciting chase scene of a conclusion.

Toy Story broke from recent tradition in that its story was nothing like the standard musical that had become the paradigm for traditional Disney animated features.

"The characters don't sing like in a Broadway-type musical," said Arnold. "But, Randy [Newman] composed and sings three

---

148 Bonnie Arnold interview with ML October 6, 1995.

songs in the film, and he sings them over emotional moments in the film or moments when something is going on in the character's thoughts."[149]

"Friend Like Me" opens the film and sets the tone for the relationship between Andy and Woody (it would also become the theme for the entire franchise of *Toy Story* films); with "Strange Things," we are inside Woody's head, as he sees Buzz taking over, and then there's "I Will Go Sailing No More," during a painful, touching moment when Buzz realizes that he is not a Space Ranger, but instead a toy (and not a flying one at that!).

More profound, character moments like this are at the heart of *Toy Story*, and more than the glistening new CGI world, this is what immediately connected with audiences.

Yes, the film is a technological marvel: the toys' plastic reflects light and takes on a wondrous tangible look, and the car chase finale has moments of eye-popping photo-realism. But that is just the "surface."

"The technology is amazing, absolutely amazing; I don't think anyone can deny that," said Arnold. "But, that's interesting for all of about five minutes. What will keep moviegoers in their seats is a good story - interesting characters, witty dialogue, and coming out of the picture learning something about yourself."[150]

The value of friendship, accepting others, and learning to accept yourself are all just some of the film's themes, all very human themes, and all of it told by toys. This careful crafting of *Toy Story* as a meaningful film, more than a CGI novelty, is what audiences loved.

When *Toy Story* opened on November 22, 1995, critical praise immediately rang out. In *Entertainment Weekly*, Owen Gleiberman wrote of the film that it "...is a magically witty humane entertainment. It has the purity, the ecstatic freedom of imagination, that's the hallmark of the greatest children's films."[151]

---

149 Ibid.

150 Ibid.

151 Owen Gleiberman, "*Toy Story* Review," *Entertainment Weekly*, November 24, 1995, ew.com (accessed March 19, 2021).

Roger Ebert wrote: "Watching the film, I felt like I was in at the dawn of a new era of movie animation, which draws on the best of cartoons and reality, creating a world somewhere in between, where space not only bends but snaps, crackles, and pops."[152]

Mr. Ebert truly hit the animated nail right on its head, *Toy Story* grossed $192 million in US and Canada, and many were immediately calling it "*Snow White* for a new generation."

At the time of its release, Michael Eisner told CNN: "'I don't think either side thought *Toy Story* would turn out as well as it has. The technology is brilliant, the casting is inspired, and I think this story will touch a nerve. Believe me; when we first agreed to work together [with Pixar], we never thought their first movie would be our 1995 holiday feature or that they could go public on the strength of it. '"[153]

Much like their film *Who Framed Roger Rabbit* from just eight years earlier, *Toy Story* was another "once in a generation" film. In addition to a tremendous win at the box office, John Lasseter received a *Special Achievement Academy Award* in 1996 for the film. Additionally, as the film starred toys, it was an immediate hit with children. However, during the holiday season of 1995, stores did not have enough *Toy Story* supply to meet demand, and there were several disappointed kids and parents.

Disney never let this happen again. In addition to a continuous run of the product, the *Toy Story* characters became a vital part of the Disney theme park experiences, culminating in the opening of attractions and entire "lands" themed around *Toy Story*.

There would also be three immensely successful *Toy Story* sequels, as well as short subjects and television specials.

Toy Story has gone on to leave its indelible mark on our pop culture and in our hearts (Buzz Lightyear's catchphrase "To infinity and beyond!" has become almost shorthand for any explanation of excellence).

---

152 Roger Ebert, "Toy Story Review," *Chicago Sun-Times*, November 22, 1995, rogerebert.com (accessed March 19, 2021).

153 Brent Schlender, "Steve Jobs Amazing Movie Adventure," September 18, 1995, money.cnn.com, (accessed March 19, 2021).

Additionally, the film was ground zero for a change in film-making and animation. With *Toy Story*, computers were seen as more than a "tool," they were now a filmmaking choice. The film answered a question that had lingered in the industry for many years: what could computers do? And could they support an entire movie?

Thanks to Pixar, the answer was yes. Other studios quickly invested in computer technology and ramped up the production of computer-animated films. Pixar, however, was first out of the gate and was (and still is) a leader in the industry. The studio would continue to partner with Disney, creating (as of this writing) twenty-three additional animated features and a number of short subjects.

With *Toy Story*, Pixar heralded the beginning of the age of computer animation. While the new technology would co-exist with hand-drawn animation for the next ten to fifteen years, computers would eventually eclipse traditional 2D animation, becoming the industry's focal filmmaking medium.

And it all started with a young animator named John Lasseter sitting wide-eyed during the infant days of computer animation and watching *Tron*. Lasseter, who would become known as "The Walt Disney of the computer generation," would eventually ascend to the role of Creative Vice President at Pixar and then Chief Creative Officer of both Pixar and Disney Animation Studios.

Even with all of this forward-thinking that *Toy Story* brought, Disney, once again, looked to animation's past for their next film, *James and the Giant Peach*.

Disney had obtained the rights to the 1961 book by author Roald Dahl, best known for his darker, cynical children's books, such as *Charlie and the Chocolate Factory* (1964).

James and the Giant Peach languished in Hollywood for several years as various filmmakers grappled with translating the book to the screen. One director, however, was familiar with bringing a more macabre children's story to the screen and was immediately attracted to it.

Henry Selick, fresh off of *The Nightmare Before Christmas*, saw *James* as the perfect follow-up and stepped up where other filmmakers had dared not tread.

"I come from this solid visual background," he said. "So, I was in love with the visual possibilities." Selick also added, "I'm always looking for something different. I like to build on our expertise in animating, but I'm always going to want differences in character and story."[154]

The director also saw the film, in many ways, as darker than *The Nightmare Before Christmas*. "[*James and the Giant Peach*] is lighter in tone, and I think it's also darker in tone. In *Nightmare*, I think the threat of no Christmas to the children of the world was kind of a lightweight threat. Oogie-Boogie [the villain in *Nightmare*] was always entertaining, even when he was threatening to cook up Santa. The overall look of it, the palette of colors was darker. But I feel because there's more lightness and sweet moments in *James*, the dark moments are more powerful."[155]

James and the Giant Peach begins in live action, telling the story of young James Trotter (played by actor Paul Terry), an orphan living with his wicked aunts, Spiker and Sponge (Joanna Lumley and Miriam Margolyes, respectively). James meets a mysterious man who gives him a bag of seeds and accidentally spills them near an old peach tree outside his aunts' house. A peach appears on the tree, which grows bigger and bigger.

The aunts take full advantage of this, charging the public admission to see the giant peach, but they forbid James to go near it. So, he sneaks out one night and enters a tunnel inside the giant peach.

This is where the film segues to stop-motion animation. Once inside the peach, James (now also transformed into stop-motion) meets a group of insects. There's the demure Miss Spider (the voice of Susan Sarandon), the gruff Centipede (Richard Dreyfuss), the Grasshopper (Simon Callow), Lady Bug (Jane Leeves), and a nearsighted Earthworm (David Thewlis). "He did a remarkable job of this basic coward who's blind and always imagines things being worse than they really are," said Selick of actor Thewlis, adding, "He did this amped up performance, a quivering voice that really fueled the animation."[156]

---

154 Henry Selick interview with ML, February 23, 1996
155 Ibid.
156 Ibid.

They all set the peach rolling out to sea, with James joining the insects on a magical journey to a place he has always dreamed of seeing, New York City.

During this adventure, the director couldn't resist a cameo from his famous previous leading man. In one scene in the film, James and the insects encounter an army of skeletal pirates. In this sequence, eagle-eyed audience members will spot a cameo by Jack Skellington. This came out of early sketches that the film's character designer Lane Smith did during pre-production. "Lane kept putting in this tall, skinny guy against these other shapes," remembered Selick. "I finally said, 'Well, he keeps looking like Jack Skellington, let's just put him in the movie.'"[157]

To tell this story, *James and the Giant Peach* not only utilized live-action and stop-motion it also incorporated CGI into some of the sequences. "Everything that's ever been done in film is in our movie," laughed Selick.[158]

More than this merging of technologies, Selick saw *James and the Giant Peach*, like all of Dahl's work, as a children's story with so much more to say. Most notably, he states that it's a story about unity. "There is the idea that cooperation among disparate creatures is possible," said Selick of his film.[159]

When *James and the Giant Peach* opened on April 12, 1996, critics praised the film's visuals. *The New York Times* critic Janet Maslin said, "Together, this prodigiously clever group has come up with expert animated effects and some boldly beautiful sights unlike anything else on screen…"[160] But this didn't help the film at the box office.

James and the Giant Peach grossed only $29 million domestically and unfortunately became another "also-ran" of the Disney Animation Renaissance.

Additionally, the film had minimal promotion behind it, as if Disney was saving all of their marketing efforts for their next, traditionally animated feature, a very non-traditional story for the studio.

---

157 Ibid.

158 Ibid.

159 Ibid.

160 Janet Maslin, "Film Review: A Poor Little Boy Befriended by Bugs," *The New York Times*, April 12, 1996, nytimes.com (accessed March 22, 2021)

The Hunchback of Notre Dame would most likely not be the choice of many people when it comes to stories that seem ripe for a Disney animated film. But the unexpected was part of the mandate for many at the studio during this time, when it came to ideas for future animated projects. And so, author Victor Hugo's unnerving and gloomy literary classic novel was chosen.

In 1482, under the title *Notre-Dame de Paris*, the novel told of Quasimodo the misshapen bellringer at Paris' Notre Dame cathedral who becomes obsessed with the gypsy Esmerelda. Hugo set this story against a sprawling backdrop of Paris, with tremendous detail given to the city's Gothic architecture.

Hugo's work had already been translated into a film several times. There was a silent film version in 1923 starring Lon Chaney and versions in 1939 starring Charles Laughton and in 1956 with Anthony Quinn.

According to Don Hahn, who would once again serve as producer, the Disney artists had ideas that would bring a new perspective to *The Hunchback of Notre Dame*. Hahn said, "In the past, certainly in Hollywood, there have been a lot of 'monster movies' about Quasimodo - this terrible guy that people view as half-human/half-animal - and we didn't want to tell that story. We felt that there's a great deal of humanity in Quasimodo."[161]

The Hunchback of Notre Dame came to Disney through the vice president of animation development David Stainton and his love of illustrated classic comic books, such as that of Hugo's novel.

"What appealed to us was the characters of the piece and the opportunity to tell a story about a character who was an outcast," said Hahn, adding that even within such a dark story, "There was plenty of opportunity for color, pageantry and even humor."[162]

Hahn's partners on *Beauty and the Beast*, co-directors Kirk Wise and Gary Trousdale, came on board and found themselves, once again, in France. "I think once we do *Cyrano* and *The Phantom of the Opera*, that will pretty much be it!" Wise joked.[163]

---

161 Don Hahn interview with ML, March 20, 1996.
162 Ibid.
163 Kirk Wise interview with ML, April 11, 1996.

The *Hunchback* team embarked on a research trip to Paris, where they had the opportunity to spend eight hours in the city with a Parisian history scholar. They also got to tour all of the nooks and crannies of Notre Dame cathedral.

This unique opportunity was the first significant spark of inspiration for the film's possibilities. Wise noted, "It's so rare on an animated film, where you can actually visit the location that the story is supposed to take place in."[164]

The photos, sketches, and artwork that the team returned with to the Disney Studio also opened up possibilities for Notre Dame to be more than a backdrop. "This is a very urban setting," said Hahn," and an opportunity to have the Cathedral of Notre Dame, one of the greatest Gothic architecture icons of civilization, almost be a character in the movie. That opportunity for visuals interested us."[165]

The massive cathedral does indeed emerge as a character in *The Hunchback of Notre Dame*, not just a "sanctuary" for the lead character, Quasimodo.

Bringing the Hunchback himself to the screen in a way that was both true to Disney and Hugo became one of the film's first major hurdles. "The one thing that we knew from the outset," said Wise adding with a laugh, "was that we didn't want to go the route where we took Quasimodo and abstracted him to the point that he became like another one of the Seven Dwarfs. You know - Happy, Dopey, Sleepy, and Quasi."[166]

Co-director Trousdale noted, "One thing we wanted to do was make him different, make him our own. Another thing is a balancing act of making him somebody who when the population of Paris says, 'My God he's the ugliest person in France,' you have to believe it, but he also has to have something about him that you can see inside; this loving quality, this appeal that's within."[167]

To add this depth to Quasimodo, particularly scenes where he is alone, Disney introduced the three characters of the gargoyles to their version of the film.

---

164   Ibid.

165   Don Hahn interview with ML, March 20, 1996.

166   Kirk Wise interview with ML, April 11, 1996.

167   Gary Trousdale interview with ML, April 11, 1996.

In his book, author Hugo does mention that Quasimodo spoke to the stone gargoyles. Disney artists took this one step further, turning them into characters: Victor, Hugo (a nod to the author), and Laverne (a random nod to the singing group The Andrews Sisters).

The gargoyles went through several name changes, including Chaney, Laughton and Quinn and Lon, Charles and Anthony, as a tribute to the actors who played Quasimodo in past films. However, legal concerns about using these names steered the filmmakers away from them.

With the gargoyles in Disney's *The Hunchback of Notre Dame*, only Quasimodo (or "Quasi," as the gargoyles call him) can talk to and interact with the gargoyles, allowing for the film to retain its level of brooding realism while adding a touch of the studio's magic.

"Hugo talks about this lonely guy living literally between heaven and hell - heavens above him and the hellish streets of Paris below - as a recluse," said Hahn. "That notion of this character all by himself, with no companions except the gargoyles, wasn't too big of a leap to say, 'Well, great, let's give him these characters that live with him in almost a Calvin and Hobbes or Harvey the Rabbit way.' If you or I were to walk into the bell tower, they wouldn't be there, but for him, they're his companions, coaches, cheerleaders, and confidants."[168]

We first meet the three gargoyles shortly after the opening scene of *The Hunchback of Notre Dame*. In a stunning introduction that begins with a striking shot of Notre Dame rising above the clouds, we are immediately pulled into the story, plunged into Medieval Paris, learn the dramatic and heartbreaking "back story" of Quasimodo and how he came to be the bellringer at Notre Dame.

In just a little over six minutes, this opening envelops us as no other Disney film has done, all of it set to one of the film's songs, "The Bells of Notre Dame," by Stephen Schwartz and Alan Menken.

Of this sequence, Hahn said that the film's directors "felt that they wanted to grab you as an audience, they wanted

---

168 Don Hahn interview with ML, March 20, 1996.

to tell you about Quasimodo and make you feel for this guy because it's a movie about him. They also wanted to grab you into the setting immediately."[169]

We also meet Clopin, the mischievous street entertainer and puppeteer who serves as the film's narrator. "We almost saw him a little bit like Joel Grey's character in *Cabaret*," said Wise adding, "In the same way that character puts a frame around that story, we used Clopin, to put a frame around *our* story."

The Walt Disney Studios in Burbank partnered with their sister studio in Paris, Walt Disney Feature Animation (France) S.A., to have the entire opening ten minutes produced there.

Hahn noted that this team was not at a loss for easy inspiration. "The neat thing about the Paris artists is they walk out their door, and there's Notre Dame!"[170]

One hundred artists at Disney's Paris-based studio completed the sequence, under the direction of co-producer Roy Conli and directors (and twin brothers) Paul and Gaetan Brizzi. They communicated with the Burbank studio with then-cutting-edge technology such as satellite and computer systems and video conferencing.

Gaetan told author Bob Thomas: "We don't want to seem pretentious, but the directors and head of layout told us that we brought a French flavor to the film."[171]

The team at the Paris studio also introduced audiences to the villain of *Hunchback*, Judge Claude Frollo, who, after a tragedy involving Quasimodo's mother, takes in the young boy, hiding him in the bell tower of Notre Dame.

This is where we meet Quasimodo, talking with the gargoyles and confiding in them that he wants so badly to leave the cathedral, where he has been sheltered by Frollo, who tells him that he would be treated like a monster in the outside world, and he should remain in Notre Dame.

This leads to Quasimodo's "I want" song, "Out There," in which he sings of his desire to lead an everyday life and be

---

169 Ibid.

170 Ibid.

171 Bob Thomas, *Disney's Art of Animation: From Mickey Mouse to Hercules,* (New York, Hyperion, 1997), p. 157.

out among the city's citizens. After this, we are taken into the streets of Paris and meet Phoebus, Frollo's Captain of the Guards, who disagrees with Frollo's cruel and discriminatory perspective toward the gypsies of Paris. We meet one of these gypsies, the savvy yet kind Esmeralda.

"Hugo crafted this story of tremendous contrasts," said Hahn, "about people who had great power and privilege, like Frollo and people without anything, like Esmerelda, or more importantly, Quasimodo. Characters like Quasimodo and Esmerelda are so archetypical and so interesting, and so simple in a sense; you have Quasimodo the innocent and Frollo, the hypocritical character in kind of a righteous shell; you have Phoebus, the Captain of the Guards, who's kind of an everyman; Esmerelda, this street-wise Gypsy girl. They're such great characters."[172]

All of the characters' stories collide at the annual Feast of Fools, a carnival-like celebration that Quasimodo desperately wants to attend. Victor, Hugo, and Laverne convince "Quasi" to sneak out of the cathedral and attend the festivities.

He gets there just in time for Clopin to welcome the crowd to what is termed "Topsy Turvy Day," in *Hunchback*'s considerable show-stopping number aptly titled "Topsy Turvy." The song features some creative and inventive lyrics, which came from Schwartz's admiration for legendary lyricist "Yip" Harburg, most famous for the songs in MGM's classic *The Wizard of Oz* (1939). The songwriter was known for how he played with words and rhyme.

"Harburg is one of my heroes," admitted Schwartz, "although I have trouble being as adept and agile with the language as he is, but the trick rhyme of: 'Scurvy naves are extra scurvy on the sixth of Janurvy,' is definitely a Yip Harburg line."[173]

The "Topsy Turvy" sequence also came with the challenge of bringing to the screen a teeming crowd in the streets of Paris. "In *Beauty and the Beast*, we would do several scenes where we would have a dozen people and having to animate even that few people by hand was a chore," said Trousdale, adding, "So,

---

172 Don Hahn interview with ML, March 20, 1996.
173 Stephen Schwartz interview with ML, July 30, 1998.

we knew to get this epic feel [in *Hunchback*], you were going to have to see these people."[174] To accomplish this, the filmmakers once again turned to computer animation.

For the film, new software was developed called "Crowd," which could design and animate a large-scale group of people, both male, and female, with different body types, program them and assign seventy-two specific movements to each one. The result is a seemingly large-scale animated group of extras that adds to the epic feel needed.

As infectiously upbeat as the "Topsy Turvy" scene is, it is followed by a sequence, during which Quasimodo had just been crowned the "King of Fools," the festival's highest honor. The crowd then turns, ridiculing and humiliating him. Frollo allows this to go on to "teach a lesson," but kind-hearted Esmerelda steps in and helps Quasimodo.

Frollo orders Esmerelda to be arrested, but she uses a "magic trick" to evade him and takes refuge inside Notre Dame. Captain Phoebus is sent after her by Frollo, but he refuses to arrest her, stating she has claimed sanctuary.

Safe inside the cathedral, Esmeralda sings the beautiful ballad "God Help the Outcasts." The song speaks to many of the characters in the film, as they are all, in one way or another, an outcast. "God Help the Outcasts" also expresses a deeper message at the center of the film: one of understanding, compassion and guidance through our faith and beliefs.

It's at the Cathedral that Esmerelda meets and befriends Quasimodo, who helps sneak her out of Notre Dame. Esmerelda's friendship and kindness provide Quasimodo with hope. In the bell tower with Victor, Hugo, and Laverne, he sings the first part of a two-part song, "Heaven's Light."

The second part of this number, "Hellfire," is sung by Frollo, in one of Disney's most dark and daring sequences since "Night on Bald Mountain" in *Fantasia*. As nightmarish, hooded figures appear from his fireplace, Frollo sings how he finds himself essentially lusting after Esmerelda.

"In the past, we have had villains who have wanted power, or money, like Ratcliffe in *Pocahontas*," said Hahn.

---

174 Gary Trousdale interview with ML, April 11, 1996.

"But, here's a guy who has all those things, he has power, he has money, but he's almost tormented because the one thing he wants is to get rid of the gypsies in Paris, but then he has tremendous feelings towards this one gypsy, Esmerelda. So, you have a character probably more complex than we've ever done."[175]

Frollo and the "Hellfire" sequence did take some audiences aback and created some controversy for *Hunchback*. Wise countered this with, "'...if we concentrated on trying to please everyone and not to offend a single soul, the films would be so watered down that we'd be making a Care Bears movie. That would be creative suicide. '"[176]

As they had been motivated since the Renaissance began, the artists at Disney were continually seeking to expand the reach of Disney animation.

Hunchback continues to do this in its story, even after these darker moments with Frollo. When the Judge finds out that Esmeralda has escaped the cathedral, he orders her to be found, having his soldiers set fire to gypsy's houses and winds up burning all of Paris to find her.

As Quasimodo watches in horror and considers what to do, the gargoyles sing their upbeat "A Guy Like You" number (which adds some much-needed levity). They give Quasimodo the courage to join forces with Phoebus to go to "The Court of Miracles" (the gypsies' secret hideout and another of the film's songs) to warn them about Frollo. However, Frollo has secretly followed them and winds up taking all of them hostage.

The Judge then chains Quasimodo back inside Notre Dame and threatens to burn Esmerelda at the stake outside. As a massive crowd gathers outside the cathedral, Quasimodo frees himself and rescues Esmerelda, resulting in a jaw-dropping action sequence in and around Notre Dame in the film's climax.

The grand scale of Disney's *The Hunchback of Notre Dame* came with an all-star array of voice talent: Tom Hulce as Quasimodo, Demi Moore as Esmerelda (with Heidi Mollenhauer providing

---

175 Don Hahn interview with ML, March 20, 1996.

176 Bob Strauus, "Courting controversy? Disney's newest animated feature 'Hunchback of Notre Dame' Takes on Sensitive Issues," *The Spokesman-Review*, June 23rd 1996 , spokesman.com (accessed March 23, 2021).

the singing voice), Kevin Kline as Phoebus, with Broadway and stage veterans Paul Kandel as Clopin and Tony Jay's deep, timbre voice as Frollo.

As the gargoyles, Jason Alexander, riding high on *Seinfeld's* success at the time, was Hugo. *Murphy Brown's* Charles Kimbrough as Victor and veteran comedy actress Mary Wickes (who had been acting in film and television for over fifty years at this point and, sadly, passed away before the film's release) as Laverne. Actress Jane Withers contributed dialogue for the character, after Wickes had passed away.

Equally impressive was the all-star cast of supervising animators who brought the characters to the screen: James Baxter (Quasimodo), Tony Fucile (Esmeralda), Kathy Zielinski (Frollo), Russ Edmonds (Phoebus), Michael Surrey (Clopin), David Pruiksma (Victor and Hugo) and Will Finn (Laverne).

These artists were at the top of their game, which critics noted when *The Hunchback of Notre Dame* opened on June 21, 1996. In *Entertainment Weekly*, Owen Gleiberman called the film a "Towering Achievement," awarding it an "A" and stating: "*The Hunchback of Notre Dame* is a beautiful and transporting experience-the best, I think, of Disney's serious animated features in the Multiplex era."[177]

In keeping with their recent efforts, Disney's marketing for *The Hunchback of Notre Dame* was in full vigor, with an array of toys and fast-food promotions. Additionally, much like *Pocahontas*, Disney transitioned the premiere of *The Hunchback of Notre Dame* into a concert-like event.

On June 19, 1996, the film premiered at the New Orleans Superdome stadium, where it was shown to the massive crowd inside via six strategically placed, gigantic movie screens. The premiere was even preceded by a parade of floats transplanted from Walt Disney World through New Orleans' famed French Quarter.

At Disney theme parks, a popular stage show, "*The Hunchback of Notre Dame*: A Musical Adventure," opened the same day as the film and ran for another six years at The Disney-MGM Studios.

---

177 Owen Gleiberman, "Towering Achievement," *Entertainment Weekly*, June 21, 1996, p.43

The film even inspired Walt Disney Theatrical Productions to produce a stage musical, which received very positive reviews and played in Berlin, Germany, and San Diego, California (in addition to touring productions).

Ultimately, Disney's animated take on *The Hunchback of Notre Dame* didn't yield the box-office results many had predicted. Hard to believe when one learns that the film grossed just over $100 million domestically, which didn't come near Disney's most recent animated hits.

For many, *The Hunchback of Notre Dame* is an underappreciated animated feature that dares to take chances in so many ways and delivers an always timely message. As Don Hahn stated, Disney's interpretation of Hugo's classic tells us, "Don't discard the outcasts in life or people because they're different, because there is great worth in those people."[178]

For their follow-up animated feature, Disney would look toward a complete change in tone. A film that was blessed by the Gods...of comedy.

---

178 Don Hahn interview with ML, March 20, 1996.

CHAPTER SEVEN

"True to Your Heart"

Hercules & Mulan

When it came time to bring the famed Greek god *Hercules* to life in Disney animation, one would think that the filmmakers would be pouring over old texts of ancient Greek mythology.

When one realizes that it's Ron Clements and John Musker, the team behind *Aladdin* co-directing *Hercules*, it makes perfect sense to learn that their inspiration actually came from classic Hollywood movies.

"We were influenced by some of the screwball comedies of the thirties and forties," said Musker, "where you have this strait-laced hero and the girl who's more sophisticated, more worldly, very sharp and kind of two-steps ahead of the guy, as in *The Lady Eve* with Henry Fonda and Barbara Stanwyck. So, we sort of modeled 'Herc' on the screwball comedy characters that Jimmy Stewart or Henry Fonda would play, in that he's sort of an innocent surrounded by cynics."[179]

Hercules would be a decidedly different take on...just about everything: Disney animation, Greek mythology, the archetypes of the hero's journey. You name it, and it was about to be skewered for laughs.

"We call it an epic comedy," said Alice Dewey, producer of *Hercules*. "So, that pretty much sums it up."[180]

"It is definitely an epic," agreed co-director Ron Clements. "It has this 'bigness' to it. But, throughout the movie, we're pulling together the 'bigness' with 'light-heartedness,' and it's

---

179 John Musker interview with ML, January 13, 1997.
180 Alice Dewey interview with ML, January 7, 1997.

an interesting combination. There's a comedic element that runs through the film, even in some of its most serious moments."[181]

"Ron and John clearly have a sense of style and wit about them that they bring to their movies," said Peter Schneider, then President of Walt Disney Feature Animation. "They're really experts in re-interpreting fable-esque stories in a unique way."[182]

Animator Anthony DeRosa, who would serve as supervising animator for the characters of Zeus and Hera in *Hercules*, summed up the production this way:

"'A Ron n' John film is not *Bambi*, *Dumbo*, or *The Lion King*, which are entertaining, restrained, more traditional Disney animation. Their movies are broader, more cartoony, caricatured, full of squash, stretch, bounce, fluidity, bigger smiles, bulging eyes. They're way out there, extreme. The previous movie I worked on was more contained, and I remember them commenting at first, 'Come on, Tony, loosen up you're not on *Pocahontas* here.'"[183]

Unlike that film and the studio's last, *The Hunchback of Notre Dame*, *Hercules* was, in no way, going to be a somber tale grounded in history or literature. This movie would be Greek mythology and Disney animation, filtered through a highly irreverent lens.

The project came to Clements and Musker in 1993, shortly after they had completed *Aladdin*. At a meeting with creative executives at the studio, the directors reviewed several projects in the early stages of development.

They came across artwork from animator Joe Haidar's story pitch for *Hercules*, and they were both intrigued. The idea of bringing mythology to life in Disney animation interested Clements and Musker. "You can design it so that it can exploit the things that animation can do, better than live-action in some ways," said Musker. "So, it seemed like a natural for animation. As far as Greek mythology is concerned, it's so rich and so visual, and the only Disney animation that had been done using this was the short 'Pastoral Sequence' in *Fantasia*."[184]

---

181   Ron Clements interview with ML, January 13, 1997.

182   Peter Schneider interview with ML, January 23, 1997.

183   Stephen Rebello & Jane Healey, *The Art of 'Hercules': The Chaos of Creation,*" (New York, Hyperion Press, 1997), p.45.

184   John Musker interview with ML, January 13, 1997.

"It just gives you so much to work with," said Dewey. "There are such great creatures like centaurs and satyrs and griffins; characters that can shape change. It's really so suitable for animation."[185]

Additionally, the filmmakers also saw the story of *Hercules* as very similar to that of many comic book superheroes. It is, essentially, the "origin story" of how he became a god and there are similarities in *Hercules* to the iconic status often bestowed on modern-day celebrities.

"He was, as we found out in our research, extremely popular, sort of the Michael Jordan of his day," said Dewey, adding, "He's kind of a common man's hero. He's half-god, half-man. So he's more accessible than some of the real Olympian gods."[186]

To root themselves in the setting of *Hercules*, the team took a pre-production research trip to Greece and Turkey. Andy Gaskill, art director for *Hercules*, said that this was extremely helpful in that they were able to have "some kind of psychological connection to the ancient world."[187]

"It turned out to really infuse the entire movie," added Roger Gould, supervisor of computer graphics on *Hercules*. "Seeing, not only the artwork, the antiques, and the temples, which were incredible, but even the natural landscape was wonderful to see. We would find a river and say, 'Oh my God. This is that river from that scene in our movie!'"[188]

But a realistic interpretation of the landscapes of Greece was not going to be the driving force behind the look of *Hercules*. In their conscious decision to differentiate this film, the directors were looking for an aesthetic that would provide the film a look that was indelibly all its own.

"In animation, one must use the medium to do things that only the medium can do," said Schneider, "which is invent fantasy characters and push the boundaries of reality. *Pocahontas* and *Hunchback* were more realistic, and now we're moving away from that in some sense. But each movie has its own style and character. We have to use whatever is right to tell the story."[189]

---

185 Alice Dewey interview with ML, January 7, 1997.
186 Ibid.
187 Andy Gaskill interview with ML, January 23, 1997.
188 Roger Gould interview with ML, January 22, 1997.
189 Peter Schneider interview with ML, January 23, 1997.

For *Hercules,* Musker looked to the work of British artist Gerald Scarfe, a cartoonist, and illustrator whose work had appeared in the British newspaper *The Sunday Times,* as well as *The New Yorker* magazine. Musker had been a longtime fan of Scarfe, who is also most famous for creating the stunning, graphic animation for *Pink Floyd: The Wall,* the surrealistic 1982 movie musical adaptation of the rock band's hit album.

Scarfe's style was one of broad caricatures and long, sweeping lines with sharp edges. At first glance, the artist's work doesn't look as if it would fit in any way with Disney animation, but Musker felt that Scarfe's flair would be the perfect look for *Hercules.*

"He draws in a very calligraphic style and an extreme style, but one that really seemed to relate to Greek vase paintings," said Musker of Scarfe. "His own analysis of Greek art was that he felt it offered a combination of power and elegance. In his drawings for our films, he did designs to capture this."[190]

Merging Gerald Scarfe's style with the norms of Disney animation and making sure that every artist working on *Hercules* was, quite literally, on the same page was a challenge and one that fell on the shoulders of Andy Gaskill, as the film's art director. "Disney has a house style," he explained. "While we try to be different from one film to the next, I think the house style is characterized by a certain balanced proportion. It's an approach to character styling that you can see going back many years in Disney films. It allows for a certain kind of expressiveness that you associate with Disney. What Scarfe did was blow apart a lot of those old proportions and formulas."[191]

Scarfe's style is so different that Gaskill was very ambivalent about the look of the film during the early days of production on *Hercules.* "I've got to be honest, when it was first mentioned, I wasn't all that excited by the idea," admitted Gaskill. "I couldn't quite see it. I didn't know how it would work. I was at a standstill for a long time."

Then, Gaskill saw early, rough-cut footage from the film. "I remember saying, 'Okay, this is going to work, and it looks

---

190 John Musker interview with ML, January 13, 1997.
191 Andy Gaskill interview with ML, January 23, 1997.

really cool!'" Gaskill admitted. "Once people started seeing that it could work, we all started running in the same direction."

Gaskill also added, "It's forced us to stretch our house style and become a lot looser than we are. It's been a real challenge for the animators, but they rose to the occasion. They've developed a whole new approach and vernacular."[192]

Gaskill came to the Disney studio in 1973 as an animator. Like many at that time, he mentored under many of the famed "Nine Old Men." Gaskill eventually left Disney to work on the animated film *Little Nemo: Adventures in Slumberland* (1989). While working on this film, he met Roger Allers, who would return to Disney to co-direct *The Lion King* and persuaded Gaskill to return to Disney, as well, to work as art director on that film.

"Generally, you have to find some simple visual equivalent for the story idea," said Gaskill of the role of an art director, adding, "It's an elusive thing to catch."[193]

Even with this artistic vision, the distinctive "Scarfe-look" of *Hercules* continually challenged Gaskill during production. "This movie really put me through my paces. It really forced me to look at things in different ways. It has changed a lot from its earliest inceptions. At the beginning, everyone thought of it as a very different animal. Over the years, it's evolved into a very loud, pushy teenager," joked Gaskill, adding, "But we love 'him!"[194]

"*Hercules* is a cartoon, a big cartoon!" summed up Eric Goldberg, who served as an animator on the film. "People enjoy the freedom associated with 'cartoony' style animation. It's very liberating to be able to do that and have the forms more pliable and more stylized."[195]

Hercules not only came with a distinct look but a tone all its own, as well. Contemporary humor and pop culture references would be lobbed throughout the film as if the Genie from *Aladdin* had written the script.

The film announces its tone very early on within its first few minutes. *Hercules* opens with solemn music and images

193 Ibid.
192 Ibid.
194 Ibid.
195 Eric Goldberg interview with ML, January 23, 1997.

of what looks like ancient Greek statues in a museum. The camera comes to rest on a vase.

Over this, we hear narration from none other than Charlton Heston, an actor instantly associated with austere Hollywood epics.

Heston begins to pontificate on Ancient Greece when one of the Muses depicted on the vase comes to life. "Will you listen to him?! He's making this story sound like some Greek tragedy!" one of the Muses declares. Another tells him, "We'll take it from here, darling!"

"You go, girl!" growls Heston

The Muses are Calliope (the voice of Lillias White), Melpomeme (Cheryl Freeman), Terpsichore (LaChanze), Thalia (Roz Ryan), and Clio (Vaneese Y. Thomas). They don't just relay the story of *Hercules*; in keeping with the tone of the film, they sing the narration, performing several of the film's Gospel-music-inspired songs like a Motown group.

"We were looking for music that seemed appropriate to our angle on the story," said Musker, adding, "which was to contemporize it a bit, and we felt that the music should help make it a little more accessible. Very early on, we saw the Muses, who are the goddesses of the arts, as really good storytellers. We thought, 'Why not have them be our Greek chorus?'"[196]

The Muses sing most of the songs in *Hercules*, written by stalwart Disney composer Alan Menken, this time teamed with another Broadway veteran, lyricist David Zippel (who had written the music for *City of Angels*).

"The Gospel Truth I" is the song that The Muses sing as they open the film and set the stage. On Mount Olympus, Zeus (Rip Torn) and Hera (Samantha Eggar) celebrate the birth of their son, Hercules, a surprisingly strong baby. Zeus and Hera present Hercules with a gift, Pegasus, a winged horse.

Also invited to the party, along with all of the other gods, is Hades, the conniving Lord of the Underworld, who secretly has his sights set on a "hostile takeover" of Mount Olympus. Hades is voiced by actor James Woods in an outstanding

---

196 John Musker interview with ML, January 13, 1997.

performance as one of the slickest, "schmoozesist" and funniest Disney villains.

"We went through practically every villain type performer in Hollywood, trying to locate just the right voice," said Nik Ranieri, supervising animator for Hades. "Of course, when you think of villains, you think of [transitions into a deep, malicious tone], 'Yes, well, hmmm,' that type of Jafar-like voice; very deep and sinister. Then, James Woods came in, and we all thought he was funny. So, we were unsure about it. Then, as we listened to it, we realized that the personality was there."[197]

"When we started the movie, we felt that there were too many of the cultured, British villains," said Clements. "We wanted a different kind of villain."[198] Ranieri added, "Usually when you first see a villain, it comes across as, 'Okay, this is the bad guy.' Then, when they speak, you definitely know that this is the villain, like Maleficent's big scene in *Sleeping Beauty*. When we see Hades, it's like that, but then, he starts off with a joke. So, right off the bat, you know that this guy is not your typical villain."[199]

Hades was Ranieri's first time animating a villain. Before *Hercules*, he served as the supervising animator for Meeko in *Pocahontas* and Lumiere in *Beauty and the Beast*. A native of Canada, Ranieri came to Disney in 1987 as an animator on *Who Framed Roger Rabbit* and was promoted to supervising animator on *The Rescuers Down Under*.

"Usually, as I'm animating something like Meeko or Lumiere, I sort of had this happy attitude," Ranieri noted. "But I really had to sort of get mean and cynical [with Hades]. I'm surprised I didn't attack my crew: 'Do it again!'," he laughed, adding, "It does sort of come across in your personality."[200]

Hades returns to the Underworld and consults with the Fates, a trio of witches voiced by Amanda Plummer, Carole Shelley, and Paddi Edwards. They warn Hades that, in eighteen years, he will be able to take over Mount Olympus, but Hercules could stand in his way.

---

197   Nik Ranieri interview with ML, January 23, 1997.
198   Ron Clements interview with ML, January 13, 1997.
199   Nik Ranieri interview with ML, January 23, 1997.
200   Ibid.

Hades realizes he needs to get rid of Hercules. He dispatches his dim-witted subordinates, Pain and Panic (Bobcat Goldthwait and Matt Frewer), to kidnap Hercules and administer a "Grecian formula," which will take away the baby's strength. The two gremlin-like sidekicks get Hercules to Earth, but they fail to distribute all of the poison, leaving the baby Hercules with his god-like strength. A mortal couple, Amphitryon (Hal Holbrook) and Alceme (Barbara Barrie) find Hercules and raise him as their own.

Here is where Hercules takes on a Superman-like vibe; Young Hercules (Josh Keaton, with Roger Bart as the singing voice) is much like Clark Kent, grappling with his uncontrollable strength. This leads Amphitryon to tell his son of his true origins, which leads Hercules to the Temple of Zeus (singing the ballad "Go the Distance," as he travels). Here, he seeks answers, and the temple comes to life to answer them. Zeus appears and tells Hercules that he can return to Mount Olympus once he proves himself a "true hero" on Earth.

Zeus reunites young Hercules with Pegasus. Together, at Zeus's urging, they fly to the Island of Idra to locate the "trainer of heroes," Philoctetes. Known as Phil, for short, he has the appearance of a satyr (half-goat/half-man) and the attitude of a crusty boxing coach. "Phil is the gruff, seen-it-all, done-it-all fight trainer," said Goldberg, supervising animator for the character. "He has to be convinced one more time to let his guard down to help Hercules. One thing I like about Phil is that, in addition to being a funny character, he does have a certain amount of pain in him. So many heroes that he's tried to train in the past have flaked out on him. So, he's given up when we meet him in the movie; he's leading a debauched life, eating too much and chasing nymphs."[201]

Goldberg, who had co-directed *Pocahontas*, returned to animating with his work on Phil. "I enjoy playing ping pong with my career," joked Goldberg, adding, "I get a lot more of my 'actor jollies' from being an animator than a director. Obviously, as rewarding as directing is, it was frustrating for

---

201 Eric Goldberg interview with ML, January 23, 1997.

me on *Pocahontas* to watch all those great animators doing these great scenes and feeling like, 'I want to animate too!'"[202]

That's precisely what he had the chance to do again and sink his teeth into a rich character like Phil, made all the richer by a vocal performance from Danny DeVito. "My earlier versions of Phil, when I was starting out playing with designs," said Goldberg, "were very much a caricature of Danny DeVito with horns, and it got a little further away from that with Gerald Scarfe's influence. Likewise, some elements of my Disney heroes crept in; a little bit of Freddy Moore, a little bit of Ward Kimball. They wanted me to take it further away from a Danny caricature, so to speak, but you've got the build to play with, and you've also got his attitude. Of course, years and years of watching *Taxi* also come into play."[203]

Also assisting with shaping the character was that Goldberg was able to sit in on DeVito's recording sessions, even, at times, making suggestions about the dialogue. "Every now and again, I would write the occasional line so that it sounded as if it were written in 'Phil-ese.' I was conscious with the character, not to have too many lines that sounded 'writerly.' If a line sounds like it should have a rim-shot after it, I tend not to want to use it."[204]

Phil trains Hercules through a song montage, "One Last Hope," as the audience sees Hercules grow up. Andreas Deja animated the character as an adult (voiced by actor Tate Donovan) in a change of pace from his consecutive work on Disney villains.

"I think Hercules was probably the most difficult character I've had to design," admitted Deja, adding, "because we started with the Gerald Scarfe influence. Some of the early drawings that I did weren't really my style, and the ones where I did go 'far out' with caricatured drawings of Hercules didn't really fit the character. He had these big, over-blown muscles and a little pin-head. They were fun to look at, but they didn't work for a character who goes through what he goes through in the movie."

Deja added, "I finally said, 'Let's go back to the Greek ideal, like the sculptures you see in museums. So, you have to have

---

202 Ibid.
203 Ibid.
204 Ibid.

a straight nose, pursed lips, and wide eyes; then I did an art deco thing with his curls."[205] Scarfe himself approved of that drawing, which hung over Deja's desk during production on *Hercules*, as a guidepost.

With his training complete, Hercules convinces Phil to leave Idra and go to the city of Thebes (dubbed "The Big Olive"). On their way, they stop to help a "damsel in distress," who turns out to be nothing of the sort. Her name is Meg.

"She's a different sort of heroine in that she's in the employ of the bad guy, Hades," said Musker. "So, she starts off seeming as if she's in the bad guy's camp, but through the development of the story, we try to show that she's a good person underneath it all."[206]

"There's a certain independence to Meg," said supervising animator Ken Duncan. "She has a pretty sharp wit and quick tongue. She says what's on her mind, which is usually pretty sarcastic and funny. She's not an innocent; she's been around the block."[207]

Duncan had been at Disney since 1989, after working over in Europe for Don Bluth. A versatile artist whose first supervising animator assignment was for the character of Thomas in *Pocahontas*, Duncan was able to adapt quickly to the specific "Scarfe-style" needed for *Hercules*.

"I tried not to think of it as a negative and get inspired by it," said Duncan. "When trying to figure out poses, I tried to think as graphically as possible." For Meg's design, Duncan looked to classic Greek shapes, shaping her torso as a column, with straight vertical lines and her hips like a pot ("With little love handles," laughed Duncan).[208]

Duncan took his cues for Meg's personality from actress Susan Egan, who provided the character's voice (she had also originated the role of Belle in Disney's Broadway production of *Beauty and the Beast*) . Egan brought strength, sly cynicism, and heart to the role. Additionally, like directors Musker and Clements, Duncan turned to vintage Holywood, as well. "I

---

205   Andreas Deja interview with ML, January 23, 1997.
206   John Musker interview with ML, January 13, 1997.
207   Ken Duncan interview with ML, January 22, 1997.
208   Ibid.

looked at '40's screwball comedies; I love those films with Jean Arthur and Barbara Stanwyck. I didn't take from anyone in particular, but just that whole independence of the women back then was really refreshing."[209]

Meg is very much in that same mold. After Hercules thinks he has rescued her from the centaur Nessus (Jim Cummings) Meg leaves Hercules and Phil, informing them that she can take care of herself.

Once Hercules and Phil arrive in the big city, Hercules is drawn into a fight with the ferocious multi-headed monster, the Hydra.

The battle is a fantastic action sequence in which Hercules attempts to defeat the Hydra by lopping off one of its heads, but each time he does, additional heads grow in their place. Toward the end of the scene, the screen is awash in Hydra heads. The creature is a marvel to behold, brought to life through computer-generated imagery.

"From day one, the directors kept saying 'Thirty Heads, we need thirty heads!,'" remembered Roger Gould, supervisor of CGI on the film. "Ron and John, the directors, wanted to create a Hydra that wasn't a three or six-headed Hydra. They said, 'What if we had a thirty-headed Hydra? What if we had something that was unbelievable in its scale? We want a Hydra that's not the size of an elephant or a rhino. What if it was the size of a skyscraper? What if it's so gigantic that Hercules has to jump on his flying horse, Pegasus, to fly in and among this jungle of necks that are attacking them?' That complexity and dimensionality were things that the computer was really good at."[210]

It's fitting that the Hydra was so massive, because computer animation took a big step forward with *Hercules*. In Disney's past animated films, CGI was used for backgrounds (as in *Beauty and the Beast*), or groups of characters (as in *Hunchback*), or to add dimension to a character (as in *Aladdin*).

The Hydra is much more. "We've created a full, acting, living, breathing character, who is competing head-to-head, literally, with Hercules," Gould said.[211]

---

209 Ibid.
210 Roger Gould interview with ML, January 22, 1997.
211 Ibid.

As imposing as the Hydra is, Hercules does manage to defeat it and, by doing so, is suddenly thrust into the celebrity spotlight, going from "Zero to Hero," a very catchy song montage from The Muses. During this, we see just how famous Hercules is, and everything from Nike to American Express is parodied. There's even a bit of self-deprecating humor, as the sequence includes a "Hercules Store," a direct poke at the popular retail division of the company, The Disney Store. Overall, the status of a celebrity is sharply lampooned, as well.

Hades also tosses a bombardment of obstacles at Hercules - sea serpents, minotaurs, wild boars - and Hercules defeats each one during this scene.

With his fame as its zenith, Hercules meets again with Zeus. Thinking that he has proven himself, Hercules finds out from his father that being a hero is more than being immortalized as an "action figure." Meanwhile, Hades discovers that Meg has fallen in love with Hercules, and she is his weakness. This initiates the villain's "hostile takeover" of Olympus. Hades unleashes the Titans, each a massive force of nature, in the film's climactic battle, in which Hercules must save Mount Olympus.

Hercules, released June 27, 1997, was once again treated as an event by Disney. The film opened on June 13 at the El Capitan Theater in Los Angeles and The New Amsterdam Theater in New York (which was being readied for the stage production of *The Lion King* that fall).

Both of these limited engagements came with stage shows featuring Disney songs and characters. In New York, the "event meter" was ratcheted up a notch, as Disney partnered with the city to stage a parade through the streets of Manhattan on June 14, 1997. "Disney's *Hercules* Electrical Parade" was held that night, re-purposing light-up floats from Disney's theme park "Main Street Electrical Parade," including newly designed *Hercules*-themed floats created specifically for the parade.

In addition to this and the engagement at the New Amsterdam, there was also the *Hercules* "Forum of Fun" held at New York's Chelsea Pier, which included games, live performances, and animation demonstrations.

Additionally, there was a flurry of *Hercules* products available that summer that seemed to mirror the parodied promotional "tie-ins" in the film itself.

And while critics praised *Hercules* (Jami Bernard in *The New York Daily News* gave the film four stars and declared: "No myth-take about it, *Hercules* is mighty strong."[212]), its box-office results were not on the heroic side that Disney had been hoping it would be. In its opening weekend, *Hercules* came in second behind the action film *Face/Off* and by its third week (as other big summer movies were released) had grossed $58 million (a far cry from the studio's recent animated features in previous summers).

The worldwide box-office totals for *Hercules* came in at $253 million, falling short of the $300 million projected. Could it be that audiences had grown weary of the months of massive marketing that accompanied every Disney film? Was every Disney animated film *really* an "event?"

Regardless of its performance, there was no denying that Musker and Clements accomplished a matchless feat with *Hercules*, a knowing, comedic take on a classic tale that still had a lot to say.

"It's about one's interior strength and not your exterior strength," said Schneider. "Hercules finds that, within him, his goodness to other people and his belief in other people is really important. It's not about being powerful and mighty and strong. It's about your basic humanity."[213]

Heroism and heart would be a central theme of The Walt Disney Studio's next animated feature, which would tell another well-known, mythic story from another part of the world.

The story of *Hua Mulan* is a legendary Chinese folk tale that dates back to somewhere in the 4th century AD. The story was first composed as a folk song, telling of a young girl who disguises herself as a man and takes her aged father's place in the army during a time of war to save her father's life.

The story came to Disney in the early 1990s, when two projects that were in development were combined. *China Girl*, about

---

212　Jami Bernard, "Musclebound for Glory," *The New York Daily News*, June 13, 1997, p. 43.

213　Peter Schneider interview with ML, January 23, 1997.

a "waifish" Chinese girl fighting a war against tyranny, was one story, and the other was a manuscript by children's book author Robert D. San Souci, based on "The Song of Fa Mu Lan."

The two scripts came together at The Walt Disney Studio as *Mulan*.

The film would signal another change in course, in several ways for Disney animation. First and foremost would be a change in where the film was produced. Feature Animation Florida, at the then Disney-MGM Studios theme park, had served as a facility to produce short subjects and assist the California studio with specific segments.

Disney's Feature Animation Florida was a fully functioning studio, but it was also an attraction at the Disney-MGM Studios theme park, called "The Magic of Disney Animation." On the attraction, a guide would take visitors through a tour of how a Disney animated film is made. Toward the end, visitors would be able to peer into windows at the animators at Disney Feature Animation Florida, hard at work on the studio's latest project.

After years of proving themselves with these projects, *Mulan* would be the first animated feature completely produced at Disney's Florida Studio. "In order for the studio to be open in the first place, it had to be a tourist attraction," noted Barry Cook, co-director of *Mulan*. "For a while, our attitude was just the thought that even if it's just a tourist attraction forever, then that's fine. It will still make money; people can still draw, and it will still work out. If something else happens, then let it. But I don't think that they were ever banking on the fact that we'd be able to make features here."[214]

With so many visitors passing by and peering down at animators during a given day, they affectionally dubbed this unique work environment "the fishbowl." "After a while, it became like moving wallpaper," said Tony Bancroft, who co-directed *Mulan* with Barry Cook. "Certainly, in the beginning, it was fun and a little freaky. You felt like you were in a little caged zoo. We used to play pranks in the beginning, and sometimes it was more fun for us to watch the people go by."[215]

214 Barry Cook interview with ML, January 20, 1998.
215 Tony Bancroft interview with ML, January 20, 1998.

"We saw one lady with a beehive hairdo," remembered Cook. "If you stretched your arms as high as you can, you couldn't have touched it. That inspired a lot of gag drawings."[216]

Cook had been with Disney Feature Animation Florida since its opening day. A native of Nashville, Tennessee, he interned at the Hanna-Barbera studio before coming to Disney to work as an effects animator on *Beauty and the Beast* and *Aladdin*.

After relocating to the Florida studio, Cook eventually directed two short subjects, *Off His Rockers* (1992) and the Roger Rabbit short, *Trail Mix-Up* (1993).

For *Mulan*, Cook was partnered with animator Tony Bancroft as his co-director. Tony, a native Californian, was attending CalArts when he landed a summer job working with animation director Ralph Bakshi. An internship with Disney in Burbank came next, and then a full-time job as one of the first animators at the Florida studio.

Tony returned to Disney in California, where he eventually served as supervising animator for Pumbaa in *The Lion King*. His impressive work on that film led him back to Florida as co-director of *Mulan*.

"We're the Rocky Balboa of feature animation," said Bancroft at the time, of the excitement around the Florida studio finally having the opportunity to produce their own full-length feature film.

Cook echoed this excitement and discussed a fable that one of the studio's animators, Alex Kupershmidt, had relayed to him, almost as a cautionary tale. "He said, 'Ya know, there's an old Russian folk tale about the hunter who came back with the eagle's golden feather,'" remembered Cook, "'and the Emperor told him, 'That's great, now go back and bring me the eagle.' Alex told me that the Emperor was now going to ask me to bring back the eagle. So, *Mulan* is the eagle that we had to go out and fetch."[217]

Everyone involved with *Mulan* was determined to bring back that "eagle."

Cook said, "Early on, we kept saying, 'Well, this would make a great live-action picture. It really could, I mean, if you treated

---

216 Barry Cook interview with ML, January 20, 1998.
217 Ibid.

the subject matter completely serious and did this as an epic story of this warrior woman, it could make a great live-action film." These words are now prophetic, as *Mulan* was re-made in live action in 2020. "But, since we're in the animation business," added Cook, "we thought, 'How can we make this work as an animated film?'"[218]

Mulan's producer Pam Coats echoed this. "We looked at it and said, 'Wow! This has the potential for a really great story.' We tracked it in terms of 'Is this an interesting story?' Then, we put in elements that are interesting in animation."[219]

The filmmakers started with the two-thousand-year-old story that inspired the film. "What you'll find is that for every generation that the story has passed down, it has changed here and there," noted Bancroft. "There are so many different versions of the tale of *Mulan* that we felt that we had enough leeway to go in different directions."[220]

"There was never any version where we said, 'This is it!'" added Cook. "They really don't know if she ever lived. Most people think that she probably did, but nobody can prove that she did."[221]

Helping to untangle the story puzzle of *Mulan* during the film's early days was artist Chris Sanders, who served as the head of the story for the film. "Chris helped us discover Mulan," said producer Coats. "He helped us discover who she was and how she makes her journey through the film."[222]

Sanders, another graduate of CalArts, came to Disney in 1987, after working as a character designer for Jim Henson's hit animated TV show, *Muppet Babies*.

With an innate sense of plotting, Sanders soon joined the story department, working on *The Rescuers Down Under, Beauty and the Beast,* and *The Lion King*. His ability to solve story challenges helped define *Mulan* early in the development of the plot.

One of these initial versions of the film had Mulan assisted

----

218 Ibid.
219 Pam Coats interview with ML, January 12, 1998.
220 Tony Bancroft interview with ML, January 20, 1998.
221 Barry Cook interview with ML, January 20, 1998.
222 Pam Coats interview with ML, January 12, 1998.

by two dragons named Yin and Yang. It was Sanders who was able to see that these sidekicks were overshadowing the main character of Mulan. "I knew almost immediately that one of them had to go," he recalled.[223] Yin and Yang were replaced by Mushu the dragon and Cri-Kee the cricket.

"I think the key to *Mulan* was indeed this unique main character and the unique position that her character is put in," said Sanders. "She's in a no-win situation. If she takes her father's place, she worse than kills him, in a certain sense, because he'd rather die than be dishonored. But she cannot stand the idea of losing him."[224]

"The main thing that we wanted was to be honorable to the Chinese culture and honorable to the person of Mulan," said co-director Bancroft of the story.

As *Mulan* was taking shape, the filmmakers also focused on the setting and embarked on a production trip to China. The film's art director Ric Sluiter remembered that the trip influenced the production of *Mulan* for some time after. "We brought back lots of little bits and pieces that came out over the years of the production. We'd have to push the mountains back a little bit in one scene, and we'd say, 'Remember those mountains?' Then we'd pull out slides and photos from the trip. There were all these feelings that we had when we came back, and we really felt that we had to get the feeling of being there into the film."[225]

This look that the artists applied to *Mulan* was "poetic simplicity," which the film's production designer Hans Bacher explained this way: "It describes what everybody wanted. We didn't want to overload the backgrounds with too much information. We wanted to create a stage for the characters."[226]

This simpler style is perfect for *Mulan*, as it reflects the work of classical Chinese artists. "In Chinese art, everything is very balanced," said Bacher. "It's like Yin and Yang. You have positive and negative space."[227]

Additionally, Bacher noted that he and his team also found

---

223 Chris Sanders interview with ML, February 7, 1998.
224 Ibid.
225 Ric Sluiter interview with ML, January 19, 1998.
226 Hans Bacher interview with ML, February 10, 1998.
227 Ibid.

inspiration in Disney's past. "The style of *Bambi* was developed by an artist named Tyrus Wong, who is Chinese," noted Bacher. "When you look at the first watercolor paintings that he did for *Bambi*, they look completely like Chinese artwork."[228]

Bacher, a German native, came to Disney in the 1980s, bringing a distinct, artistic talent that would influence the visual development of *Aladdin* and *The Lion King*. With *Mulan*, Bacher, as production designer, worked closely with art director Ric Sluiter to ensure that the film had a consistent style that carried through all elements.

"There is a team of over four hundred people working on this film," said Bacher. "And, in the end, the film has got to look as if it came from one artist."[229]

That particular look of "poetic simplicity" meant that all involved with *Mulan* would have to get comfortable with a significant filmmaking change. The team behind *Mulan* decided not to use tone mattes when making the film. This is artwork, created by the effects animators, that lend shadows and depth to the characters. Not using tone mattes would help give the film the "flatter," more straightforward look the artists wanted. "We fought really hard to prove to them that we could put these characters on a background with atmosphere and no tone mattes," said Sluiter.[230]

Sluiter, who hails from Toronto, Canada, worked for several years as an electrician before attending Sheridan College and studying art. He joined Disney in 1989, contributing to *Beauty and the Beast* and *The Lion King*.

For *Mulan*, both Sluiter and Bacher also incorporated the work of Disney artist Chen-Yi Chang, who designed characters and costumes for the film. "[Chen-Yi] comes from a background of Chinese brushwork," added Bacher, "real simple 'S'-shapes, one line leading into another, simple, graphic, elegant shapes and so to get that, you have to design each character with a lot of rules. It's like a schematic formula that has to be laid out and embedded into each artist. Chen-Yi is a designer, not an animator,

---

228   Ibid.

229   Ibid.

230   Ric Sluiter interview with ML, January 19, 1998.

so the artists had to take his shapes and make them animatable."[231]

It was fitting that so much thought was dedicated to the look of *Mulan*, as the film opens like an unfurling piece of artwork, being created before the audiences' eyes. What looks like bamboo brush art is "painted" across the screen, revealing an image of the Great Wall of China.

The serene mood soon changes, as the security of the Great Wall is breached by the Hun army led by the film's villain, Shan-Yu, voiced by the deep, ominous voice of actor Miguel Ferrer. "His voice carries an intelligence behind it," said Pres Romanillos, supervising animator for Shan-Yu, "so he gave the character more credibility, and he becomes more than just a hulk-ish figure."[232]

Still, the imposing character did take its toll on the animator, who admitted with a laugh, "I didn't realize it at the time, but my brow would always be furrowed, and I would go home, and my wife would ask me what I was angry at."[233]

With the attack, the Emperor (Pat Morita) dispatches his aide, Chi-Fu (James Hong), to carry out conscription that one man from each family must serve in the Imperial Army.

As this is happening, in a small village, the only child of the Fa family, Mulan (voiced by Ming-Na Wen, with the singing voice of Lea Salonga, who had sung for Princess Jasmine in *Aladdin*) nervously awaits her meeting with the Matchmaker. This turns disastrous due to a mishap with Mulan's good luck cricket, Cri-Kee. The incident brings shame to her mother, Fa Li (Freda Fo Shen), Grandmother Fa (voiced by two legends: June Foray as the voice and Marni Nixon as the character's singing voice), and her father Fa Zhou (Soon-Tek Oh).

It's with her father that Mulan is the closest. Fitting that Mark Henn served as supervising animator for both characters in the film. "He's very traditional, on the surface," said Henn of Fa Zhou, "yet deep down, he recognizes Mulan's uniqueness and the specialness of his daughter."[234]

---

231 Hans Bacher interview with ML, February 10, 1998.
232 Pres Romanillos interview with ML, January 19, 1998.
233 Ibid.
234 Mark Henn interview with ML, January 20, 1998.

Soon, Chi-Fu comes to the village announcing that one male from each family must be drafted into the army to help battle the Huns. Fa Zhou, the male in his household, accepts, even though he is older and in poor health.

Knowing that her father will not make it through the war, Mulan sneaks away that night. She disguises herself by cutting her hair, dons her father's battle armor, and rides away on her horse, Khan, to join the army. When Grandmother Fa learns of this, she pleads to their ancestors to watch over Mulan.

The spirits of the ancestors awake in the nearby temple. They realize they must send a guardian out to watch over Mulan. The First Ancestor (voiced by *Star Trek*'s Mr. Sulu himself, George Takei) awakens Mushu, a small dragon, who has been demoted from guardian. The fast-talking Mushu sees an opportunity here to get his guardian status back. Cri-Kee joins Mushu, and the two set off to find Mulan.

One of the world's most famous comedians, Eddie Murphy, made his animation acting debut, providing the voice of Mushu. "We didn't know how it was going to go over," said Mushu's supervising animator, Tom Bancroft, of Murphy providing the character's voice, "because we were designing this very serious look at Chinese culture and family honor and here we were throwing in this very urban voice. But, then, I was with it, because of the contrast between this character and this culture and all the other characters, I thought that it would work great and that there would be a lot of chemistry."[235]

It was when Murphy started recording his dialogue that Mushu began to take shape. "At first, they were writing for the character and what they felt that the needs of the story were," noted Tom. "Eddie recorded that, but he was struggling with it. So, then he would read it the way we had it, and then he would ad-lib and say, 'Well, let me try that another way,' and then he would do it his way. And it would always come out so much funnier, whether it was a funny line or not because he'd put these inflections in it and make these straight lines sound pretty funny. So, they went back and re-wrote almost

---

235 Tom Bancroft interview with ML, January 20, 1998.

all of Mushu's lines and added some gags and made it more 'Eddie-esque.'"[236]

Tom found himself in a unique position, not only animating this distinct Disney character but also in the fact that *Mulan* became somewhat of a family affair for him, as co-director Tony Bancroft is his twin brother.

Tom came to Disney the same year his brother did and worked on many of the Disney studio's significant features and shorts at the Florida studio. Mushu represented his first supervising animator opportunity, and Tom said that working with his brother was a benefit in that their perspectives on the character were aligned. He noted that this made taking direction from his sibling all the easier.

"As twins, our likes and dislikes have always been similar, so animation-wise it was the same," said Tom. "If I wasn't crazy about it, I pretty much knew that Tony would have changes. And his changes I pretty much always agreed with."[237]

Of this unique working relationship, Tony added, "My brother and I have worked on things together our whole life - comic strips, comic books, you name it. In the past, though, he would criticize my work, and I would criticize his." Laughing, Tony added that in his role as co-director, "Now, I'm just criticizing his, and he can't do anything about it."[238]

Thanks to this symbiotic, sibling working relationship, Mushu emerges as the film's scene-stealer from the moment he comes on screen. The "travel-sized" dragon, along with Cri-Kee, helps Mulan get to the army camp, where she convinces the other recruits that she is a man, adopting the more "manly" name of Ping.

"We had to create Mulan as a believable character as herself and then create her trying to be a believable character as Ping when she joins the army and disguises as a man," said Mulan's supervising animator Mark Henn. "The acting challenge of that was very exciting."[239]

The first three soldiers Mulan meets in the camp are

---

236 Ibid.
237 Ibid.
238 Tony Bancroft interview with ML, January 20, 1998.
239 Mark Henn interview with ML, January 20, 1998.

the disparate trio of Yao (Harvey Fierstein), Ling (Gedde Watanabe), and Chien-Po (Jerry Tondo).

Broose Johnson and Aaron Blaise shared supervising animator duties for the three soldiers. "It really is like two actors bouncing off one another," said Johnson of their working relationship. "We'd usually wind up with something far more enjoyable than was planned." [240]

"We did work more closely than two typical animators," added Blaise, "but we didn't work as closely as we thought we would. It was just about trusting the other guy."[241]

Yao, Ling, and Chien-Po each have distinct personalities. Blaise says of Yao, "The way I had always envisioned him was someone who always thinks with his fists, kind of a hothead, opens his mouth before he thinks and wants to start throwing punches, but he's always outmatched."[242]

Blaise also served as supervising animator of Ling, who is usually lighting the fuse for Yao's explosive personality. "His character basically became the instigator. One thing he loves more than anything is getting Yao started, and the funny thing is, he usually winds up on the receiving end of Yao's punches somehow."[243]

Blaise, who hails from Vermont, was hired by Disney after graduating from the Ringling College of Art in Sarasota, Florida. With *The Lion King*, Blaise was promoted to supervising animator for the character of Nala.

Broose Johnson, Blaise's partner on *Mulan*'s "Gang of Three," as the characters came to be known, was another graduate of CalArts. Johnson came to Disney in 1987, just in time for the Renaissance. He worked in clean-up and as an assistant animator before supervising the character of Chien-Po in *Mulan*.

Johnson noted that the peaceful, meditative Chien-Po balances the other two. "The last thing he's going to do is think with his fists. He's relaxed, really centered; he's our Buddha."[244]

---

240 Broose Johnson interview with ML, January 19, 1998.
241 Aaron Blaise interview with ML, January 19, 1998.
242 Ibid.
243 Ibid.
244 Broose Johnson interview with ML, January 19, 1998.

During their training, Captain Shang leads Chien-Po, Ling, Yao, and Mulan. Ruben Aquino served as supervising animator for Shang, as well as Mulan's mother, Fa Li. An interesting dynamic about Shang (voiced by actor B.D. Wong, with the singing voice of Donny Osmond) is that he is appointed by General Li (James Shigeta), who is also Shang's father. "He's really excited and very eager to take on the responsibilities that he's been given," said Aquino of Shang. "That's a more human side of him, that, when you see him again outside the tent talking with the soldiers, you don't really see again because there he has to put on the mask of a commanding officer."[245]

A native of Okinawa, Aquino had worked at Disney for sixteen years when he started work on *Mulan*. During that time, he contributed animation to every Disney feature from *The Black Cauldron* through *The Hunchback of Notre Dame*. Although he majored in architecture in college, he found animation compelling. "You have to be pretty motivated and love the art form," said Aquino. "You have to love performing, not really in front of an audience, but entertaining through your drawings. You have to have that knack of 'hammy acting.'"[246]

Aquino would find himself acting out scenes in front of a large mirror he kept in his office. "The mirror helps me to break the dialogue into phrases and helps me figure out what my main poses might be," he said. "Then within poses, I can figure out sub-poses so that I get a little bit of texture within the acting. This way, there's a little bit of rhythm, variation, and it's not so predictable."[247]

This detailed acting is seen in Shang as he leads the Imperial Army into battle with the Huns. When the two armies meet up, it's on a snow-covered mountainside, where a seemingly endless hoard of Hun soldiers and an avalanche are brought to life through CGI in an impressive action sequence.

The entire Hun army, effects and even the avalanche, were created in the computer and then enhanced to blend seamlessly with the 2D animation and the look of "poetic simplicity" found in the rest of the film.

---

245 Ruben Aquino interview with ML, January 20, 1998.
246 Ibid.
247 Ibid.

Eric Guaglione, the supervisor of digital production of *Mulan*, said, "Every time we'd go into a meeting and talk about the graphics and the actions, we'd also talk about how to stage something compositionally and graphically, as well as keeping the images balanced and, to me, that's what this whole film has been about. Every time I thought about how a CGI element fit into this film, I had to think about that again: 'Don't go overboard with this, make sure it's in keeping with the rest of the film."

Guaglione also added, "We wanted to do everything to integrate the CGI into the film without you being able to detect it."[248]

"We tried to think of [the Hun army] as being a real thinking character, even though what we wind up doing are things with masses of character in them," said Rob Bekuhrs, who served as supervising animator for the digital production sequences. "We still have individuals in there; they should have individual actions. They shouldn't necessarily stand out either, and that's somewhere where you have to strike a balance between a really dynamic character and a whole bunch of characters that act as a group."[249]

A program called "Atilla" was explicitly designed for the computer animation in *Mulan*. In addition to this, the effects artists researched a number of the battle effects during what they dubbed "Destructo Day."

David Tigdwell, the supervisor of visual effects animation on *Mulan*, explained, "I told everyone, 'Whatever you have that you want to destroy or set on fire or explode, just bring it in and we'll film it.' It got messy, but it was fun. That's helpful because sometimes you can find the simplest little key to an effect."[250]

Something that wasn't as easy to solve or find a detail for during "Destructo Day" was the avalanche sequence. For this scene, the effects artists had to play with the "reality" of an avalanche.

"The story told us to do one thing, but the logic of the avalanche told us to do another," said Tidgwell. "Avalanches don't have all the sliding snow behind them in the way that the story has to have. There must have been fifty different ideas on what the back part of the avalanche should look like. "[251]

---

248 Eric Guaglione interview with ML, January 20, 1998.
249 Rob Bekurs interview with ML, January 20, 1998.
250 David Tigdwell interview with ML, January 20, 1998.
251 Ibid.

During the battle that leads to the avalanche, it is the actions of Mulan/Ping that save the army. However, during this, she is wounded, her disguise is revealed, and Shang and the army are forced to leave Mulan behind.

Mulan learns that Shan-Yu is plotting an assault on the Imperial City. With Mushu and Cri-Kee in tow, Mulan sets out to the city to warn the soldiers. To save the Emperor (and China), she winds up joining the battle herself and faces off against Shan-Yu during the film's climax.

Mulan features songs by Mathew Wilder and *Hercules'* David Zippel. "Honor to Us All," one of the first songs in the movie is sung as Mulan nervously meets with the Matchmaker; "I'll Make a Man Out of You" is Shang's song (along with the soldiers) as he attempts to get the army ready for war; "A Girl Worth Fighting For," is sung by Yao, Ling, Chien-Po and the troops as they march off to battle and "True to Your Heart," performed by the pop group 98 Degrees and Stevie Wonder, plays over the ending credits.

It's *Mulan*'s ballad, "Reflection," sung by the title character at the beginning of the film, that speaks to the character's journey and the other characters' journeys in the film.

"She discovers that she's not this person she thought that she was - this perfect Chinese maiden, this bride - that they want me to be," said director Tony Bancroft. "When she discovers this, that is when her father is called off to war, and then she goes on her journey to save her father's life, and it's through that journey that she really changes. What I think is so great about this film is that she changes how society views a woman. She doesn't change who she is at all; she remains consistent throughout the story. It's the characters that she comes up against who change to see things her way."[252]

These differentiators about *Mulan* signaled a change in direction for Disney from what had become their "formula" for their previous animated films. In addition to how dissimilar the main character's journey was, the pacing, the subject matter, and how the film incorporated the musical numbers was a break from the traditional paradigm.

---

252 Tony Bancroft interview with ML, January 20, 1998.

Additionally, when *Mulan* was released to theaters on June 19, 1998, it arrived with a much quieter marketing campaign than the studio's previous animated features. As both *Hunchback* and *Hercules* had fallen short of their projected performances, there was no "event vibe" surrounding *Mulan*. There was no premiere in Central Park or parade down Fifth Avenue. *Mulan*'s marketing budget was $30 million (half that of *Hercules*). To debut the film, Disney opted for a low-key premiere at The Hollywood Bowl.

"'It was better to let the movie lead the way,' said Richard Cook [then], chairman of Disney's Motion Picture Group."[253]

The movie's "tie-in" advertising (such as that with McDonald's) didn't begin until just days before *Mulan*'s release.

"'We wanted to get the message of the movie out there first before selling the ancillary product,' said Schneider, admitting that promotional hoopla can 'send the wrong message.'"[254]

This all went perfectly with the central message of the film *Mulan*, as producer Coats noted. "The overriding theme as Shakespeare would put it is be true to yourself," she said. "You succeed in life by figuring out who you are and being true to that and not being true to what someone expects from you or tells you to do."[255]

Critics were very responsive to this and praised *Mulan*. Richard Corliss in *Time* magazine said that the film was "...a strange and beguiling new breed of Disney animated feature." He added, "...this is strong and supple entertainment, not a girlish cartoon in the style of *The Little Mermaid*, in which a girl becomes a woman. Here, a girl becomes a man."[256]

Mulan grossed $120 million domestically and $304 million worldwide. An extremely respectable box-office performance.

However, it wasn't the highest-grossing animated film made in 1998. That title would go to Disney's next major animated release just five months later: the second feature film from the studio that had taken animation "to infinity and beyond."

253 Claudia Eller and James Bates, "Bridled Optimism," *The Los Angeles Times*, June 12, 1998, latimes.com (accessed March 25, 2021).

254 Ibid.

255 Pam Coats interview with ML, January 12, 1998.

256 Richard Corliss, "An Ode to Martial Smarts, *Time*, June 22, 1998, content.time.com (accessed March 25, 2021).

CHAPTER EIGHT

"Two Worlds, One Family"

A Bug's Life & Tarzan

How do you follow up *Toy Story*?

The film had grossed $373 million worldwide. At the time, it was the twenty-first highest-grossing film, sold 21.5 million copies in its first year of release on VHS, a direct-to-video sequel was planned, children (of all ages) were obsessed with the characters, and Pixar had "gone public" on the New York Stock Exchange.

No pressure.

Amidst all of this success, at Pixar Animation Studio, as the focus now shifted to the future and the studio's next full-length animated feature, anxiety began to set in.

"'Are we going to be a one-shot wonder?' producer Darla Anderson wondered."[257]

Animator Andrew Stanton, who would co-direct the next feature with John Lasseter, realized, just before the release of *Toy Story,* that the film might be a success, and thought, 'Oh my gosh! We may get to make another movie!'"[258]

Brainstorming meetings started between Stanton and Lasseter, who met with animator Peter Docter and Joe Ranft, head of the studio's story team, to develop future animated features.

"We started bouncing around potential ideas, some of which were jokes," said John Lasseter. "Then, we hit upon something with the Aesop fable, *The Grasshopper and the Ants*. We knew

---

257 John Canemaker, *Two Guys Named Joe*, (New York, Disney Editions, 2010), p.12.
258 Ibid, p.12.

immediately that it was perfect for the medium because of the way the insects and their microscopic world are built."[259]

Lasseter also found motivation in his own home and his five sons, who, at the time, were young and enjoyed exploring their backyard, catching bugs and placing them in jars with holes poked in the lids. Said Lasseter, "The insect world is just fascinating, and it became very inspiring."[260]

Stanton and Ranft took *The Grasshopper and the Ants* story as the launching point and began crafting a script initially entitled *Bugs*. Stanton remembered: "It was like going from freshman class of 'How to Make a Movie' with *Toy Story* to senior thesis."[261]

When work started on this "senior thesis" that would become *A Bug's Life*, Stanton worked in animation for a decade, starting his career with the animation studio, Kroyer Films.

He applied at Disney three times but kept getting rejected, which led him to Pixar in 1990, where he was hired as the Studio's second animator (Lasseter was the first). After being part of the team that worked and reworked the script for *Toy Story*, Lasseter asked Stanton to co-direct *A Bug's Life*.

Stanton and Ranft took Aesop's simple fable of how a grasshopper spends a summer enjoying themselves while an ant works diligently and stores food for the winter. The grasshopper then has to beg the ant for food come winter in a parable about the virtues of hard work and responsibility.

As they refashioned this familiar story into *A Bug's Life*, Stanton and Ranft worked on the concepts of a "bug circus" and crafted the grasshoppers as the film's villains.

An early version of the story centered on Red, an ant, the ringleader, looking for work for his circus. It was Stanton who, instead, shifted the focus to be an ant from a colony who mistakes the circus performers for warriors and hires them to help protect the colony from the grasshoppers.

From here, it was Ranft who, with his innate storytelling and comedic skills, injected the plot with humor. Some of his earliest storyboards and ideas for the plot remained intact in the finished film, as he served as a cheerleader through the

---

259   John Lasseter interview with ML, September 28, 1998.
260   Ibid.
261   Pixar.com, "Filmakers Round Table: *A Bug's Life*.

plot's challenges. Stanton recalled of Ranft: "He had a way of making you feel like anything was possible, and any problem could be overcome. He brought out the best in you."[262]

Ranft joined Disney in 1980, working as a writer and storyboard artist, and eventually mentored under Eric Larson. Here, he worked on the story for such features as *Oliver & Company*, *Beauty and the Beast*, and *The Lion King.*

During this time, Ranft's talents as a performer came to light as he studied and performed with the noted improvisational group The Groundlings, bringing this instinctive comedy to the stories he touched.

In 1991, Pixar hired him to head up their story department. He worked on *Toy Story* at Pixar, and his storytelling abilities were also called upon by other studios. He served as story supervisor for *The Nightmare Before Christmas* and *James and the Giant Peach.*

Lasster said: "Well, story is the most important thing. Period. In our films. And getting the story department solid and bringing in experienced people really, they're the ones who roll up their sleeves and keep hammering away at the story and its long, hard journey period of reworking and reworking and reworking. It's a collaborative effort, and Joe was a big part of building that."[263]

Sadly, Ranft passed away in 2005, at the age of 45, in a car accident in California. His passing left Pixar and many in the animation industry reeling. Ranft leaves behind a remarkable legacy with his talent, especially with *A Bug's Life* and a specific character in the film.

As storyboards came together for *A Bug's Life*, Ranft provided the voice for Heimlich, the caterpillar, on the film's temporary soundtrack (the artists and animators will often do this before actors are cast). Lasseter recalled, "In creating the character Heimlich, Joe, who is just a very funny person, did this hilarious, high-pitched-German-'mama's boy'-voice. We were just cracking up."[264]

---

262 John Canemaker, *Two Guys Named Joe*, (New York, Disney Editions, 2010), p.14.
263 Bill Cody, "John Lasseter Talks *Cars 2* and the Memory of His Friend and Collaborator, Joe Ranft," June 22, 2011, comingsoon.net, (accessed March 28, 2021).
264 John Lasseter interview with ML, September 28, 1998.

As casting for the film began, the filmmakers started to look for an actor to provide Heimlich's "permanent" voice for the film, but none seemed to match Ranft's performance. One night, Lasseter brought a rough-cut "story reel" of *A Bug's Life* home to show his family. "Every time Joe said Heimlich's line, my wife giggled," he remembered.[265]

The next day, Lasseter told Ranft that he had the part and, it was the story artist, not a well-known comedian or actor (as would usually be the case with a film's comic relief) voicing Heimlich in *A Bug's Life*.

There was another unexpected "twist" that occurred during the production of the film. DreamWorks, SKG Animation, the studio co-founded by Jeffrey Katzenberg, announced that they had entered into a partnership with the computer animation production company, Pacific Data Images, to produce their own full-length animated feature.

The film would be entitled *Antz* and...it would also be about the insect world.

Controversy immediately started to swirl. Was it just coincidence that both Disney and Pixar would have similar projects in the works, so close after the Katzenberg-Disney "split?" As reported by Peter Burrows in *Newsweek*, at the time, that's how it seemed:

"...Pixar executives don't believe that Katzenberg found out about the *Bugs* project while at Disney. Indeed, some are even willing to believe DreamWorks' version of the facts that Katzenberg got the idea for *Antz* from Nina Jacobsen, a former Disney executive (now back at Disney) who pitched the idea while working for DreamWorks at the time."[266]

What truly stung and added to tensions was when release dates began to be announced. Disney and Pixar had a stake in the ground with *A Bug's Life* slated for Thanksgiving weekend of 1998. *Antz* was scheduled for spring of 1999.

However, several months into 1998, DreamWorks announced a change in *Antz*' release date, and the film would

---

265 Ibid.

266 Peter Burrows, "*Antz* vs. *Bugs*: The inside Story of How DreamWorks Beat Pixar to the Screen," *Business Week*, November 23, 1998, Bloomberg.com (accessed March 29, 2021).

now hit theaters on October 2, 1998, over a month before *A Bug's Life* would bow, beating the film to the box-office punch.

As animation historian and author John Canemaker noted, "How and why two rival studios happened to be producing CGI features, with ants, that would both premiere in the fall of 1998 remains a matter of smoldering anger among Pixarians."[267]

As it would turn out, the only fundamental similarities between the two films were that they were both computer-animated views of the insect world.

Antz, decidedly slanted from a tonal perspective toward an adult audience with a voice cast that included Sharon Stone, Sylvester Stallone, Gene Hackman, Christopher Walken, Jennifer Lopez, and, in a significant voice casting coup, Woody Allen as the main character, an ant named "Z."

Z is a worker ant who trades places with a soldier ant and unwittingly becomes a hero in the film. With a PG-rating and some comedically darker moments, *Antz* carried with it mature themes around the power of the individual and the cost of war and violence.

This was in stark contrast to the somewhat similar but lighter tenor and visuals found in the story of *A Bug's Life*. The film begins at "Ant Island" and tells the tale of a colony of ants led by Princess Atta (Julia Louis Dreyfus) and her mother, the Queen (Phyllis Diller). They find themselves persecuted by a colony of grasshoppers, led by the malicious Hopper (Kevin Spacey).

Hopper and the grasshoppers force the ants to harvest food for them. Enter the film's main character, an inventive member of the ant colony, Flik (Dave Foley), who accidentally spills their latest crop into the water with his latest invention, a grain harvester.

"Our hero is such that he is a really unlikely hero," said Lasseter of Flik. "He's more like an everyday guy. He has a huge heart and always means well. Like us, in our own lives, we tend to get ourselves into predicaments that we didn't mean to. It's how you deal with those predicaments that measure your character."[268]

267 John Canemaker, *Two Guys Named Joe*, (New York, Disney Editions, 2010), p.14.
268 John Lasseter interview with ML, September 28, 1998.

Flik's character is truly put to the test when Hopper demands twice as much grain to make up for the loss. "Hopper is extremely smart," Lasseter noted of the film's villain. "He is probably the smartest character in the film. From the beginning, he knows what the secret to the ants' strength is. He works just to keep them 'down,' to keep them without any self-confidence. He's so much more powerful than them and really exploits that and oppresses them."[269]

As Atta and the other ants fear that they won't meet Hopper's demands, Flik volunteers to venture off to the city and find some bugs who will come back, fight the grasshoppers, and protect the colony.

When he gets to the city, we see some creatively funny duplicates of our human world (skyscrapers are discarded food boxes, a mosquito in a bar orders a "Bloody Mary"). It's here that Flik finds a group of insects he thinks are mighty warriors but are, in fact, out of work circus bugs looking for their next gig. And, they're quite the crew: there is the ringleader PT Flea (John Ratzenberger, now Pixar's "good luck charm"), Slim, the walking stick (David Hyde Pierce of *Frasier*), Heimlich the caterpillar (Ranft), Francis, a male ladybug (comedian Denis Leary), Manny, a magician praying mantis (Jonathan Harris, Dr. Smith on TV's *Lost in Space*), his assistant Gypsy, a gypsy moth (Madeline Kahn), Dim, the rhinoceros beetle (*Everybody Loves Raymond*'s Brad Garrett), his trainer Rosie, the black widow spider (Bonnie Hunt) and acrobats Tuck and Roll, twin pill bugs (comedian Michael McShane).

When the supposed warriors come back to the ant colony, both the circus bugs and Flik realize their mutual misunderstanding (during a hysterical sequence, originally storyboarded by Ranft). The ants' "second-grade class" puts on a play that depicts the potential battle that's to come.

Realizing what they may be facing, the circus bugs, trying to leave, are attacked by a bird, and in the process of escaping from it, they rescue Dot (Hayden Panettiere), Atta's little sister. They gain the respect of the colony, and the troupe agrees to continue to stay to help battle the grasshoppers.

---

269 Ibid.

"Part of what makes a great movie is character growth," said Lasseter. "With Flik, he grows quite a bit, but more importantly, everyone around him, because of his influence, also grows a tremendous amount. That's a lot like everyone's lives. In your own life, you don't realize all the people that you come in contact with - your friends, your loved ones - how much you affect them. It's a really apt emotional core to the film that really fits with everyone's everyday lives."[270]

Rounding out the cast of this "insect epic" was Richard Kind as Molt, Hopper's second in command, Roddy McDowall as Mr. Soil, the ant thespian, and Edie McClurg as colony physician, Dr. Flora.

Technically, *A Bug's Life* came with its challenges, as the filmmakers indeed sought to bring the miniature insect world to life. With *Toy Story*, the artists re-created the look of plastic; here, the computer animation had to bring to life our natural world believably.

Early in production, the artists watched "bug cam" footage (film of blades of grass and flowers from an insect point of view). "They found that a single clover looked like an enormous tree. Cracked mud looked like the Grand Canyon. But most impressive was the translucency of the bug world."[271]

This gave a "stained-glass" look that inspired *A Bug's Life's* bright color palette.

Unlike *Toy Story*, *A Bug's Life* would also involve bringing large crowds of ants and other insects to the screen. Added to this was the additional hurdle of animating them during a battle sequence at the film's climax.

In all, there were 400 crowd scenes, and each character was animated with unique movement. The film was another tremendous technological leap for the quickly growing realm of computer animation.

When *A Bug's Life* opened in theaters on November 20, 1998, critics praised this colorful attention to detail.

Writing in *The San Francisco Chronicle*, Peter Stack gave the film "...six thumbs up and a crawling ovation." He wrote: " *A*

---

270 Ibid.
271 Pixar.com, (accessed March 29, 2021).

Bug's Life is one of the great movies - - a triumph of storytelling and character development, and a whole new ballgame for computer animation. Pixar Animation Studios has raised the genre to an astonishing new level."[272]

Los Angeles Times critic Kenneth Turan declared: "What *A Bug's Life* demonstrates is that when it comes to bugs, the most fun ones to hang out with hang exclusively with the gang at Pixar."[273]

The last critique was a direct jab at DreamWorks' *Antz*, which *A Bug's Life* bested at the box office when the dust settled from the "great animated insect battle of 1998."

Antz was the number one movie at the box office for two weeks; when it opened in October of '98, its final domestic tally was $90 million. *A Bug's Life* also remained in the number one spot at the box office for its first two weeks grossing $162 million domestically.

While once again steering away from selling the film as "an event," Disney fully embraced *A Bug's Life* in its marketing and promotion, with no lack of toys and related products on store shelves.

At Disney theme parks, the characters from *A Bug's Life* were featured in the attraction "It's Tough to be a Bug" at Disney's Animal Kingdom theme park in Florida (where it's featured inside its centerpiece, The Tree of Life). The attraction was also at Disney's California Adventure at the Disneyland Resort, which also showcased "A Bug's Land," an entire section of the park themed around the film (the land closed in 2018).

A Bug's Life was also creatively unique, daring to do something no animated film had attempted up to this point: include "bloopers" during the ending credits. Patient moviegoers were treated to what looked like actual outtakes from the film's production, with the bugs flubbing their lines or laughing while delivering a line.

These "bloopers" were created in such a way that they genuinely looked as if they had happened during filming (when in fact, they were recorded and animated to appear that way).

272 Peter Stack, "*Bugs* Has Legs/Cute Insect Adventure is a Visual Delight," *The San Francisco Chronicle*, November 25, 1998, sfgate.com, (accessed March 29, 2021).
273 Kenneth Turan, *The Los Angeles Times* review, (accessed via Rottentomatoes. com, March 29, 2021).

Lasseter recalled: "'We picked shots and the characters from the film so that it had the feel that it was actually part of the film. Then we went to our last recording session with each of the actors. We talked to them about the idea of creating the outtakes, and they went nuts. They loved it. Our actors are so good at improvisation they came up with the great ideas on their own.'"[274]

The "bloopers" were such a surprise for audiences and became such a hit that Disney and Pixar used them to help promote *A Bug's Life* after being released to theaters. In December, approximately a month after the film's release, Disney and Pixar inserted all-new "bloopers" into the film's ending credits. They began a new advertising campaign around this, enticing audiences to see the movie again.

"You work on these movies for four years," reflected Lasseter just before *A Bug's Life* opened. "These are our babies. We labor over every frame, and we try to make the best movie that we can in every way. I always equate it to having a child and then raising it. At a certain point, your son or daughter graduates from high school and goes to college. You give them to the world and hope that you did okay. That's very much like these movies. When we get to the release date of these films, we realize that this movie doesn't belong to us anymore. It belongs to the world, and you really hope that you did okay in raising your child."[275]

Seven months after *A Bug's Life*, Disney had another animated "child" that was going to graduate, and this one would bring with it a long legacy that went well beyond the studio.

Tarzan of the Apes by Edgar Rice Burroughs was first published in a magazine in 1912 and as a novel in 1914. The story was of a young child, raised by apes in the jungle who grows into manhood not knowing the outside, civilized world. It captured readers' imaginations.

So famous was Burroughs' novel that, in 1918, Hollywood translated it into a silent film. Re-makes and different film versions followed. MGM studios' series of *Tarzan* films were

---

274 Jeff Howard and Dave Neill, "*A Bug's Life* Bloopers Explained By Director," The Las Vegas Sun, December 18, 1998 , lasvegassun.com (accessed March 30, 2021).

275 John Lasseter interview with ML, September 28, 1998.

the most popular. These debuted in 1932, starring Olympic swimmer Johnny Weissmuller as Tarzan. The MGM films loosely adapted Burroughs' work but gave the character traits such as speaking in broken English and the now famous "Tarzan yell," that became part of the Ape Man's persona.

The character of Tarzan continued to be remade and adapted through the years in such films as *Greystoke: The Legend of Tarzan Lord of the Apes* (1984) and 1998's *Tarzan and the Lost City.*

Tarzan eventually surfaced as an animation project for The Walt Disney Studios in the mid-90s, and Kevin Lima, fresh off directing *A Goofy Movie,* was approached to co-direct. "When they first brought up the idea, I thought, 'Why make this movie?'" he admitted. "We found out later that it's the second most made movie of all time."[276]

Lima was partnered with Chris Buck to co-direct *Tarzan.* The film would mark Buck's debut as a director. The Kansas native had been working as an animator at Disney since 1978. "I came here on *Fox and the Hound,*" Buck remembered. "Things were okay, but nothing was really happening yet."[277] Leaving the studio for freelance work, Buck also taught animation classes at CalArts from 1988-93. Returning to Disney full-time after that, he served as supervising animator of three characters in *Pocahontas*: Grandmother Willow, Percy, Ratcliffe's pet dog, and Wiggins, the villain's sidekick.

During the early days of *Tarzan*'s production, Buck and Lima began to pour over Burroughs' original work, and possibilities began to surface.

"Here was a chance to make Tarzan move like he does in the book," said Buck. "There's always a guy swinging on a vine, or walking around, in a live-action film. This is a man who was raised by the apes and doesn't really know human locomotion. He knows how to move like the apes."[278]

"I don't think anyone has seen Tarzan the way that Edgar Rice Burroughs has envisioned Tarzan," said Glen Keane, who served as supervising animator for the title character.

---

276   Kevin Lima interview with ML, January 22, 1999.
277   Chris Buck interview with ML, January 22, 1999.
278   Ibid.

"Primarily because you could never find a human actor who wouldn't die in the process of filming because Tarzan has to move like no human being can move. He is a man who is a genius of adaptation. He has developed the skills of an animal in the jungle, and he moves like an animal. So, this was a character who really had to be animated in order to realize Burroughs' vision."[279]

In addition to a new perspective on the character of Tarzan, Disney's version of Burroughs' story would be purposefully different from the studio's recent string of animated hits.

"We said, from the very beginning, 'Tarzan cannot sing!'" said Lima. "We do not want this character to open his mouth and burst into song about how he loves living in the jungle. That's something that we just couldn't see happening."[280]

"We began to question whether the characters really had to sing," added Buck. "Then, the year that we started working on the film, *Toy Story* came out, and they were very successful with not having the characters sing, but instead using background songs. We realized that does work and that the audience accepts it."[281]

The *Tarzan* team turned to pop music enlisting Phil Collins to write the songs for the film. *Tarzan*'s producer Bonnie Arnold, who also produced *Toy Story*, was familiar with music fitting differently into a story. She noted that, early on, they knew that Collins' talents would be perfect for the film: "We felt that his sense of rhythm was the right link for something that was set in the jungle. It was an interesting marriage of his abilities as a songwriter with his sense as a percussionist."[282]

Even with several decades as one of the world's most popular singers (along with seven number one hit singles), Collins admitted that crafting the songs for *Tarzan* was a new experience. He stated:

"One of the biggest challenges is length. A song on a record can be anything from three to six minutes, but when you're writing for an animated film, you have to be more succinct.

---

279 Glen Keane interview with ML, January 22, 1999.
280 Kevin Lima interview with ML, January 22, 1999.
281 Chris Buck interview with ML, January 22, 1999.
282 Bonnie Arnold interview with ML, January 22, 1999.

Two-and-half or three minutes is the max. And lyrically, you can't come back and repeat the chorus. There has to be some kind of story movement."[283]

Collins would perform his songs for the film, which would play on the soundtrack at certain moments, to accentuate the story's emotion. As this story of Disney's *Tarzan* (adapted by screenwriters Tab Murphy, Bob Tzudiker, and Noni White) began to take shape, the filmmakers looked to remain faithful to the source material and also resonate with contemporary audiences.

"The funny thing about Tarzan is that he's not Superman, but he is super-human," noted Arnold, adding, "That's something that really appealed to us, as well as the reoccurring theme of family. The directors and I felt that was an element that was true to the original story and yet had a lot of contemporary relevance. If you think about it, Tarzan is this kid who is adopted by another family."[284]

Arnold also added that the filmmakers immediately saw opportunities for the magic that only Disney animation can realize: "The idea of exploring Tarzan's relationship to the animals was very appealing to us because that is probably Disney's strongest suit - talking animals and the relationships between animals," said Arnold. "That's a piece of fantasy that I think everyone wonders about - what would it be like if you could talk and communicate with animals?"[285]

"Our apes talk," added Lima. "There's that communication ability between Tarzan and this family that he grows up with. That opened up a big door for us that we would discover and explore in this whole world."[286]

Tarzan opens with Collins' dramatic ballad, "Two Worlds." We are introduced to baby Tarzan and his mother and father during a dramatic montage in which a shipwreck strands them in the jungle.

The other family in the film is that of the gorillas in the jungle and the heartbreaking moment when the female gorilla, Kala looses her baby to the fierce leopard, Sabor.

---

283 Howard E. Green, *The Tarzan Chronicles*, (New York, Hyperion Press, 1999), p.169.
284 Bonnie Arnold interview with ML, January 22, 1999.
285 Ibid.
286 Kevin Lima interview with ML, January 22, 1999.

Soon after, a baby's cry interrupts the quiet of the jungle, and Kala goes to investigate. She discovers the infant, Tarzan, who has just lost his own parents to Sabor.

The scene in which Kala and Tarzan first meet is played quietly, without dialogue, in a sweetly crafted sequence, where we see both characters immediately forming a bond. "The relationship between Kala and Tarzan is so strong and is this great bond throughout the movie," said Russ Edmonds, supervising animator for Kala, adding, "My character winds up going through an emotional roller-coaster in this film."[287]

Edmonds came to *Tarzan* after animating Phoebus in *The Hunchback of Notre Dame*. Originally from New York, Edmonds, like many of his peers, came to Disney in the 80s from Cal Arts and was able to be part of the immense growth at the studio.

The animator brought his talents and gave tremendous depth to Kala. He admitted that a large part of this came from a significant life event in his family while working on *Tarzan*. "During production, my father passed away," remembered Edmonds. "When I came back from the funeral, all of this emotional, gut-wrenching stuff came across my desk. That's when I was able to use my experiences back home."[288]

The voice of Kala was one of Hollywood's most prestigious and talented actresses, Glenn Close. "That threw me off,'" admitted Edmonds. "It was like, 'Okay, we're going to give you this giant ape, and we want it to have this tiny little voice.'" Listening to Close's recording sessions, the animator found a new dimension to Kala, thanks to the actresses' performance. "She brought all the softness to the character. Her voice *became* the character," said Edmonds.[289]

Kala rescues Tarzan from an attack by Sabor. She brings the baby to live with the apes, despite opposition from her husband, Kerchak the silverback ape leader (actor Lance Henriksen with Bruce W. Smith serving as supervising animator). He fears the dangers that this child may bring.

Kala comforts and protects Tarzan, singing the lullaby "You'll Be in My Heart" to him. As Tarzan grows up, he notices

---

287 Russ Edmonds interview with ML, January 21, 1999.
288 Ibid.
289 Ibid.

how different he is from the other apes and wants desperately to fit in.

Thankfully, young Tarzan (voiced by child actor Alex D. Lintz) has two best friends. One is the "tomboy" ape Terkina, Terk for short (voiced by comedian Rosie O'Donnell), who acts as a surrogate "older sister," of sorts. The character was brought to the screen by supervising animator Michael Surrey. After animating Timon in *The Lion King* and Clopin in *The Hunchback of Notre Dame,* he had become quite adept at sidekicks.

"The great thing about sidekicks is that they do give you a variety of acting," said Surrey. "Your villain or your main character has to be inside a certain range. Sidekicks are much broader. In the case of Terk, she goes from being sarcastic to supportive to angry with Tarzan throughout the film, and it's nice as an animator to get that variety."[290]

Surrey, a native of Canada, came to Disney as an assistant animator on *Beauty and the Beast* and was promoted to supervisor with *The Lion King.*

For Terk, Surrey had a rich vocal performance with Rosie O'Donnell. However, while the animator did incorporate the comedienne's mannerisms into Terk, he didn't want it to dominate the character. "You don't want it to be Terk as Rosie. You want it to be Rosie as Terk," Surrey noted. "It has to be about the character. There are a lot of similarities between Rosie's on-screen performances and the character, which is what you want to grab from and put in there because it's appealing. It's dangerous, though, because you don't want to start writing the scenes for how they work for Rosie. You have to think about how they work for Terk."[291]

Along with Terk, Tarzan's other best bud is the neurotic elephant Tantor (voiced by Wayne Knight, Newman from *Seinfeld,* with Sergio Pablos serving as supervising animator).

During a montage, we see the ape-man grow up and hone his ability to observe, imitate, and adapt. He grows into a unique creature who can glide through the jungle with unparalleled agility.

---

290 Michael Surrey interview with ML, January 21, 1999.
291 Ibid.

The sequence is all set to the infectious and exhilarating Phil Collins song "Son of Man," which adds tremendous energy to the scene.

"Phil has become the emotional voice of Tarzan throughout the story," added Lima. "When the songs kick in, they are dealing on a different level. They're expressing this inner voice. It's really an interesting way to deal with the music."[292]

This emotion builds as Tarzan even gains the acceptance of the other gorillas, including Kerchak, after he grows into adulthood (now voiced by Tony Goldwyn) and defeats Sabor.

Then, other humans arrive in the jungle.

An expedition led by Professor Archimedes Q. Porter, a primatologist (voiced by actor Nigel Hawthorne with Dave Burgess as supervising animator), has come to the jungle to study gorillas. With Porter is his daughter, Jane. (as in "Me Tarzan...You Jane").

"She's a spirited girl. She's very inquisitive and very enthusiastic," said Ken Duncan, who served as supervising animator for Disney's fresh take on Tarzan's love interest. "Her personality, in going to the jungle, is a young woman with a very broad imagination of what she's going to see. In the beginning, unfortunately, it's a little different from what she imagines. So, that positive perception she had changes a little bit. It's actually Tarzan who allows her to see the way the jungle really is. It makes her more of a textured character than we've seen in past films."[293]

Duncan joined the *Tarzan* production only one week after finishing work as supervising animator for Meg in *Hercules*. "Meg was very street-wise, and Jane doesn't have that quality at all, which was interesting in doing the design, as I was trying to break away from Meg," recalled Duncan. "I really tried to get into [Jane's] personality. She's a very innocent person, in a very bright-eyed way. She's not a stupid person, just very innocent. When I designed her, I tried to think of her in that way."[294]

Also shaping this inquisitive personality was Minnie Driver, who provided Jane's voice. The actress's physical performance

---

292 Kevin Lima interview with ML, January 22, 1999.
293 Ken Duncan interview with ML, January 22, 1999.
294 Ibid.

while recording proved to be a great inspiration. "She really had these exaggerated poses," noted Duncan. "When she was listening to the directors, her neck would really stretch out, and when she talked, she had these really big mouth shapes. So, it was really just a matter of looking at her."[295]

Jane's curious spirit leads to her meeting Tarzan as he rescues her from a group of feral baboons. After this, Tarzan meets the other humans, including Clayton, the British big-game hunter, who has accompanied the expedition. Clayton attempts to befriend Tarzan, but only for sinister reasons, as he has plans to capture the apes.

Clayton's nature is ambiguous at first, but his villainous side is seen as his true intentions emerge. "The biggest difference between Clayton and a lot of past Disney villains is that his villainy is less obvious," said the character's supervising animator Randy Haycock. "I had to keep it subtle and less obvious because the other characters don't know that he's a bad guy until later in the film. So, he had to have a certain duality to his personality. The audience has to be clued in on it so that they accept it when he turns, but it has to be subtle enough so that it's not too obvious to the other characters."[296]

Haycock, who hails from Colorado, had been working in the animation industry since 1990 and at Disney since 1992, found Clayton's personality in the character's voice, provided by actor Brian Blessed, who demonstrated a larger-than-life personality when he came to his recording sessions.

"We started talking about what made Brian so charismatic," said Haycock, "and we realized that was what we needed to get into the character. Even some of his features - Brian Blessed has a huge smile, with these big teeth and dimples - so I made sure that I got that into Clayton's smile so that we could get some of that charm that Brian has into the personality."[297]

Producer Bonnie Arnold laughed when remembering Brian Blessed: "He did his audition, and we all just sat there scared. When he left, we all looked at each other and said, 'He is Clayton!'" Arnold added, "He is so suave and so charming that

---

295 Ibid.
296 Randy Haycock interview with ML, January 23, 1999.
297 Ibid.

he could tell you anything, and you'd believe him. He'd tell us these stories during the voice sessions. We'd come out of these sessions and say to one another, 'Did you guys believe that?!'"[298]

Blessed performance as Clayton sets up a conflict within Tarzan. He becomes torn between the ape family that he feels he has now betrayed and this new human world that has somewhat betrayed him.

This internal conflict provided Glen Keane with fertile ground for Tarzan. "We were trying to define our characters with one-word descriptions," he said. "Tarzan's was 'driven.' This is a man who's driven to find himself. At the beginning, he realizes that he's a gorilla, and that's who he believes that he is. Then, in the second act, he realizes that he's a man, as he finds himself a part of the human world. In the end, he real-izes that 'It's me. I'm Tarzan.'"[299]

Keane looked to express this in Tarzan's movements, a combination of primate and human. "The first mistake that we were making was to interpret the animal movements too closely so that Tarzan moved just like a gorilla," recalled Keane. "As soon as we did that, he didn't seem intelligent. We had to take him a step further. You could take your original inspiration from the movement of a gorilla or a panther, but then you had to add a human intelligence to it."[300]

Keane found inspiration from his son's passion for "extreme sports" like rollerblading, snowboarding, and skateboarding. "I started thinking of Tarzan like that.," admitted Keane. "He has to be moving through the jungle, always on the edge. Putting him in danger is something that makes him feel alive. I started to think of him as a 'tree-surfer.' He surfs the branches, which became like a freeway for him to move along."[301]

The jungle that Tarzan glides effortlessly through came to life thanks to a computer software program called "Deep Canvas" created specifically for the film to enrich the jungle backgrounds.

---

298   Bonnie Arnold interview with ML, January 22, 1999.
299   Glen Keane interview with ML, January 22, 1999.
300   Ibid.
301   Ibid.

With "Deep Canvas," an artist paints a background, except here, it's painted on the computer through a "digitizer tablet." "Deep Canvas" regenerates the same painting "pixel for pixel" and subtly changes where each brush stroke is from frame to frame. The program is, literally, a "moving painting." "We are actually re-painting the background for each frame by just moving the brush strokes a little bit," explained Eric Daniels, who served as head of the CGI unit for *Tarzan*.[302]

Daniels created "Deep Canvas" with Disney programmers Tasso Lappas and George Katanics to meet the filmmaking "blue sky" ideas discussed early in production. "The technique grew out of a lot of different, conflicting desires on this film," said Daniels. "The first thing I did was sit down with all of the other department heads and cleared my mind of everything I knew about computer graphics and just listened to what they wanted to see."[303]

One vision for *Tarzan* was the concept of the "ultimate jungle" which sprang from an early pre-production trip that the team took to Africa. "We all had the same experience of being in that jungle together," said *Tarzan*'s art director Dan St. Pierre. "For me, I felt that there were elements there that had to be in the movie."[304]

What the artists didn't want, however, was to reproduce specific locales. "We didn't have one particular thing that we could point to and say, 'That's it,'" said co-director Buck. "It's not that we didn't want that. It just didn't happen right away."[305] "The idea wasn't to create a realistic world," producer Arnold added. "But to create a believable world."[306]

The world of *Tarzan* is not just believable but emotional and dramatic as the film heads into its climax, as Tarzan confronts Clayton to save the "Two Worlds" he has come to know.

"He's a child, who is trying to find himself," said Keane of Tarzan. "And the thread of our story follows a very human, natural quest that we all go on."[307]

---

302   Eric Daniels interview with ML, January 21, 1999.
303   Ibid.
304   Dan St. Pierre interview with ML, January 25, 1999.
305   Chris Buck interview with ML, January 22, 1999.
306   Bonnie Arnold interview with ML, January 22, 1999.
307   Glen Keane interview with ML, January 22, 1999.

Critics and audiences connected with this. Roger Ebert awarded the film the highest honor of four out of four stars, writing: "I saw *Tarzan* once, and went to see it again. This kind of bright, colorful, hyperkinetic animation is a visual celebration."[308]

Opening on June 18, 1999, *Tarzan* was the number one movie at the box office, impressively beating out *Star Wars Episode I: The Phantom Menace*, which had ruled the minds of moviegoers that summer, since opening the month before.

By the end of its run, *Tarzan* grossed $170 million domestically and remained very much "in the conversation" throughout that summer. This success had to do with a healthy marketing push (again, not on the "event" scale). Collins' song "You'll Be in My Heart," spent nineteen weeks on the adult contemporary charts, was inescapable on the airwaves, and eventually won the Oscar for Best Original Song.

In addition to "Two Worlds," "You'll Be in My Heart," and "Son of Man," Collins contributed two additional songs to the film: "Trashin' the Camp" and "Strangers Like Me."

Collins recalled his experiences for *Tarzan* by saying:

"'...I pushed myself into a much more dramatic area than I would normally go. This, of course, proved necessary as the film went through so many emotional and romantic changes. I ended up having written the kind of songs I'd never written before. Writing songs for this movie pushed me into different areas and caused me to do something better than ever. In a way, I felt I'd grown up a bit as a writer.'"[309]

His songs would also feature prominently in the entertaining and energetic "*Tarzan* Rocks!" stage show at Disney's Animal Kingdom theme park that featured acrobats and extreme sports as it relayed the film's story in a concert-like setting. The show closed in 2006.

Collins also expanded and wrote new songs for a Broadway stage musical of *Tarzan*, which was sadly not as successful as previous Disney theatrical outings. It closed a little over a year after opening in May of 2006.

---

308 Roger Ebert, *Tarzan* Review, Rogerebert.com, (accessed March 30, 2021).

309 Howard E. Green, *The Tarzan Chronicles*, New York, (Hyperion Press, New York 1999), p. p.182.

Despite this, Disney's version of *Tarzan* has been embraced by many. The most significant "stamp of approval" came during the film's production, when Danton Burroughs, grandson of Edgar Rice Burroughs and Secretary-Treasurer of Edgar Rice Burroughs, Inc., wrote a letter to Glen Keane.

In it, he praised Keane's work, after having just seen a "rough cut" of Disney's *Tarzan*, and wrote: "If my Grandfather were alive, he would embrace you for your keen awareness of his creation."[310]

Looking back at *Tarzan*, co-director Lima noted that it resonated with audiences because it was, in many ways, similar to his other animated film, *A Goofy Movie*. An unexpected analogy, but the universal similarities are there. "If you really look at the movies, they're about the same thing," Lima said. "Ultimately, they're about family and patching relationships. All of those themes sort of play through."[311]

Disney's next film would explore similar themes in another partnership with Pixar. This time, the studios would team up for a sequel and a *blockbuster* sequel at that.

---

310   Ibid, p. p.74.
311   Kevin Lima interview with ML, January 22, 1999.

CHAPTER NINE

"When She Loved Me"

Toy Story 2 & Fantasia 2000

Toy Story 2 was going to be produced...but almost never made it to theaters.

In 1994, Disney had scored a surprise hit with a "direct to video" sequel to 1992's *Aladdin* entitled *The Return of Jafar*. It would not open in theaters, but instead, the animated film debuted on home video (VHS). Produced by Walt Disney Studios Television Animation, *The Return of Jafar*, Disney's first "direct to video" feature, was made for $5 million and grossed over $300 million in worldwide video sales, making it one of the best-selling films on home video.

The success of *The Return of Jafar* began a trend at Disney, and the studio sought out other opportunities for "direct to video" sequels. *Toy Story* rose to the top of this list.

"It was just a business decision early on," said John Lasseter, who directed *Toy Story* and would co-direct the sequel with Ash Brannon and Lee Unkrich.[312]

There was even the thought that the filmmakers could keep the budget low for the "direct-to-video" sequel. Pixar had a "video backlot"—animation from the original stored on hard drives. Initial plans called for re-using some of it for *Toy Story 2*.

"We had a lot to live up to," said the sequel's producer, Helene Plotkin. "We knew how much the characters meant to people."[313]

But, with tighter budgets and limited technical and creative

312 John Lasseter interview with ML, August 27, 1999.
313 Helene Plotkin interview with ML, August 9, 1999.

freedom, many at Pixar wondered if they would do justice to the groundbreaking original. "We were handed a lot of restrictions, initially," remembered Jim Pearson, art director for *Toy Story 2*. "Despite that, we always thought of this as something that was as good as a full-blown theatrical release. We never thought of it as just direct-to-video. We said, 'This is a movie.'"[314]

Then came a "work-in-progress" screening for *Toy Story 2* in 1997. Reaction to it was so strong that direction changed quickly, and the sequel would now be a theatrical release.

In January of 1999, Lasseter came aboard the sequel as co-director after already serving as executive producer.

The filmmakers took great pains to make sure that *Toy Story 2* wouldn't join a long list of disappointing follow-ups and studied Hollywood's most successful and acclaimed sequels.

"Most sequels are just re-hashes of the first film," said Lasseter. "They aren't really special in any way, kind of a 'been there and done that.' In film history, however, there have been sequels that take off from the original and became as good if not better than the original. *Godfather II* is one that I would put on that list, and *Empire Strikes Back* is another. I was really inspired by them. They evolve the characters, and they have the notion that, 'here's a sequel that's different and yet it has a lot of what made the first film great.'"[315]

Co-director Ash Brannon also points to the sequel to Francis Ford Coppola's seminal mafia opus as highly influential. "We actually looked at *Godfather II* as the inspiration for the story," he said. "There you have a sequel that's really a movie unto itself. We felt that the characters could really continue to grow."[316]

Studying animation at both Douglas Anderson School of Visual Arts in Florida and CalArts in California, Brannon began his career as an animation trainee on *The Little Mermaid* at Disney before transitioning to Pixar, where he served as a story artist on *Toy Story* and *A Bug's Life*.

Brannon was thrilled to see that others had faith enough

314   Jim Pearson interview with ML, August 19, 1999.
315   John Lasseter interview with ML, August 27, 1999.
316   Ash Brannon interview with ML, August 19, 1999.

in *Toy Story 2* to promote it to a theatrical release. "The story deserved the treatment that it's getting now," said co-director Ash Brannon. "We all knew that this wasn't going to be a run-of-the-mill sequel."[317]

The plot of *Toy Story 2* centers around the culture of toy collecting, which had hit its zenith during the 1990s, just before the sequel's release. Prices skyrocketing on ebay for playthings once so easily discarded was a culture just waiting to be explored.

Lasseter, a massive toy collector himself for many years, could relate to this. "To put it simply, I was more like Andy than Sid, as a kid," said Lasseter, referencing the destructing toy villain from the original *Toy Story*. "I didn't blow up toys."[318]

The filmmaker was one of those rare kids who took care of his toys even from a young age. "Unfortunately, my GI Joes didn't survive. I think my mom gave them away at some point," admitted Lasseter. "But, I told her, 'Never, ever give away my Hot Wheels.' So, to this day, I still have them, and I was at the exact perfect age when Hot Wheels first came out. I got all the first year Hot Wheels, and that was my life for a long time. I still have all that original stuff."[319]

Lasseter has such a passion for these Hot Wheels and keeping them as pristine as possible that he recalled how, one time, it led to a tense moment at home. "I came home once, and my little boys had found daddy's box of Superchargers [Hot Wheels] and track. They filled their room with it. And I'm sure all collectors, especially those who have kids, have experienced this. It's sort of like, [he then segues into an imitation of someone on the verge of a nervous breakdown], 'Oh...I'm so glad...you're playing...with Daddy's toys. Those are...uh... daddy's toys, ya know?'"[320]

This obsessive passion found in toy collecting circles became the major plot catalyst in *Toy Story 2*. "One thing that came up during production was that when we were growing up, none of us knew there was any value to our toys," said the film's producer,

---

318   John Lasseter interview with ML, January 18, 1997.
319   Ibid.
320   Ibid.

Karen Robert Jackson. "The only value was that you played with it." She added, "To think that kids are looking at toys for value is kind of distressing. We're not trying to tell people what's right or wrong in the film. But, it is an interesting dilemma that has been created around something that used to be simple."[321]

The *need* inherent in collectors for finding a particular toy to complete a set is at the center of the sequel. "I'm absolutely convinced that collectors have something born in them," said Lasseter. "People either have it, or they don't. And people who are not collectors just don't understand the *need*."[322]

In *Toy Story 2*, it turns out that there is a need for Woody the cowboy, as he is not just "a child's plaything," he is also a highly sought-after collectible.

The film opens with a dazzling, science fiction action sequence featuring Buzz Lightyear (Tim Allen) facing off against his enemy Emperor Zurg (the voice of co-writer Andrew Stanton). Things seem dire for Buzz until we see that it's a video game that Rex (Wallace Shawn) is playing, and we are back in Andy's room.

It's summer, and Andy is about to leave for camp and wants to take Woody (Tom Hanks) with him, but he accidentally tears the cowboy's arm while playing with him and is forced to place Woody on a shelf with a dusty, forgotten penguin squeak toy named Wheezy (Joe Ranft).

"Woody starts questioning how long he's going to last," said Lasseter. "If he continues to rip, does that mean that Andy's not going to love him as much? To relate it to an adult world, it's like worrying about growing old and dying."[323]

Andy's family is having a yard sale. When Wheezy is placed with the items for sale, Woody attempts to rescue him and winds up being stolen by insidious collector Al McWhiggin (Wayne Knight), who also owns the toy superstore "Al's Toy Barn."

This sets the other toys, Buzz, Hamm (John Ratzenberger), Slinky Dog (Jim Varney), and Mr. Potato Head (Don Rickles), out on a mission to rescue Woody.

When they do, they leave behind Bo Peep (Annie Potts) and

---

321 Karen Robert-Jackson interview with ML, August 9, 1999.
322 John Lasseter interview with ML, January 18, 1997.
323 Ibid.

one of the new additions to the playroom, Mrs. Potato Head (Estelle Harris). "Obviously, in the first film, Mr. Potato Head had been looking forward to the day that Mrs. Potato Head comes into his life," said Plotkin. "Now that she has, we had to make a choice – should we make them this couple that quarrels and nags each other or, should we do the opposite, and make them so lovey-dovey that's it almost sickening for everyone else? We decided to make them super-sweet because it was just such a great contrast to Mr. Potato Head's orneriness."[324]

Al takes Woody to his house, where the collector intends to repair Woody and sell him. It seems that the cowboy is a very highly coveted collectible and was once the star of his own show, *Woody's Round-Up*, a black and white, marionette, *Howdy Doody*-like kids show from the "50s. It even had its own theme song (performed by the group Riders in the Sky).

Woody also had other co-stars on the show, such as Jessie, the yodeling cowgirl (Joan Cusack), Bullseye, his faithful horse, and the cantankerous prospector, Pete (Kelsey Grammer).

"One of the fun things about him is that he's a toy that is still 'mint in the box,'" said co-director Lee Unkrich of Prospector Pete. "He's never been out of his box, and the other characters have to push him around the room like he's an old man in a wheelchair."[325]

The stars of the *Round-Up* have also been stored away at Al's, waiting for Woody to complete the collection.

All of this is startling and new to Woody, who is utterly unaware of his sidekicks or his past stardom, until Jessie, Bullseye, and Pete show him videotapes of his old *Woody's Round-Up* show. These scenes are stunning in how they re-create the grainy black-and-white look of '50s television.

"We looked at old Kinescopes [an early form of recording television shows, which resulted in poor picture quality] of *Howdy Doody* and *Andy's Gang*," said art director Pearson, adding, "The way that the film looks is largely the work of one of our technical directors, Oren Jacobs. There's this 'bloom' that you get on anything that is lit on the old Kinescopes. Oren

---

324 Helene Plotkin interview with ML, August 9, 1999.
325 Lee Unkrich interview with ML, August 27, 1999.

nailed that. Then we added scratches and skips. It's a beautiful job. It looks completely convincing."[326]

Al plans on selling the entire *Woody's Round-Up* set of characters to a toy museum in Japan, where they will all live forever in pristine condition behind glass.

Learning what he was and what he is now creates a tremendous internal conflict for Woody. "He has his mid-life crisis in this film," said producer Jackson. "He has to decide whether to live life as a toy if that means that eventually, a boy might actually discard you or he can have the fountain of youth and live forever on a shelf in mint condition, which means that you can't play with a boy anymore. He has to choose between bringing joy to millions or bringing joy to one child."[327]

Making this decision even more difficult is when Jessie relays the story of her past to Woody. It turns out that she was once owned by a young girl named Emily, who once loved and played with her but eventually grew up and gave Jessie away to charity.

"Jessie is one of the most important characters in influencing Woody's fate," said co-director Brannon. "She's a toy who, a long time ago, also belonged to a kid, but the kid grew up and abandoned her. It's almost as if she's a jilted lover."

Jessie's heartbreaking arc brought impressive depth and emotion to the sequel, making her a favorite among many during the production and eventually audiences, as well. "The animators were bribing their supervisors so that they could work on this character," laughed Plotkin.[328]

Adding to the complexity of Jessie's personality is the song "When She Loved Me," performed by Sarah McLachlin and written by Randy Newman, who returned for the sequel. The music added so much to the scene's emotion as we watch Jessie's life transition from days playing with Emily to being cast aside in a cardboard box on the side of the road.

While Jessie is relaying her life story and Woody grapples with his identity crisis, Buzz, Hamm, Rex, Mr. Potato Head, and Slinky Dog continue on their undertaking to rescue Woody.

---

326   Jim Pearson interview with ML, August 19, 1999.

327   Karen Robert-Jackson interview with ML, August 9, 1999.

328   Helene Plotkin interview with ML, August 9, 1999.

Attempting to get to Al's apartment, they wind up at the nearby Al's Toy Barn store after closing, hoping to find Al himself.

Buzz meets up with "Utility Belt Buzz," a "2.0" version of himself on display. It turns out that the new Buzz is exactly like he was in the original and suffers from the delusion that he is an actual Space Ranger. "Utility Belt Buzz" sees Andy's Buzz as a threat and ties him up in one of the toy boxes.

Mr. Potato Head, Hamm, Rex, and Slinky Dog survey the rest of the "Toy Barn" in a remote-control car. Here they meet up with a shelf-full of one of the world's most popular toys, Barbie, all of whom are having a party. Ironically, Pixar wanted Barbie to be in the original *Toy Story* until Mattel (the company that owns and manufactures Barbie) decided they didn't want the character to be a part of the film.

When *Toy Story* became a blockbuster and a sequel was planned, Mattel approached Pixar. "They came to us and said, 'Well...ya know...if you want to use Barbie in the sequel, you're welcome to," said Lasseter with a chuckle.[329]

It's Tour Guide Barbie (voiced by Jodi Benson, the voice of Ariel and the official voice of Barbie) who agrees to help Andy's toys navigate the mammoth Toys R Us-like Al's Toy Barn.

During the tour, Barbie takes the toys down the Buzz Lightyear aisle and notes, "Back in 1995, short-sighted retailers did not order enough dolls to meet demand." This was a sly jab at the real-life Buzz Lightyear action figure shortage when the first film was released.

Buzz eventually catches up with the rest of the gang. They make their way to Al's apartment through the elevator shaft, where they are reunited with Woody, who reveals to his friends that he's not going back to Andy's and, instead, wants to stay with the *Round-Up* gang and live the rest of his days in the museum, until Buzz convinces him otherwise.

"He's the one who tells Woody the other side of the story," said Lasseter. "This time, he gets to tell Woody, 'You are a toy, you're not a collectible. You are a child's plaything!' So, it's been kind of fun to turn the tables on the two characters."[330]

---

329 John Lasseter interview with ML, January 18, 1997.
330 Ibid.

Woody does realize this and wants to bring the *Round-Up* gang home with him, but it turns out that Pete has been a turncoat, and he *wants* to go to the museum. He foils the plan, and soon Al returns, loading *Woody's Round-Up* toys into boxes to ship them to Japan.

A kinetically choreographed action sequence through the airport follows: Buzz and the toys rescue Woody, Jessie, and Bullseye, bringing everyone home to Andy's room, just in time for him to return home from summer camp.

Much like the original, throughout the action and humor of *Toy Story 2*, there are some powerful messages at work, as the sequel explores the ideas of self-identity and placing the needs of others above oneself.

With *Toy Story 2*, Pixar proved once again that even as computer-generated imagery was advancing to the point that nearly anything was possible, it was still the heart and emotion that was more essential to the success of the film than technical advancements.

"We like to think of ourselves as storytellers and artists and not computer 'techies,'" said co-director Unkrich, who had a career as an editor before coming to Pixar in 1994 on a temporary assignment, where he would stay for another twenty-five years, co-directing or directing a number of the studio's biggest films. "Story and character are really number one to us, and we've always tried to tailor the computer tools to aid in that process."[331]

"If we hire an animator, the last thing I want is for that person to be spending their time worrying about technical issues," said Glen McQueen, supervising animator for *Toy Story 2*. "They should only be worrying about the performance of their characters."[332]

This is precisely what everyone responded to when *Toy Story 2* was released on November 24, 1999. The movie review website "Rotten Tomatoes" sums up what almost every critic at the time noted, stating that *Toy Story 2* is: "That rare sequel that arguably improves upon its predecessor. *Toy Story 2* uses

---

331 Lee Unkrich interview with ML, August 27, 1999.
332 Glen McQueen interview with ML, August 19, 1999.

inventive storytelling, gorgeous animation, and a talented cast to deliver another rich moviegoing experience for all ages."[333]

The sequel made $80 million alone in its opening weekend, ending its run with $245 million at the domestic box office. Many consider it one of the best movie sequels of all time, and *Toy Story 2* earned a place alongside the two films that served as its inspiration, *The Godfather Part II* and *The Empire Strikes Back*.

On Christmas Day, '99, about a month after *Toy Story 2* was released, Disney and Pixar included "bloopers' (like those in *A Bug's Life*), over the ending credits, featuring Woody, Buzz and the gang.

As computer animation continued its ascension, Pixar continued to emerge as not just the pioneer but a significant player in the filmmaking industry. The studio was doing this by remaining focused not on the technology but the hallmarks of filmmaking: story and character. And the studio did this with its inimitable style.

"One of the reasons that Pixar has had the successes they've had is that they do concentrate on a good story," added art director Pearson. "It's in the 'Disney mold' to a certain extent because Disney has always had good stories and good characters. But, we take a slightly more irreverent approach."[334]

With *Toy Story 2*, Disney and Pixar had finally done what no one else had been able to do at this point: create a successful sequel to a hit animated film.

And yet, another sequel was next for Disney animation. This time, it would be to one of the studio's most prestigious films and one that was a personal labor of love for Walt Disney himself...*Fantasia*.

To realize how a sequel to this film came about, an understanding of the original is needed.

Fantasia was released on November 13, 1940 and was unlike anything ever seen. It came from Walt's love of merging music with animation. His series of popular *Silly Symphony* short subjects, which began in 1929, is an early example of this.

---

333 Rottentomatoes.com (accessed March 30, 2021).
334 Jim Pearson interview with ML, August 19, 1999.

In the late thirties, hard as it is to believe, Mickey Mouse's box-office popularity was beginning to wane, and Walt started looking for a comeback vehicle for his beloved star. He looked to *The Sorcerer's Apprentice*, a 1797 poem by Johann Wolfgang von Goethe about the title character who finds himself in trouble when he misuses magic.

The poem had been set to music by composer Paul Dukas, and Walt thought that this would be perfect for Mickey. He met with Leopold Stokowski, conductor of The Philadelphia Orchestra, to potentially conduct the music.

From that very positive and exhilarating meeting came *The Concert Feature*, which was eventually retitled *Fantasia*.

Fantasia would not have a plot or a traditional cast of characters. Instead, a master of ceremonies, film critic and composer Deems Taylor, would be on screen, standing in front of an orchestra, introducing each musical segment.

Each one would feature animation set to a piece of classical music, as interpreted by the Disney artists: "Toccata and Fugue in D Minor" by Johann Sebastian Bach featured surrealistic shapes and images; "The Nutcracker Suite" by Pyotr Ilich Tchaikovsky jettisoned the familiar Christmas story in favor of anthropomorphic dances by fish, flowers, and fairies; there was "The Sorcerer's Apprentice" bringing us Mickey in his, now iconic sorcerer hat and robe trying to keep control of out-of-control brooms; Igor Stravinsky's "Rite of Spring," brought us the formation of the earth, complete with dinosaurs; "The Pastoral Symphony" by Ludwig van Beethoven brought to life characters from Greek mythology; Amilcare Ponchielli's "Dance of the Hours" became a comic ballet for hippos, elephants, ostriches and alligators and "Night on Bald Mountain & Ave Maria" by Modest Mussorgsky depicted a clash of good and evil with one of the studio's darkest characters, the mountainous Chernabog.

With such a non-traditional motion picture format, Walt saw *Fantasia* as more than a film and wanted it treated as a concert. The film was distributed as a "roadshow attraction" (released to a limited number of theaters for a certain period), it came with an intermission, was released in "Fantasound" (a pioneering version of today's surround sound so commonplace in movie theaters), and programs were provided to audiences.

Walt's enthusiasm for *Fantasia* was boundless, and he had plans for the film to live on after this original version and return like a recurring concert, or even something more, something new.

"'It is our intention to make a new version of *Fantasia* every year,' said Walt Disney in 1940. 'Its pattern is very flexible and fun to work with – not really a concert, not a vaudeville or a revue, but a grand mixture of comedy, fantasy, drama, impressionism, color, sound and epic fury.'"[335]

Sadly, the world in 1940 had other plans. While film critics praised *Fantasia* (music critics weren't as kind), the film did not fare well at the box office (the onset of World War II in Europe prevented distribution there, which also hindered the movie's grosses). By the end of its run, *Fantasia*'s combined receipts from each roadshow made $325,000, less than *Pinocchio*, which was released earlier the same year.

Walt put plans for another *Fantasia* on a shelf, and the studio moved on to other projects.

It would take, of all things, the turbulent 1960s for *Fantasia* to be re-discovered. It was during this time that filmmakers began to experiment, particularly with visuals and music in movies. This was most evident in films like the Beatles' animated *Yellow Submarine* and director Stanley Kubrick's *2001: A Space Odyssey* (both 1968).

In 1969 (three years after Walt Disney's death), *Fantasia* was re-released to theaters (complete with a psychedelic poster that spoke directly to audiences of the time). Suddenly, appreciation for the film from a new, younger audience began to emerge.

"Animator Art Babbitt was asked by some young people who saw the film for the first time if he and his colleagues had used drugs when they made the film 30 years before. 'Yes, I was on drugs,' Babbitt replied, "Ex-lax and Pepto Bismol!'"[336]

And now, the world once again had other plans for *Fantasia*. The film was seen as the Disney masterpiece that everyone had missed during its initial run.

---

335 John Culhane, *Fantasia 2000: Visions of Hope*, (New York, Hyperion, 1999). P.10.
336 Leonard Maltin, *Of Mice and Magic*, (New York, New American Library, 1980) p.341.

Through the 70s and 80s, *Fantasia* would continue to be re-issued to theaters through several changes, including a newly recorded digital soundtrack at one point and complete restoration for the film's 50th anniversary in 1990.

Roy E. Disney, Walt's nephew, who was nine when *Fantasia* was initially released, held a torch for the film through all of these re-releases. "I thought it was exciting. There were a lot of things happening all the time," said Roy E. Disney of *Fantasia*. "I also loved it because I knew that it was conceived as an endless idea. You could keep reinventing it and going back to it."[337]

In 1984, shortly after Michael Eisner joined Disney as CEO, and Roy E. Disney had just taken over as vice chairman of the board and head of the animation department, the two had lunch together. During that lunch, Disney surfaced the idea of a sequel to *Fantasia*.

"I saw a look in Michael's eyes when I told him about *Fantasia*, and he said, 'Yeah, that's kind of an interesting idea,'" remembered Disney. "So, I tucked away his reaction and thought, 'That was interesting, I can't imagine previous administrations reacting that way.'"[338]

Seven years later, in 1991, fifty-one years after *Fantasia* was initially released, the film came out on home video, as the studio began issuing their classic animated films on VHS. *Fantasia* went on to sell an impressive 8 million copies worldwide.

Roy E. Disney took action, as he remembered: "I wrote Michael a little note and said, 'Not only should we do the second *Fantasia*, but *now* we can afford it!'"[339]

That same year, serving as executive producer, Roy E. Disney would realize his Uncle Walt's dream, and production would begin on a sequel to *Fantasia*.

There was no one better suited for this. Having grown up in the Disney family (his father, Roy O. Disney, and his Uncle Walt started the company), Roy E. Disney had a front-row seat to the growth and the ups-and-downs of the company even

---

337 Roy E. Disney interview with ML, January 21, 1999.
338 Ibid.
339 Ibid.

before he officially came to work there in 1954, as an assistant film editor on the *True-Life Adventures* documentaries

As a boy, Roy listened closely to the sound of his father's car pulling up to the house each evening. If the car "slammed" into the driveway, young Roy knew that dad and Uncle Walt had argued that day, and he would quickly head for another room.

Roy had seen the company that bears his name from so many different perspectives.

"Growing up around Walt and my father, anything was possible," said Disney, adding, "There's that sense that possibilities are endless, so nothing surprises you."[340]

As the follow-up to *Fantasia* went into production, Roy watched the Disney studio ride an incredible wave of success that emerged from a draught in animation not that long before. "It's just been a hell of a ride," said Disney with a smile. "I keep telling people, 'I don't know why they pay me to do what I do. It's just too much fun.'"[341]

Within this ride, Roy E. Disney noted that the weight of how to begin to piece together a follow-up to one of the studio's most highly respected films was heavy, "from the point of view that *Fantasia* is a beloved piece of work, for a lot of reasons and by a lot of different constituents."[342]

Walt and his artists had ideas for numbers for a second *Fantasia* as far back as 1940 (one was Richard Wagner's "Ride of the Valkyries") and then in the 80s, a *Fantasia*-like film entitled *Musicana* was put into production at Disney, but both projects were eventually shelved until 1991.

It was then that Roy E. Disney brought his first two members of the production onboard: Don Ernst as producer (he had served as co-producer of *Aladdin*) and Hendel Butoy (co-director of *The Rescuers Down Under*), to helm several of the sequel's segments.

"As we were coming off of *The Rescuers [Down Under]*, I had mentioned that if we ever do another *Fantasia*, I'd love to be involved with it, in some way," remembered Butoy. "I figured it would never happen. Three months later, I get a phone call

---

340 Ibid.
341 Ibid.
342 Ibid.

from Roy. He's the one who eventually said, 'I think it's time. I think that the artists here have proven themselves. They've done work that's shown that they can do it. We should just go ahead. '"[343]

The sequel's production would be unlike any other, taking almost a decade to reach the screen. This didn't signal any type of trouble but instead was by design so that the second *Fantasia* could take its time.

"There was no urgency to the film," noted Disney. "There was the ability to slide people off of one show and have them for a little while and then slide them into the next show, without everybody else missing beats along the way."[344]

With this, the sequel went through several title changes, from *Fantasia Continued* and a potential release date in 1997, before its eventual title of *Fantasia 2000*, which placed the film to be released to commemorate the 60th anniversary of the original *and* the turn of the century.

Initially, *Fantasia 2000* was a hybrid of new segments, along with several returning from the first film, which had been Walt's initial vision for a follow-up. *Fantasia 2000* was to include half of the segments from the original. Still, as production evolved and more new components were produced, this became a challenge and led to some difficult decisions, in which the initial segments were cut from the sequel.

"The most difficult for me was to lose the whole 'Night on Bald Mountain' scene," admitted Disney, "It's just such a classic piece of animation. To see that go was tough. But the only way that you could use that piece was at the end. We tried it once, actually, in the middle, without 'Ave Maria.' It doesn't work. Anyone who has seen the movie would have just felt cheated. It's interesting because the film has changed. I've gone forever saying that nothing has changed. But the cutting and the pacing of what we do today is just so much faster."[345]

In the end, only one of the original segments, the centerpiece "The Sorcerer's Apprentice," would remain in *Fantasia 2000*, with newly produced segments rounding out the sequel.

---

343   Hendel Butoy interview with ML, January 22, 1999.
344   Roy E. Disney interview with ML, January 21, 1999.
345   Ibid.

Fantasia 2000 opens with an otherworldly air. In what looks to be a stage, floating in space, an orchestra, led by conductor James Levine, arrives and begins to tune-up. Sail-like screens float in, with images from the first *Fantasia* playing on them. The echoey voice of Deems Taylor's narration from that first film is heard.

And we are taken into the first segment, Ludwig van Beethoven's "Symphony Number 5," with what is arguably the four most famous notes in music history ("Da-da-da-daa"). The sequence reveals abstract, triangular shapes that mimic both butterflies and bats, culminating in a swarm against a backdrop of light that seemingly drips and flashes through clouds.

Animating one of history's most famous pieces of music didn't come easy. "Thomas Schumacher explains, 'We approached several artists for ideas on the piece. The problem was not a failure of the artist, but a failure of the process to be able to articulate an idea without taking it all the way. The realm of the visual is mysterious. When you 'see' it, you know what you have, but before that, it's all theoretical abstractions is not an easy collaborative process. '"[346]

It was director Pixote Hunt who was able to solve this. He noted that during an early meeting, "'...Roy Disney looked at me and he said, 'We want you to take this piece of music and GO DREAM.'"[347]

This dream-like (at times nightmarish) sequence and the familiar tones of "Symphony Number 5" immediately pull the audience into *Fantasia 2000*, paying homage to the original style and introducing something new at the same time.

Steve Martin then comes on screen, introducing the sequel and providing some history on how *Fantasia 2000* came to be. Unlike the original, there is no central host for the sequel. Instead, a variety of celebrities are in the film to introduce the different segments, in live action "interstitial" scenes directed by Don Hahn.

After setting the stage, Martin introduces violinist Itzhak Perlman, who segues us into the next segment, "Pines of

346 John Culhane, *Fantasia 2000: Visions of Hope*, (New York, Hyperion, 1999). P.23.
347 Ibid, P.25.

Rome" by Ottorino Respighi. The music is the backdrop for a "whale ballet," of sorts, as whales are summoned by a nova and not only burst from the water, they take flight, soaring into the night sky.

The segment's director, Hendel Butoy, explained how these visuals came about: "With just a verbal concept, we went to story sketch artists. I said, 'I don't know what we're going to do, but let's just think about it. Let's make it a fantasy of some kind.' One of our artists then went and drew what a child might see in the shapes of clouds in the sky. She drew one sketch that had a whale in the clouds. From that sketch, we said, 'Well, that's an image that we've never seen before.'"[348]

The artists then grappled with the concept of how to make the whales take flight and still look somewhat naturalistic. "We played around with where it was that they should leave the water," recalled Butoy. "When it was first storyboarded, we did it at the very beginning. Right now, the way it is, the whale reaches up and then falls back into the water. In early versions, the whale just reached up and kept going. But, as we kept playing with the story, we noticed that you got a much better sensation of flight when you first had the feeling of what it was like to be underwater. The whales should swim around and look natural in their own habitat, then come out of the water. There was a better contrast than to just go with them flying."[349]

Fantasia 2000 then transitions to New York City for "Rhapsody in Blue" by George Gershwin (introduced by Quincy Jones).

Directed by Eric Goldberg, the animation in the segment is designed in the style of Goldberg's artistic hero, caricaturist Al Hirschfeld, whose work came to influence *Aladdin*, thanks to Goldberg.

The sequence started life as a "stand-alone" animated short subject that Goldberg had been working on. He had approached Hirschfeld about utilizing his style and setting it against Gershwin's "Rhapsody in Blue."

---

348 Hendel Butoy interview with ML, January 22, 1999.
349 Ibid.

Eric storyboarded the short, pitched it, and was given the green light to move into production. While this was happening, *Fantasia 2000* was concurrently underway, and those working on the film noticed that the sequel needed a boost of energy.

"There were parts of it that were dragging," remembered Goldberg. "Roy [Disney] turned to me after a screening and said, 'You think 'Rhapsody' is going to be done in time?' So, all of a sudden, it became a *Fantasia* piece."[350]

Set in 1930's Manhattan, the segment focusses on four characters and stories: Duke, a construction worker, who dreams of being a jazz musician; Joe, an out-of-work loner who dreams of employment, "Flying John" (caricatured after noted animation historian John Culhane, also the inspiration for Mr. Snoops in 1977's *The Rescuers*), who dreams of getting the most out of life, despite his stuffy socialite wife and a little girl who dreams of being with her parents, while getting dragged around the city by an extreme nanny.

"It's about everybody chasing their dream and realizing their dream," noted Goldberg.[351]

'Rhapsody in Blue" became a true Goldberg family affair. Eric directed it with his wife Susan, serving as art director (additionally, their daughter Rachel served as the inspiration for the young girl's character in the sequence). Best of all, the segment is how they originally conceived it. "We got something on the screen that really feels like our vision," said Goldberg. "And, we did it with the studio's blessing."[352]

The next segment, introduced by Bette Midler, is set to "Piano Concerto No. 2," by Dmitri Shostakovich and tells the tale of "The Steadfast Tin Soldier" by Hans Christian Andersen. The story had almost been adapted by Disney in the late thirties and early forties when the Disney studio began to work on their Hans Christian Andersen film that never came to be.

Conceptual artwork created for this unproduced film was still in the studio's Animation Research Library when Disney's publishing branch decided to use some of the art created for

---

350 Eric Goldberg to ML, September 9, 1999.

351 Ibid.

352 Ibid

"The Steadfast Tin Soldier" in a new children's book, published in 1991.

Hendel Butoy, who was assigned to direct "Piano Concerto No. 2" (in addition to "Pines of Rome") for *Fantasia 2000,* had purchased the book and providence stepped in.

"Roy brought in the music and asked, 'Is there anything worthwhile here?'" remembered Butoy. "I took the book out, as I was listening to the music, and the structure of the music and the story seemed to go together, so we decided to pull out all of the original sketches. We put the sketches together as a story reel, and everybody looked at it. It was unanimous: we should do this. It was just kind of serendipitous that those sketches were done back then, and now it's come around. It's one of those happy coincidences."[353]

The titular tin soldier finds himself falling in love with a beautiful ballerina doll and facing off against a villainous jack-in-the-box. The soldier is cast out of the children's bedroom, where he experiences adventure after adventure in the "real" world.

The segment keeps the darker tone of Andersen's original story intact and, as an added challenge, the animators on "Piano Concerto No. 2" and all of the segments in *Fantasia 2000* had to craft personalities without the benefit of dialogue

Said Butoy, "In some cases, when I was talking with the animators, we'd have to say, 'Here's what they would say if they could talk.' We'd have to create our own dialogue just to be able to communicate what the character was trying to say. But this is animation in its purest form because making a drawing believable is all about making a character look like it's thinking.

"If you notice, even in dialogue animation, the times that you believe a character most is when the character stops moving and just pauses for a bit because you get the sense that the character is thinking before he's going to do something. In this case, it really applies. You don't have the 'crutch' of dialogue."[354]

Personality comes through without any dialogue in the next segment (introduced by James Earl Jones, with a cameo by Eric Goldberg). "Carnival of the Animals" by Camille Saint-Saens is

---

353 Hendel Butoy interview with ML, January 22, 1999.
354 Ibid.

the backdrop for the tale of a flamingo who gets a hold of a yo-yo, much to the chagrin of his snobbish peers.

The concept for the fast-paced segment came from artist Joe Grant, who, at the time, was 91-years-young and still working at the studio, contributing conceptual artwork. Joe is one of the studio's legends, who worked on the first *Fantasia*, making him the only artist to have worked on both films! "I credit Joe Grant with the high concept," said Goldberg, who, in addition to "Rhapsody in Blue," also directed "Carnival of the Animals." "Various people had tried doing different versions of that idea," said Goldberg.[355]

Original versions harkened back to the "Dance of the Hours" segment of the original *Fantasia*. This didn't provide Goldberg with fertile, creative ground.

"I needed a reason for [the flamingo] to have a yo-yo," he said. "Originally, he just finds it and all of the other flamingos chase him, not unlike the ostriches chasing the one with the grapes in 'Dance of the Hours.' I felt that it was too similar to 'Dance of the Hours,' so I decided to change the dynamic and just make him the goofball that just doesn't want to get in line. He just wants to do his yo-yo tricks and be left alone, thank you very much. Of course, the others don't like that because they have a mob mentality."[356]

Goldberg animated a majority of the segment himself, in addition to directing it. Once again, he worked with his wife Susan, as art director for "Carnival" who created a very distinct palette. "I call it the Hawaiian shirt take," she said. "With today's technology, we have a tendency to make colors very muted. Flamingos are out there, so I figured we would go for the extreme."[357]

"It's not done the traditional way," added Eric. "The entire piece, flamingos, backgrounds - are all hand water colored. It gives it a softer, rendered look that you normally don't get with an outline around the character or tone matte with a shadow."[358]

---

355 Eric Goldberg interview with ML, September 9, 1999.
356 Ibid.
357 Susan Goldberg interview with ML, September 22, 1999.
358 Eric Goldberg interview with ML, September 9, 1999.

The "Carnival" crew did research, studying both flamingos at the San Diego and LA Zoos. They also studied the movements of director Mike Gabriel, a yo-yo aficionado, who had co-directed *Pocahontas* with Eric.

It's appropriate that the joy of "Carnival of the Animals" is followed by the return of "The Sorcerer's Apprentice" from the original *Fantasia* as the next segment (fittingly introduced by magicians Penn and Teller).

After, Mickey Mouse attempts to find Donald Duck, as the following number is his big moment. "Pomp and Circumstance" by Edward Elgar. It is the backdrop for the story of "Noah's Duck." Donald plays Noah's assistant and is trying desperately to get two of each animal onto the ark before the flood. However, there's just one that he can't find – Daisy Duck. With shades of *Sleepless in Seattle*, the two characters spend the musical segment just missing each other.

It's fitting that Disney's most famous fowl would be featured so prominently in *Fantasia* 2000, as Mickey had been the centerpiece of the original.

" The whole thing being done in pantomime really lent itself to Donald," said the segment director Francis Glebas. "It was actually like doing a silent film, only it was much trickier, because if we made a little change, the music didn't change, so you had to come up with new 'bits of business' to stick in where the old 'business' was."[359]

Glebas also added, "What's really interesting is that it really 'reads' as Donald Duck even though there's no dialogue. That was a real trick. We began to realize that the more you 'smash' Donald and make things go wrong for him, that it was funny. Then, at one point, I realized, 'Wait a minute, we have to make sure that he really deserves it.'

"The thing about Donald is that he's that piece of us that tries, against our better will, to do something that he shouldn't be doing, and that's why he deserves to be 'smashed.' That's what was funny. So, there was this really fine line. We had to make sure that it was woven in."[360]

---

359 Francis Glebas interview with ML, January 22, 1999.
360 Ibid.

Also merging with this "cartoony" sensibility is a tremendous amount of heart, particularly in "Pomp and Circumstance'" crescendo, when Daisy and Donald are finally reunited.

From this uplifting moment, *Fantasia 2000* segues into its darker finale, "The Firebird Suite," by Igor Stravinsky. Introduced by Angela Lansbury, the segment tells the very dramatic story of a beautiful sprite awoken by an elk. As she begins to bring life to the forest, she accidentally wakes the destructive force of the Firebird, a mammoth bird made of flames and lava, who emerges from a nearby volcano and goes on a destructive spree.

"The 'Firebird' finale knocks people off their chairs, literally," said Roy E. Disney, remembering an early preview screening of the sequence. "I could see the audience quite clearly, and, at one point, there were three women who jumped off of their chairs. It was astonishing!"[361]

The segment was directed by twin brothers Paul and Gaetan Brizzi, who were already established in the animation industry when Disney approached them in 1989 to buy their independent animation studio in France to spearhead the studio's Paris facility. "Disney wanted us to come up with new ideas and new ways to do animation," said Gaetan. "We wanted to push animation in other areas of art and into other areas of expression."[362]

The brothers worked on some of Disney's prominent films at the Paris studio (most notably *The Hunchback of Notre Dame*), but they eventually came to work at Disney's Burbank studio. "We wanted to be part of this whole Renaissance movement," added Paul. "There is a difference in culture between America and Europe. We wanted to combine European ideas with American entertainment."[363]

The Brizzi brothers most definitely accomplished this with the impressive "Firebird Suite." "Our goal was to create a visual poem, using the expressions of the characters to convey this," said Paul, adding, "It's a tribute to nature and how it can be

---

361 Roy E. Disney interview with ML, January 21, 1999.
362 Gaetan Brizzi interview with ML, January 19, 1999.
363 Paul Brizzi interview with ML, January 19, 1999.

so beautiful and so powerful and dangerous and unpredictable. It's really a message of hope, especially at the end of the millennium."[364]

Paul added that this hopeful feeling found in the film should stay with the viewer after they see *Fantasia 2000*. "They should feel as if they have just gone into an eclectic world of ideas, of art, of expression. It should all feel like a beautiful dream that you don't want to wake up from."[365]

Gaetan added that the hope *Fantasia 2000* provided also carried over to the artists who worked on the film and the possibilities for animation. "I think this reminds people that this is an art form," he said, adding "and maybe this movie could attract people to museums and to galleries. It's almost our duty as artists to innovate without being too intellectual or too personal, but instead, making the audience more open."[366]

In the spirit of the original, *Fantasia 2000* had a very untraditional release. The sequel had its premiere on December 16, 1999, at Carnegie Hall in New York, part of a five-city concert tour. *Fantasia 2000* then opened on New Year's Day 2000, at the start of the new century, exclusively at IMAX theaters, where it was to play for a four-month limited engagement through April 30. This was followed by a brief hiatus, after which *Fantasia 2000* returned to theaters everywhere on June 15, 2000.

The first full-length feature to play in IMAX theaters, *Fantasia 2000* set a record for the highest-grossing IMAX film (at the time). Even with its unique, platformed release, *Fantasia 2000* generated $60 million domestically at the box office.

Fantasia 2000 had been a part of so many Disney artists' lives that some found it hard to believe that, just before the film's release, it was finally coming to theaters. "I started working on the film in '92," said Glebas. "That was the year my son was born, and when it comes out in theaters, he'll be able to read my name in the credits!"

Butoy, one of the first brought on to the film celebrated twenty years with Disney just before *Fantasia 2000* came

---

364 Ibid.

365 Ibid.

366 Gaetan Brizzi interview with ML, January 19, 1999.

to theaters, and said, "My hope is that anyone who watches this film goes through the same spectrum of emotion and excitement and thrill that we had coming up with the ideas and the images."[367]

Critics appreciated the film history that *Fantasia 2000* represented. Roger Ebert wrote, "...as exactly what it is *Fantasia 2000* is splendid entertainment, and the IMAX system is an impressive co-star."[368]

Others were non-plussed. *Empire* magazine's David Parkinson called it a "...mixed bag of delights."[369]

As the shepherd for his Uncle's vision, Roy E. Disney said, while *Fantasia 2000* was in production: "We're going to have to endure the critics. They're all going to say, 'How dare you mess with a masterpiece?' and all of the other things that they accused the first film of. But, when you see the film, it's like listening to the music through entirely new ears."[370]

He summed up the whole *Fantasia 2000* experience by saying, "It's interesting, when we were putting the film together, in terms of the order of the pieces, and we looked back at the original, you could see this emotional journey that you go on. It happens in this film, too."[371]

With the grand, epic production of *Fantasia 2000* complete, the film brought Disney history full circle.

As the decade and the century closed out, many felt that the Disney Animation Renaissance also came to an end. However, there were two films on the horizon that were still a part of this period, as they had both been in production almost as long as the Renaissance itself.

---

367 Hendel Butoy interview with ML, January 22, 1999.

368 Roger Ebert, "Review: *Fantasia 2000*," December 31, 1999, rogerebert.com (accessed April 4, 2021).

369 David Parkinson, "*Fantasia 2000* Review," *Empire* magazine, January 1, 2000, Empire.com (accessed April 4, 2021).

370 Roy E. Disney interview with ML, January 21, 1999.

371 Ibid.

CHAPTER TEN

"Perfect World"

Dinosaur & The Emperor's New Groove

"Making this movie was like jumping off of a cliff," admitted co-director Eric Leighton when discussing Disney's computer-animated feature *Dinosaur.* "I hadn't really touched a computer before this film, and I'm not very good at video games, but it was a challenge and a good one. To me, that meant a potential for growth."[372]

Disney would once again look to break new ground for their next production, pushing animation and technology forward.

Dinosaur began life as an idea from visual effects artist and legend Phil Tippet, a master of stop-motion animation.

In 1986, Tippet worked on *Robocop* with director Paul Verhoven and approached him about partnering on a dinosaur movie using stop-motion animation. The two brought in screenwriter Walon Green (*The Wild Bunch*) to write the screenplay.

"That version would have been a lot more violent," laughed Leighton.[373]

Tippet and Verhoven eventually left the project, but it was that version, however, that initially brought the film to The Walt Disney Studios, as it was pitched to Jeffrey Katzenberg and went into development in 1988 at the studio's live-action division.

From here, the "dinosaur movie" went through many iterations. When *Jurassic Park* ruled the box-office in 1993, Disney decided to move away from stop-motion and other practical effects and make the film digitally.

---

372 Eric Leighton interview with ML, January 20, 2000.
373 Ibid.

Here, the film moved over to Disney's Feature Animation Studio and went through several changes. At one point, the film was to be a combination of digital dinosaurs with miniature sets. This idea was eventually scrapped, and the miniature sets were replaced with live-action backgrounds.

At another point in the production, the characters were to speak only in voice-over (audiences would essentially be hearing the dinosaurs' thoughts). "That just wasn't emotional or engaging enough for these majestic animals," remembered *Dinosaur* co-producer Baker Bloodworth.[374] In the end, it was decided to allow the dinosaurs to speak.

To fully realize the film and compete in the expanding realm of computer-generated imagery, Disney created a complete "in-house" digital studio to produce *Dinosaur* and future digital productions.

This studio was "The Secret Lab" at Disney and was built by and for *Dinosaur*

It was a merger of The Walt Disney Company and Dream Quest Images, a visual effects company that had created effects for such films as 1989's *The Abyss* (for which they won the Academy Award). Disney purchased the Santa Monica-based Dream Quest Images in 1996 and moved the studio to Burbank and Disney Feature Animation. This laid the groundwork for "The Secret Lab," which was formed in 1999.

"We had to do what no other filmmaking crew has ever had to do," added Bloodworth. "We had to hire three hundred and fifty artists, which took a year and a half. Then, we had to try and figure out how to make a movie that no one has ever made before."[375]

Ironically, co-director Leighton was well-versed in stop-motion animation, having worked as an animator on the effects for *Robocop 2* (1990), as well as *Tim Burton's The Nightmare Before Christmas*.

He was partnered with Ralph Zondag, another veteran of traditional animation, who started his career as an animator on *The Care Bears Movie* in 1985. He came to Disney in 1995

---

374 Baker Bloodworth interview with ML, January 20, 2000.
375 Baker Bloodworth interview with ML, January 20, 2000.

after making his directorial debut on another dinosaur movie, Amblimation's *We're Back! A Dinosaur's Story* (1993).

Zondag noted that CGI wasn't initially embraced by many in the industry. "There was definitely a fear [of computers] for years, especially from animators. I think part of that fear was just not understanding it. I think what's happened is that technology has strengthened over the years. As it gets stronger, it starts attracting really talented artists, which makes it that much better. The possibilities with it then become endless. It opens up a new door for storytelling."[376]

When *Dinosaur* was in production, one of the film's animators, Eamonn Butler, said that it was the "rubber-hose days of computer animation"[377] (in reference to the 1920s and '30s, when black-and-white animated characters moved their arms and legs like rubber hoses in those early films).

The artists bringing the dinosaurs to the screen in *Dinosaur* had to create software written for the film, with names like "tear program" (to allow a character to cry) or the self-explanatory "fur program," as well as realism of the dinosaur's skin.

No detail could be left unexplored, as the dinosaurs in *Dinosaur* wouldn't just be a part of several sequences. They would be in the *entire* film, in *every* scene.

"This film is entirely set during the Cretaceous times," added Leighton. "Unlike *Jurassic Park*, which had about sixty scenes with dinosaurs, we've got somewhere between fourteen to fifteen hundred scenes."[378]

"We had to give the characters realism and a certain amount of weight that you need to sell the believability of the character and yet still provide the entertainment for the film," said Mike Belzer, one of the *Dinosaur*'s supervising animators.[379]

"I knew the job was dangerous when I took it," laughed Neil Eskuri, *Dinosaur*'s supervisor of digital effects, who added: "We constantly had to break new bounds," He also noted, "We were working with software that hadn't even gone out to the market yet. We would develop certain functionality or technique, then

---

376   Ralph Zondag interview with ML, January 20, 2000.
377   Eamonn Butler interview with ML, January 18, 2000.
378   Eric Leighton interview with ML, January 20, 2000.
379   Mike Belzer interview with ML, January 18, 2000.

there'd be a new cut, and everything we developed wouldn't work. It was always two steps forward and one step back."[380]

Adding another level of technical difficulty were the live-action backgrounds that were interacting with the computer-generated dinosaurs. The artists had to take live-action footage of such locations as Death Valley and scan them into the computer. These were then combined with the digital animation of the dinosaurs. "We had to always think that the characters were always there," said visual effects supervisor Neil Krepela of the challenge of merging these elements.[381]

To aid with this, the artists adjusted the live-action scenes through technical "trickery," at times combining two separate locations in the computer.

Adjusting elements brought about difficulties in making sure that nature didn't start to look too digitally created. "The biggest challenge for us was the amount of interaction the characters had with water," admitted Eskuri. "We all know what water looks like. We've seen it our entire lives."[382]

To add realism, the filmmakers did extensive research about dinosaurs and the world when they roamed the earth. "We all wanted to take a wayback machine for our pre-production trip," laughed art director Cristy Maltese. "Instead, we looked at a lot of books and took trips to museums."[383]

Producer Bloodworth also noted that they got creative with their research, bringing an elephant into the studio: "We were able to reference their movements in terms of how a ten-ton character would walk, stretch and essentially move. That was very significant."[384]

During one of these sessions, the animators had the opportunity to ride the elephant they observed. "That's one of the perks of working at Disney," said Belzer excitedly, "you're animating one day and riding an elephant the next!"[385]

---

380   Neal Eskuri interview with ML, January 20, 2000.
381   Neil Krepela interview with ML, January 18, 2000.
382   Neal Eskuri interview with ML, January 20, 2000.
383   Cristy Maltese interview with ML, January 19, 2000.
384   Baker Bloodworth interview with ML, January 20, 2000.
385   Mike Belzer interview with ML, January 18, 2000.

Paleontologists were brought in to consult on *Dinosaur*, but the artists stopped just short of letting the film become too realistic.

"This is not a scientifically accurate film," added Bloodworth," and we would never pretend that it is. We are telling a story, and we are taking creative license to make our characters interesting. But we know people are ready to tear us apart. In some sense, you do care about that because it is someone's opinion. On the other hand, paleontologists and scientists really don't agree on what happened. History, here, is not entirely final."[386]

As this was an animated film, there was an artistic as well as naturalistic inspiration for *Dinosaur*. For help in creating the backgrounds, art director Maltese turned to the work of artist Frederic Edwin Church for inspiration. Church is best known for crafting large, stunning landscape paintings of mountains, sunsets, and waterfalls. Although working in the 19th century, his work seemed to fit perfectly in *Dinosaur*. "There's a translucence quality that Church had," noted Maltese. "That we kind of think of as prehistoric."[387]

Additionally, the animators had to bring dinosaurs back to the screen and make sure they had personalities.

"These dinosaurs are our actors," added producer Pam Marsden. "They're not just effects in the film; they're not screaming, charging dinosaurs, in the way that we usually think of them. These are dinosaurs with personalities, emotions, and motivations."[388]

"A photo-realistic dinosaur certainly has power to it," said Leighton. "We wanted the story to match that as much as possible. We wanted a feeling of reality, of trueness, to the story."[389]

The film *Dinosaur* most definitely brings these emotions during its opening sequence, which begins with a startingly realistic scene devoid of dialogue. A mother Iguanodon cares for her egg in her nest. A vicious Carnataurus then attacks, knocking the egg out of the nest.

---

386 Baker Bloodworth interview with ML, January 20, 2000.
387 Cristy Maltese interview with ML, January 19, 2000.
388 Pam Marsden interview with ML, January 18, 2000.
389 Eric Leighton interview with ML, January 20, 2000.

We then follow the egg as it goes on its adventure, bobbing down a river and taken by a Pterodactyl, who takes it in flight, dropping it into the jungle.

Here, the egg hatches, and a baby Iguanodon emerges, rescued by a family of lemurs, led by Plio (the voice of Alfre Woodard) and Yar (Ossie Davis). Despite Yar's objections, the lemurs raise the young dinosaur, whom they name Aladar.

Years later, adult Aladar (D.B. Sweeney), now growing up among the lemurs, spends time with his best friend Zini (Max Casella) and his adopted sister Suri (Hayden Panettiere). However, he knows he is different.

After a violent meteor shower (with some impressive effects) causes a massive explosion and shockwave. Aladar, Plio, Yar, Zini, and Suri escape, but, sadly, the rest of the lemur community doesn't survive.

Once they flee, they join a herd of dinosaurs, led by the stubborn Iguanodon Kron. They are all trying to find their way to the safety of the valley and their nesting grounds. "Kron isn't really the villain," added Marsden, "he's just the leader of a herd who can't adjust to the changes that the meteor wrought. He's very much a soloist. Aladar comes in with the idea that as a community, they can be safe. In a way, Kron is pretty sympathetic. He's just doing things the way that he's always done them."[390]

Kron, who clashes with Aladar, is voiced by Samuel E. Wright, returning to a Disney animated feature in a much different performance from Sebastian, the crab in *The Little Mermaid*.

"He has this great stage presence and this great ability to project," said Butler (Kron's supervising animator) of Wright. "He's also got great control over the sounds and the way he creates sounds. We asked all of our actors to create animal sounds while we were recording the dialogue. He was doing a lot of roaring and shouting. We were getting worried that he might get hoarse or lose his voice. He kept saying he was fine. It turns out he has this trick that he does, where he could vibrate the back of his palette and doesn't use his voice box at all. All of that came from his stage training."[391]

---

390   Pam Marsden interview with ML, January 18, 2000.
391   Eamonn Butler interview with ML, January 18, 2000.

Other familiar voices can be "heard in the herd." Julianna Margulies (of TV's *ER*) is Neera, Kron's sister, who becomes Aladar's love interest, Della Reese as the wise, slow-moving Styracosaurus, Eema and Dame Joan Plowright as the elderly Brachiosaurus, Baylene.

"As an animator, you always dream of working with a voice that has a little bit of character," said Baylene's supervising animator, Belzer. "Joan was all about that. There was just so much color in her voice."[392]

"We had been trying to cast this hundred-ton character for a long time," added co-director Leighton. "It went through a lot of phases. Once we put Joan's voice to the character, it just came alive."[393]

As the herd continues to make their trek to the nesting grounds, they're hunted by two Carnotaurus. It's Aladar who rallies the herd to "stand together!" against the Carnataurus so that they can make it to the nesting grounds.

Throughout this story, *Dinosaur* strives to be more than simply a groundbreaking technical feat but instead looks to comment on universal themes. "Adapting, understanding that things can change and that you can get through it, as long as you're open to it, is probably the strongest theme that's in the picture," said Zondag.[394]

When the film opened on May 19, 2000, critics immediately responded favorably to *Dinosaur*'s astonishing visuals. Each comment on how the film provides the well-worn "feast for the eyes" was balanced with a observation on how all of this somewhat collapses under the weight of an underwhelming script.

In *The Los Angeles Times*, Kenneth Turan voiced his frustration with this, writing: "*Dinosaur* astonishes, and disheartens as only the most elaborate, most ambitious Hollywood products can. A technical amazement that points computer-generated animation toward the brightest of futures, it's also cartoonish in the worst way, the prisoner of pedestrian plot points and

---

392   Mike Belzer interview with ML, January 18, 2000.
393   Eric Leighton interview with ML, January 20, 2000.
394   Ralph Zondag interview with ML, January 20, 2000.

childish, too-cute dialogue."[395]

Turan concludes his review with a thought echoed by many at the time; that while *Dinosaur* is a visual marvel, it's missing an element seen in some other recent films: "President Abraham Lincoln, or so the story goes, wanted to find out what the victorious General U.S. Grant was drinking and send it to the rest of his commanders. In the same way, it's too bad they can't bottle what John Lasseter is drinking and send it to the gang at Disney despite their peerless visual magic they need it, they really do."[396]

Audiences may have felt the same way. After many years and iterations before arriving on screens, *Dinosaur* made only $137 million domestically at the box office.

The film had come with a sustained marketing campaign and was the centerpiece of a popular attraction at Disney's Animal Kingdom theme park. Originally called "Countdown to Extinction," the attraction was renamed "Dinosaur!" in 2000 to coincide and align with the film.

By then, however, *Dinosaur* was seen as a disappointment by many, noting that, while the film was a visual marvel, it was a far cry from the string of animated successes that Disney had been experiencing now for over a decade.

Like *Dinosaur*, another project at Disney animation had meandered through its production over most of the 90s before making it to the screen.

The Emperor's New Groove has snowballed in its appreciation since its initial release in December of 2000. Today's legions of fans count it among their Disney favorites but may not realize that the film started life much differently than we know it today.

Roger Allers, co-director of *The Lion King*, remembered:

"'I had finished *Lion King* and was looking around to see what to do next. Disney was starting to push to do things set in other cultures. Tom Schumacher [executive vice president for Walt Disney Feature Animation] called me in, and he had three pictures up on the wall: representations of Inca, Aztec, and Mayan cultures. For the Incan culture, there was a picture

---

395 Kenneth Turan, "What Would He Say," *The Los Angeles Times*, May 19, 2000, latimes.com (accessed May 3, 2021).

396 Ibid.

of these amazing stone buildings and Machu Picchu, the city atop a mountain in the clouds. I said, 'I'd love to try to develop something around the Incas.' I started looking for an idea.'"[397]

From this initial concept in 1994 came *Kingdom of the Sun*, an animated film inspired by the novels *The Prisoner of Zenda* by Anthony Hope and *The Prince and the Pauper* by Mark Twain, all set against Incan culture.

The film would tell the story of a greedy, self-centered emperor, Manco (voiced by David Spade), and a peasant Pacha (Owen Wilson), who look so much alike that they decide to switch places, as the Emperor is bored with his life.

The film's villain, Yzma (Eartha Kitt), concocts a plan to summon a god to destroy the sun. When Yzma finds out about the Emperor/pauper swap, she turns the Emperor into a llama and threatens him with revealing the pauper's true identity. Meanwhile, the pauper falls in love with the Emperor's fiancé Nina.

Kingdom of the Sun was also going to include the voice talents of actress Carla Gugino as Nina, Laura Prepon as Mata, a humble llama herder, and Harvey Fierstein as Huacua, a talking rock talisman who served as Manco's advisor.

The film was coming together as an epic, Disney-animated fable in the mold of many Renaissance hits. It was even slated to be a traditional musical. Like *Lion King* and *Tarzan*, one of the biggest names in pop music was brought on with Sting joining the film and composing a number of songs.

There was a pre-production trip to Peru, early conceptual art, character design, storyboards, and animation.

Then, early "work in progress" screenings of *The Kingdom of the Sun* didn't yield positive results. "The story wasn't quite coming together," the film's producer, Randy Fullmer remembered, "The first two years we were working on this film, people were pouring out their hearts and souls, trying to make a good movie. We eventually just took a step back and said, 'We are really on the wrong track.'"[398]

---

397 Bilge Ebiri, "We'll Never Make that Kind of Movie Again,' An Oral History of The Emperor's New Groove, a Raucous Disney Animated Film That Almost Never Happened," Jan 27, 2021, vulture.com (accessed May 5, 2021).

398 Randy Fullmer interview with ML, August 9, 2000.

In 1997, Mark Dindal was brought on to *Kingdom of the Sun* as co-director with Allers. Dindal had just completed directing the film *Cats Don't Dance* for Turner Feature Animation but had begun his career at Disney in the early eighties.

"I started about five months after Don Bluth and company had left, so there was a very small group here," said Dindal, adding, "There were still some of the veteran animators here, and I was able to talk to them and get some insight. So, in spite of the fact that the movies made at the time weren't all that fulfilling, there were things here that I'm glad I had an opportunity to experience."[399]

Dindal worked on such projects as *The Fox and the Hound* and *The Great Mouse Detective*. He left to pursue other projects but returned to Disney to work on *The Little Mermaid* and an animated segment in Disney's 1991 live-action film *The Rocketeer*.

It was after this that Dindal left for Turner Feature Animation and *Cat's Don't Dance*. The film did not fare well at the box office but caught the attention of animation fans and many in the industry with its unique sensibilities.

This included Randy Fullmer, who brought Mark on to *Kingdom of the Sun*. "He knows how to delegate, entrust and empower artists," said Fullmer of Dindal. "He lets artists bring their creative ideas to the table. When you trust artists like that, they really take off. Mark intuitively knows this."[400]

By 1998, *Kingdom of the Sun* still wasn't coming together, and there was a summer 2000 release date looming. "It never quite clicked," admitted Dindal. "Each time we tried to work out a problem, Peter Schneider and Thomas Schumacher would ask us to think outside the box-think broader strokes, not just little changes. Finally, we came to a point where we decided to think beyond where we were."[401]

A challenge with *Kingdom of the Sun* was that the story, set in a specific time and place, was getting mired down in details. As Fullmer remembered: "One day, literally, we had an argument about whether it was right to put a wheel in the movie. The

399 Mark Dindal interview with ML, August 11, 2000.
400 Randy Fullmer interview with ML, August 9, 2000.
401 Mark Dindal interview with ML, August 11, 2000.

Spanish were the ones who brought over the wheel [to South America], and since the Spanish hadn't arrived yet, could we really have a cart with a wheel on it? At the end of the day, we realized that we were heading in the wrong direction."[402]

A tough decision was made. With dialogue and music recorded and more than a third of the film animated, *Kingdom of the Sun* was shut down, and the movie would be taken in a different direction.

The story was completely overhauled, and only two of the characters would remain. This led to another tough decision around the music and, sadly, all of the songs Sting had written and re-written for the different iterations of the film were taken out.

"He is so atypical of what you think a rock star is," said Fullmer of Sting. "He was a real trooper. He watched us throw out some really good songs. Then, we had the painful moment, where we had to call Sting up and explain that we were making significant changes. He wanted to know if we could still use the songs, and at first, we thought that maybe we could, but then we realized that particular song structure wouldn't fit, and we could see that, as well."[403]

It was also around this point in the production that Allers decided to leave the film. He recalled:

"I could have stayed on as a directing partner, but I just didn't think I could do it. I had put so much into it. I mean, it was four years developing, and the movie was like one-third animated. It was just going to be too disheartening for me. I had no resentment towards anybody who took over the film. I myself had worked with another director on the early versions of *Lion King* before he was taken off, and I was teamed up with somebody else. It happens so often."[404]

Now re-titled *Kingdom IN the Sun*, the film moved forward with Dindal as a solo director, and the tone of the film morphed into that of comedy with more cartoonish sensibilities. "It's now more like Eric Clapton's 'Unplugged,'" Fullmer

---

402 Randy Fullmer interview with ML, August 9, 2000.

403 Randy Fullmer interview with ML, August 9, 2000.

404 Bilge Ebiri, "We'll Never Make that Kind of Movie Again,' An Oral History of The Emperor's New Groove, a Raucous Disney Animated Film That Almost Never Happened," Jan 27, 2021, vulture.com, (accessed May 5, 2021).

said, describing the new version. "We said let's just strip it out, give it a very clean, graphic look and turn it into more of a character piece."[405]

"These movies are meant to be pliable and meant to be changed," said Tony Bancroft, who had co-directed *Mulan* and would return to the role of supervising animator for *Kingdom in the Sun*. "It takes time in animation to really work over the story. We work with a very limited time frame, where we're telling pretty epic tales in 80 minutes. Sometimes it's like putting the genie back in the bottle."[406]

As the artists were working through this story, there was something new that had developed outside of Disney and the film industry: the increasing preponderance of the Internet. Today, it is so commonplace for trials and tribulations of movie productions to be such a large part of our social media-centered world. For the artists at Disney in the late '90s, this was still unchartered territory, as stories of *Kingdom of the Sun*'s unsettled production began to surface on "the web." "It's frustrating that things leak out," said Fullmer. "It's as if an artist decides to work on a painting for five days and someone comes along and critiques it on day one."[407]

Bruce W. Smith, another of the film's supervising animators, added, "A lot of what happened was very normal in the process of making an animated film. It's just never been captured on the Internet like this before. But, from our point of view, this was all very natural and wasn't all that alarming."[408]

In early 2000, the film's title changed to *The Emperor's New Groove*. With a tone more akin to Warner Bros.' Looney Tunes cartoons, the film centers on Emperor Kuzco (David Spade, one of the two returning cast members from the original). The audience meets Kuzco as the film opens through some irreverent voice-over from the character.

A llama sits in a jungle, drenched from a rainstorm. We learn that the llama was once an Emperor, in fact, the Emperor who is telling the story, Kuzco. "You go back aways, ya know

---

405 Randy Fullmer interview with ML, August 9, 2000.
406 Tony Bancroft interview with ML, August 11, 2000.
407 Randy Fullmer interview with ML, August 9, 2000.
408 Bruce Smith interview with ML, August 14, 2000.

before I was a llama, and this will all make sense," says Kuzco in voice-over. Baby Kuzco appears on the screen. "Alright, now see that's a little too far back," he adds.

Then the opening song, "Perfect World" (one of two songs Sting created for *Emperor's New Groove*) is performed by "Theme Song Guy" (a Vegas-lounge club-like singer, voiced by Tom Jones), who sings all about Kuzco in a fast-paced sequence that shows immediately just how spoiled Kuzco is and how so many cater to his every whim.

As Kuzco starts to dance, an elderly man gets in the way and "throws off his groove." Shockingly, Kuzco has the old man (voiced by veteran Disney vocal talent John Fiedler) thrown out the palace window.

"We did struggle over likeability," said Nik Ranieri, supervising animator of Kuzco. "A few scenes were cut early on because many felt that Kuzco was too nasty. The idea being that the more nasty he is at the beginning, the more of a personality change that he goes through."[409]

Ranieri had to re-animate a number of scenes several times, as there were concerns during production that the character would turn off audiences too quickly at the start of the film.

One sequence, in particular, became a source of debate among the artists while they were making *The Emperor's New Groove*. Ranieri remembered, "In one scene, Kuzco is checking out his potential brides. As he walks past this line of girls, he's saying, 'Hate your hair! Hate your face! Yikes!' And all the girls are pretty, so it was showing what a jerk he is, but some people got really offended by it. I thought, 'Of course you're supposed to be offended, he's an idiot!'"[410]

Michael Eisner came to the rescue of the scene and felt it should be left in the film after watching an early rough-cut of *The Emperor's New Groove*. "Ah Michael, I owe him a lot," laughed Ranieri. "He suggested James Woods for Hades and now this."[411]

As insensitive as Kuzco is, he's not the film's villain. That is Yzma, his advisor, who secretly has her eye on the throne. "We wanted a character who had evil intent but also had some

---

409 Nik Ranieri interview with ML, August 10, 2000.
410 Ibid.
411 Ibid.

redeeming and charming qualities," said Fullmer of Yzma. "She, like the other characters in the film, is going along her own path, based on her own obsessions."[412]

"There was a fear that she was a little too close to Cruella DeVil," admitted Dale Baer, Yzma's supervising animator. "But, I think Yzma stands out on her own."[413]

When *The Emperor's New Groove* was in production, Baer had almost thirty years' experience in animation. He joined Disney in 1970, working on *Robin Hood* and *The Rescuers*. He left to work at other studios and even opened his own studio, Baer Animation Company, in the 1980s. Baer also taught animation as part of the faculty at CalArts.

He returned to Disney in 1998, working on *The Emperor's New Groove* and Yzma. Baer found what helped differentiate the villainess was legendary actress and singer Eartha Kitt. In addition to Spade, Kitt was the only other member of the voice cast to return from the original inception of the film.

"She's incredible," Baer said. "Not just watching her recording sessions but listening to them; you got a very distinctive picture in your mind. It just made coming up with ideas for her scenes that much more fun. She put so much into the performance that you wanted to do it justice."[414]

One of Kuzco's first acts in the film is firing Yzma, along with Kronk, Yzma's beyond-dimwitted muscular henchman (*Seinfeld*'s David Puddy himself, Patrick Warburton). "This character is a lot like Puddy," said Bancroft, Kronk's supervising animator. "They're both in the big, dumb-guy mold."[415]

After the firing, Kuzco's ability to be overly insensitive is only illuminated more when he meets with Pacha (John Goodman), a kind, mild-mannered peasant who has been summoned to meet with Kuzco. It seems that Kuzco has plans for the small village Pacha lives in. The Emperor wants to build "Kuzcotopia," his "ultimate summer getaway, complete with water slide!"

Pacha is beyond shocked that his home will be destroyed for

---

412 Randy Fullmer interview with ML, August 9, 2000.
413 Dale Baer interview with ML, August 14, 2000.
414 Ibid.
415 Tony Bancroft interview with ML, August 11, 2000.

such a selfish reason and that Kuzco doesn't care. The Emperor has Pacha ushered out.

From here, Yzma enacts her plan to take over as Empress herself. With Kronk, she devises a scheme to ascend the throne. Inviting Kuzco over for dinner, Yzma looks to poison Kuzco, but when Kronk mistakenly uses the wrong formula, the Emperor is accidentally transformed into a llama.

Yzma instructs Kronk to knock Kuzco out, place him in a sack and dispose of him outside the palace grounds.

As dark and devious as these scenes sound, they contain some of the film's funniest moments, thanks to the character of Kronk. With his obsession with cooking the perfect dinner (particularly his spinach puffs) and creating and humming his own *Mission Impossible*-like theme song while sneaking Kuzco out of the city, the character quickly emerged as the scene-stealer of the film.

"He wasn't given very good advice when someone told him to pursue a career as a villain's sidekick," laughed Bancroft when discussing the character of Kronk. "He's a really good-hearted guy, definitely more brawn than brain, but still a good guy."[416]

Kronk can't bring himself to "do in" Kuzco and accidentally places the sack with him in it on Pacha's cart, and the peasant unknowingly takes llama Kuzco with him, when he goes home to his expectant wife Chicha (Wendie Malick) and his two kids, Chacha and Tipo (Kellyann Kelso and Eli Russell Linnetz).

Here, when the "talking llama" is discovered to be the Emperor by Pacha, he decides to cut a deal with Kuzco: he will get the Emperor back to the palace (and a potential antidote to turn him back to a human) in exchange for Kuzco agreeing to build his "Kuzcotopia" elsewhere.

Bruce W. Smith, who served as supervising animator for Pacha, had the task of crafting the one character in the film, who served as the selfless, innocent, sane compass amid the cartoon cacophony around him.

John Goodman, the actor behind Pacha, brought warmth to his performance that informed the character. Said Smith,

---

416 Ibid.

"We taped certain recording sessions. We would study those and see exactly what John Goodman brought to the character, in the form of facial expressions, subtle acting that would enhance the character's mannerisms. We analyzed them over and over, really trying to dissect what would make this character interesting."[417]

Los Angeles native Smith joined Disney as an animator on *Who Framed Roger Rabbit*. He went on to work at other studios, such as Paramount, where he directed 1992's *Bebe's Kids* and at Warner Bros., directing the Looney Tunes character animation in the hit live-action/animated *Space Jam* (1996).

He returned to Disney as supervising animator for Kerchak in *Tarzan* before joining *The Emperor's New Groove*, where he welcomed the film's change of pace. "The humor is way beyond anything that Disney has done," Smith said. "This film is like something from the Zucker brothers, like *Airplane*, with its non-sequiturs. That's never been done in an animated film, to this degree."[418]

This screwball, overtly cartoonish tone is on full display as Kuzco and Pacha attempt to make their way back to the palace, with Yzma and Kronk in pursuit, after Yzma realizes that Kuzco is still alive.

On this chase, we see several familiar yet seemingly fresh, iconic cartoon tropes, such as the angel and devil on the shoulders, a dotted-line tracing characters journeying across a map, and a character struck by lightning, stopping them burnt to a crisp in mid-air.

The climactic finale back at the palace is a rapid-fire succession of humor, involving a running gag around Yzma's secret lab and a creatively choreographed sequence in which Kuzco keeps drinking the wrong formula and transforming into different animals.

However, through it all, Kuzco moves from selfish to selfless, first looking to betray Pacha's trust, then coming to the realization that he cannot. Pacha, meanwhile, doesn't give up on the self-centered llama. A connection and friendship

---

417 Bruce W. Smith interview with ML, August 14, 2000.
418 Ibid.

develop between the two as *The Emperor's New Groove* grows a heart within its comedic frame.

"I like the challenge of getting emotion out of the characters that are done without realism in mind," noted Dindal. "There's a dimension to the characters, and all the animators apply the traditional rules to them. But, when you take something that's far out in the imagination and still get a heartfelt moment, it's an interesting combination."[419]

The Emperor's New Groove opened in theaters on December 15, 2000. Several critics were pleasantly surprised by the film's irreverence.

Writing in *Variety*, Robert Koehler stated: "Disney's new generation of animators has quietly staged a Palace revolt with *The Emperor's New Groove*. The holiday release may not match the groovy business of many of the studio's other kid pix, but it will be remembered as the film that established a new attitude in the halls of Disney's animation unit."[420]

Jay Boyar, in the *Orlando Sentinel*, wrote: "I admit I feel a little guilty to be praising a production whose aims are so thoroughly modest, but I laughed all the way through this movie."[421]

Unfortunately, the critical support didn't help buoy *The Emperor's New Groove* (which came with a very sparse marketing campaign) at the box office. The film finished its run with a very discouraging $89 million domestically.

The Emperor's New Groove did receive an Oscar nomination (For Sting's song "My Funny Friend and Me," which played over the ending credits) and also gave way to a TV series, *The Emperor's New School*, and a direct-to-video sequel, *Kronk's New Groove* (2005).

But it was two years after *The Emperor's New Groove* first hit theaters when the film gained some notoriety with the release of the 2002 documentary, *The Sweatbox*, co-directed by John-Paul Davidson and Trudie Styler, who is Sting's wife. Styler, a documentary filmmaker, was granted access to the production of *Kingdom of the Sun* when Sting came onboard the project.

---

419 Mark Dindal interview with ML, August 11, 2000.

420 Robert Koehler, *The Emperor's New Groove* Review *Variety*, December 10, 2000, Variety.com, (accessed May 5, 2021).

421 Jay Boyar, "A toon just for fun," *Orlando Sentinel*, December 15-21, 2000, p.22.

The documentary was intended as a behind-the-scenes look at how an animated feature film is made but became more of an at-times painful, first-hand look at how the original movie unraveled and eventually became *The Emperor's New Groove*.

The title, *The Sweatbox*, comes from a name given to the screening room during the early days of animation, which had no air conditioning, causing animators to sweat while reviewing rough-cut versions of their work.

The documentary featured interviews with all involved with the making of the film and even featured completed pencil animation from *Kingdom of the Sun*. The documentary premiered at the Toronto Film Festival in September of 2002 and played in Los Angeles and Orlando as part of the Florida Film Festival.

As of this writing, the documentary has not been made available on home video, but an unauthorized version has surfaced online.

With it's underground, "Hey, did you ever see it?" vibe, *The Sweatbox* is a component that has allowed *The Emperor's New Groove* to grow in popularity through the years.

Like *The Nightmare Before Christmas*, the film has developed multitudes of supporters who recognize just how unique, memorable, and clever *The Emperor's New Groove* is and refuse to allow it to slip into obscurity. With its sharply written one-liners, the film has become endlessly quoted (say the name Kronk to any Disney-fan, and they will immediately break into a low, Patrick Warburton voice). The *Emperor's New Groove* has also become a favorite in the GIF and Meme circles on social media.

Merchandise (nonexistent at the time of the release) has even become available. All the newfound love that continues to grow each year justifies the work of artists who struggled through the highs and lows of *The Emperor's New Groove* and broke new ground with the film.

"We loved the cartoon aspect of it all," said animator Smith.[422]

---

422 Bruce W. Smith interview with ML, August 14, 2000.

Fullmer added, "Most of the animators have said that they've been waiting ten years to work on a film like this."[423]

In those ten years, Disney animation had been transformed. As its Renaissance period came to a close, the studio looked ahead to a new century and another period of transformation.

---

423 Randy Fullmer interview with ML, August 9, 2000.

CHAPTER ELEVEN

"Small Wonders"

After the Renaissance

It was the end of an era. The Disney Animation Renaissance had concluded, and the studio faced two decades during which a lot would change.

A lot.

There were indeed challenging times ahead for Disney. Six months after *The Emperor's New Groove*, The Walt Disney Studios ventured out into uncharted waters for animation by producing an action-adventure film with *Atlantis: The Lost Empire*.

From the team of Don Hahn (producer) with Kirk Wise and Gary Trousdale (as co-directors), the film, released in June of 2001, did not perform well at the box office. Additionally, the film was bested by *Shrek*, which would be the first significant blockbuster for Jeffrey Katzenberg and DreamWorks, with the studio emerging as Disney's primary competitor.

Additionally, *Atlantis: The Lost Empire* signaled the start of a string of successive setbacks, such as *Treasure Planet* (2002) and *Brother Bear* (2003). In 2001, The Secret Lab, with only one film to their credit, *Dinosaur*, was closed by Disney.

A bright spot during this time was the success of 2002's *Lilo and Stitch*, which was a small story that connected with audiences through its offbeat, anti-hero Stitch.

In 2003, history seemed to be repeating itself when Roy E. Disney announced his resignation from the company, as he disagreed with the direction in which the company was heading. *USA Today* reported at the time: "Upon quitting the board, the last active Disney family heir called for the resignation of CEO Michael Eisner, saying 'It's time for new blood.'"[424]

Roy E. Disney even started a website, "SaveDisney.com," dedicated to the cause of changing the leadership and revitalizing The Walt Disney Company.

In January of 2004, Disney announced the closure of its Feature Animation Studio in Florida. In addition to *Mulan*, *Lilo & Stitch* & *Brother Bear* had also been produced in Florida. Another animated feature, *My Peoples*, was in production (but never finished) at the Florida studio when it closed.

The newspaper *The St. Petersburg Times* stated at the time of the closing that Disney had reduced its animation staff from 2,200 employees in 1999 down to 600 and that the animation studios in Paris and Tokyo would also be closing.[425]

In 2004, a year after the closing of these animation studios, Disney released *Home on the Range*, which many consider a true low point for the studio. The animated western had gone through an unsettled production and several iterations before coming to theaters, where it was unanimously panned by critics and ignored by audiences.

Home on the Range also became the "poster child" for what many considered to be the disappointing state of Disney animation at the time and how far the fall had been from the days of *The Lion King* just ten years before.

The film also signaled something that many thought would never happen: the end of traditional, two-dimensional animation at Disney. The growing possibilities, power, and popularity of computer animation were pointing toward a new horizon that many felt couldn't be denied any longer. Disney announced in 2004 that all of their future feature films would be produced in computer animation and that they were converting to a full CGI studio.

The first of these would be 2005's *Chicken Little*, Disney's first fully computer-animated feature, which didn't realize the box-office hopes many had for the film.

---

424 Michael McCarthy, "War of Words Erupt at Walt Disney," *USA Today*, & Bob Child, AP, December 2, 2003, usatoday30.usatoday.com (accessed May 5, 2021).

425 Associated Press, "Disney Pulls its Animators from Orlando," *The St. Petersburg Times*, January 13, 2004, news.google.com, (accessed May 5, 2021).

The move toward computer animation seems to stem from the fact that, running parallel to the continuous setbacks at Disney, Pixar Animation Studio was experiencing a Renaissance of their own with massive hits like *Monsters, Inc* (2001), *Finding Nemo* (2003), and *The Incredibles* (2004).

While these films were in production, however, the relationship between Disney and Pixar grew contentious, resulting in Pixar eventually looking for another studio to potentially distribute their movies.

In 2005, Michael Eisner, who, as CEO, had guided Disney through two decades of unprecedented growth in all areas of the company, announced he would step down. Bob Iger, who was then president of The Walt Disney Company, was named the new CEO.

Under this new leadership, turbulent times would level off: Roy E. Disney re-joined the board, and negotiations with Pixar began, eventually leading to Disney acquiring Pixar in 2006. John Lasseter was named Chief Creative Officer of both Pixar and Disney Feature Animation, which was renamed Walt Disney Animation Studios in 2007. With this change, an upswing began.

The first animated feature released by Disney under Lasseter's watch was 2007's *Meet the Robinsons*. Despite a strong story, the film, unfortunately, continued the box office setbacks. This was followed by 2008's *Bolt*, which also unfortunately, underperformed.

This was followed by a surprising move: a return to traditional, 2D animation for *The Princess & The Frog* in 2009. The film, loosely based on *The Frog Prince* fairy tale, would feature the studio's first Black Disney Princess. *The Princess & The Frog* brought back several talented artists who had been let go as the studio moved toward CGI. It did well initially at the box office, but as the uber-blockbuster *Avatar* was released by 20th Century Fox the following week, *The Princess and the Frog* quickly lost box office steam.

After this, Disney would once again venture into fairy-tale territory with their 50th animated feature, *Tangled* (2010), a re-telling of the *Rapunzel* fable, which had been in various states of production at the studio for almost a decade.

Told using computer animation, *Tangled* received praise for its story, characters, and music, all of which connected with audiences, earning the film $200 million at the domestic box office, making it the tenth most successful film of 2010.

Critics couldn't help but note that the film was a return to form for Disney. In the *New York Times*, critic A.O. Scott wrote that watching the movie was "...like entering a familiar old neighborhood that has been tastefully and thoroughly renovated."[426]

The following year, Disney returned to traditional animation and A.A. Milne's beloved characters with the 2011 film *Winnie the Pooh*. Opening the same weekend as *Harry Potter and the Deathly Hallows-Part 2*, Disney was most definitely the "also-ran" at the box office. *Winnie the Pooh* made a dismal $26.7 million, and the studio went back to CGI for all of their subsequent films.

Concurrently, during this period, Pixar released hit after hit: *Cars* (2006), *Ratatouille* (2007), *Wall-E* (2008), *Up* (2009), and the eagerly awaited *Toy Story 3* (2010).

The merging of Disney and Pixar "under one roof" and one leader, Lasseter, proved successful. Stories and productions seemingly got stronger, evidenced by 2012's *Wreck-it Ralph* from Disney.

The film delivered solidly on video game nostalgia, but as *Entertainment Weekly*'s critic Keith Staskeiwicz noted: "...the real success of the film is its emotional core and the relationship between the two misfits."[427]

The following year, Disney Feature Animation would return to a status that they hadn't experienced in almost two decades: that of a blockbuster film.

Frozen, all puns intended, took everyone by storm when released in 2013. Based on Hans Christian Andersen's *The Snow Queen* (which Walt had considered as a follow-up to *Snow White and the Seven Dwarfs* in 1937), *Frozen* was a mega-blockbuster, the likes of which Disney hadn't seen since the heart of the Renaissance in the mid-90s.

The film went on to win the Oscar for Best Animated Feature, a first for The Walt Disney Studios, and *Frozen* went on to make $1 billion worldwide.

---

426   A.O. Scott, "Back to the Castle, Where it's All About the Hair," *The New York Times*, November 23, 2010, nytimes.com, (accessed May 5, 2021).

427   Keith Staskeiwicz, "*Wreck-It Ralph*," *Entertainment Weekly*, November 9, 2012, ew.com (accessed May 5, 2021).

The film also served as a re-awakening of sorts for audiences. A new generation found that the film had incredible "re-watch-ability" and "re-sing-ability" (notably the Oscar-winning favorite "Let It Go"). Store shelves were bare of *Frozen* product and lines to meet the film's main characters Anna and Elsa, at Disney theme parks rivaled some of the most popular attractions.

Disney animation was back in the zeitgeist again.

A string of animated features, each critically or commercially successful, followed: *Big Hero 6* (2014), *Zootopia*, *Moana* (both 2016), and the sequel *Ralph Breaks the Internet* (2018).

Pixar during this time continued to produce solid hits as well, such as *Brave* (2012), *Inside Out* (2016), and *Coco* (2017), as well as a string of sequels to some of their most famous films: *Cars 2* (2011) and *Cars 3* (2017), as well as *Monsters University* (2013), *Finding Dory* (2016), and *The Incredibles 2* (2018).

Pixar was not without its struggles. After a non-stop line-up of hits, their difficult production of *The Good Dinosaur* failed to ignite the box office in 2015.

A significant change came for Pixar two years later, in November of 2017, when it was announced that John Lasseter would be taking a leave of absence amid "missteps."[428] Laura Bradley in *Vanity Fair* reported: "Though his announcement did not acknowledge any specific misdeeds, a subsequent article from *The Hollywood Reporter* indicated that Lasseter had an alleged pattern of sexual misconduct...."[429] [430]

In June of 2018, Disney announced that Lasseter would be leaving the company at the end of the year. Peter Docter, who had directed *Up* and *Inside Out,* took over Lasseter's duties at Pixar. Jennifer Lee, who had co-directed *Frozen,* stepped in as Chief Operating Officer at Disney.

Lasseter's exit was a shock wave, considering how he had been the architect for Pixar and a driving force in Disney

---

428 The Hollywood Reporter Staff, "John Lasseter Taking a Leave of Absence from Pixar Amid 'Missteps'," *The Hollywood Reporter*, November 21, 2017, hollywoodreporter.com (accessed May 5, 2021).

429 Laura Bradley, "Pixar's John Lasseter Takes Leave of Absence After citing "Misteps" in Vague Memo," *Vanity Fair*, November 21, 2017, vanityfair.com (accessed May 5, 2021).

430 The Hollywood Reporter Staff, "John Lasseter's Pattern of Alleged Misconduct Detailed by Disney/Pixar Insiders," *The Hollywood Reporter*, November 21, 2017, hollywoodreporter.com (accessed May 5, 2021).

animation's rebound over the past decade.

Amidst this news, Disney and Pixar went into 2019 with successful sequels to two of their biggest films: *Toy Story 4* and *Frozen II*, each making well over $400 million at the domestic box office.

In February of 2020, Bob Iger stepped down as CEO of Disney with Bob Chapek named as his replacement.

That same year, as the COVID-19 pandemic ravaged the world, animation from Disney would prove to be a soothing balm of relief for many. Thanks to their streaming service, Disney+, introduced in November 2019, a good number of the studio's animated films are available in the comfort of homes. Additionally, Disney+ allowed more recent efforts, such as *Onward* and *Soul* (both 2020) and 2021's *Luca*, from Pixar, and Disney's *Raya and the Last Dragon* and *Encanto* (both 2021), to find an audience.

Over thirty years since the Renaissance began with *The Little Mermaid* in 1989, animated features continue to be developed at Disney.

The Walt Disney Studios had come a long way on a fable-like journey worthy of their animated films. From the days in the 1980s, in which Disney animation struggled to keep even a "toe hold" in our collective consciousness, to today when the announcement of a new Disney animated feature is met with a heightened eagerness that sets social media aflame, it has been an inspirational comeback story.

These recent blockbusters, such as 2013's *Frozen* and the renewed exuberance for all things Disney animation, owe so much to Disney's Animation Renaissance of the 1990s.

For those who were at the studio at this time and contributed significantly by scaling new artistic heights, what was it like to be a part of Disney's Animation Renaissance?

"When we did *Mermaid*, I was giving a talk, and someone asked me, 'What's your goal at Disney?'," remembered animator Ruben Aquino, who retired from Disney in 2013. "I told them that I would love it if I could be part of making Disney films as good as they used to be. We may not have achieved the level of animation that they achieved in the 'Golden Age, but actually, on a lot of levels, I think we have recaptured some of that past glory."[431]

"These are the kinds of times that all of us dreamed about in the seventies," noted art director Andy Gaskill, who is now with Alcon Entertainment.[432]

Peter Schneider, who left Disney in 2001 to form his own theater company, echoed this enthusiasm when discussing the animation Renaissance: "It's been nothing short of exhilarating. It has been the most satisfying artistic experience of my life."[433]

"It was in the back of our minds that, maybe, we could make films like they did back in the 'Golden Days' as they called it," said Hendel Butoy, who now teaches at the School of Visual Arts and Design at Southern Adventist University. "The thrill of it is that people out there really do enjoy this art, and I think we always had this sense that people would like this if it was done right. We just felt, back then, that we'd never get that chance to make it happen. Now that it's happened, it's terrific to see people respond to it the way that they have."[434]

"I've been a part of all the big, animated films that have been produced here [at Disney]. I'm real proud of that, and I feel I've been a part of making history and a future for animation," said *Mulan*'s co-director Tony Bancroft, who left Disney in 2000, after which he formed his own animation studio and also worked at several other studios. He continues to work in animation, is the animation program director at Azusa Pacific University, and co-hosts "The Bancroft Brothers Podcast" with his twin brother Tom.[435]

Director John Musker, who retired in 2018 and no longer has to explain his movies to servers at restaurants, added, "At one point, they were considering charging higher admission prices [for animated films] because people weren't going to them and they couldn't afford to keep making them. Then, gradually it turned around. Now, it's fun to have your movies

---

431   Ruben Aquino interview with ML, January 20, 1998
432   Andy Gaskill interview with ML, January 23, 1997
433   Peter Schneider interview with ML, January 23, 1997
434   Hendel Butoy interview with ML, January 22, 1999
435   Tony Bancroft interview with ML, January 20, 1998

play worldwide and really move into the mainstream."[436]

Glen Keane left Disney and has directed the Oscar winning short subject 2017's *Dear Basketball* (a partnership with the late Kobe Bryant) and also directed the Oscar nominated feature *Over the Moon* for Netflix. He noted that he believed that the medium had been elevated during the Renaissance, saying: "I've always felt that animation is an art form, and just like the subtle smile on the Mona Lisa, it's not just reserved for that painting; let's do that in animation too."[437]

Don Hahn, who would direct two definitive documentaries about Disney's Animation Renaissance, 2009's *Waking Sleeping Beauty*, which documents the growth at the studio in the 90s and 2020's *Howard*, about the life and career of Howard Ashman, said, "As we grow with each picture, we've been able to try out different parts of our talents and stretch ourselves artistically. It's been a pretty neat journey; seeing it go from this 'also ran' corner of the film industry to something that's really in the spotlight right now."[438]

Roy E. Disney, who we sadly lost in 2009, said in a 1999 interview that he felt that audiences were waiting for Disney's animated comeback: "Maybe the public wanted it to happen, in a way. I think, maybe, they missed it."[439]

Walt Disney and his artists built their animated features from the ground up, giving to the world a new art form: the full-length animated feature film. Over fifty years later, artists who spent their lives passionately studying those classic Disney films waited through declining decades for their time and their turn to expand upon all that came before them.

They knew what Walt knew, back in 1940 when he was making *Fantasia* and said of animation: "We have worlds to conquer here."

The artists who were part of Disney's Animation Renaissance certainly conquered them.

---

436   John Musker interview with ML, January 13, 1997
437   Glen Keane interview with ML, March 16, 1995
438   Don Hahn interview with ML, March 20, 1996
439   Roy E. Disney, interview with ML, January 21, 1999

Bibliography

Books

Beck, Jerry, *The Animated Movie Guide*, Chicago: Chicago Review Press, 1995.

Canemaker, John, *Paper Dreams: The Art and Artists of Disney Storyboards*, New York: Hyperion,1999.

---, *Before the Animation Begins: The Art and Lives of Disney Inspirational Sketch Artists*, New York: Hyperion, 1996.

---, *Two Guys Named Joe*, New York: Disney Editions, New York, 2010.

---, *Walt Disney's Nine Old Men & The Art of Animation*, New York: Hyperion, 2001.

Culhane, John, *Disney's Aladdin: The Making of the Animated Film*, New York: Hyperion, 1992.

---, *Fantasia 2000: Visions of Hope*, New York: Hyperion, 1999.

Finch, Christopher, *The Art of Walt Disney: From Mickey Mouse to The Magic Kingdoms*, New York: Abrams, 1995.

Gabler, Neil, *Walt Disney: The Triumph of the American Imagination*, New York: Alfred A. Knopf, 2006.

Grant, John, *Walt Disney's Encyclopedia of Animated Characters*, New York: Hyperion, 1993.

Green, Amy Booth and Howard Green, *Remembering Walt: Favorite Memories of Walt Disney*, New York: Hyperion, 1999

Green, Howard E., *The Tarzan Chronicles*, New York: Hyperion, 1999.

Hollis, Tim and Greg Ehrbar, *Mouse Tracks: The Story of Walt Disney Records*, Jackson: University Press of Mississippi, 2006.

Johnston, Ollie & Frank Thomas, *The Disney Villain*, New York: Hyperion, 1993.

Maltin, Leonard, *Of Mice and Magic*, New York: New American Library, 1980.

---, *The Disney Films*, New York: Disney Editions, 2000.

Rebello, Stephen & Jane Healey, *The Art of 'Hercules': The Chaos of Creation*, New York: Hyperion, 1997.

Smith, Dave, *Disney A to Z*, New York: Disney Editions, 2006.

Solomon, Charles, *Enchanted Drawings: The History of Animation*, Avanel: Wings Books, 1994.

Thomas, Bob, *Walt Disney: An American Original*, New York: Hyperion, 1994

---, *Disney's Art of Animation: From Mickey Mouse to Beauty and the Beast*, New York: Hyperion, 1991.

---, *Disney's Art of Animation: From Mickey Mouse to Hercules*, New York: Hyperion, 1997.

Articles

Avins, Mimi, "Ghoul World," *Premiere*, September 26, 1993, p.24.

Bernard, Jami, "Disney Scores with a Fanta-Sea of Love," *New York Post*, November 15, 1989, Section 2.

---, "Disney's *Lion King* Roars Out of Africa," *The New York Daily News*, June 11, 1994, p.17.

---, "Musclebound for Glory," *The New York Daily News*, June 13, 1997, p. 43.

Boyar, Jay, "A toon just for fun," *Orlando Sentinel*, December 15-21, 2000, pp. 20, 22.

Carroll, Kathleen, "*Oliver* is a Grimm Disney Tale," *New York Daily News,* November 18, 1988, p.57.

Culhane, John, "*Oliver & Company* Gives Dickens a Disney Twist," *The New York Times*, November 13, 1988, p.44.

Daly, Steve, "Ghost in the Machine," *Entertainment Weekly*, October 29, 1993, pp. 28-31.

Darling, Lynn, "An Animated Twist on Dickens," Newsday, November 18, 1988, p.13.

Ebert, Roger, "Runaway Hit from a Rabbit," *The New York Post*, June 22, 1988, p.23.

Gallo, Hank, "A Twist in Disney's Future," *The New York Daily News*, November 17, 1988, p.43.

Gelmis Joseph, "Snappy Mice, Zippy Mickey," *New York Newsday*, November 16, 1990, Section II.

Gleiberman, Owen, "Towering Achievement," *Entertainment Weekly*, June 21, 1996, pp. 43-44.

Klass, Perri, "A *Bambi* for the '90s Via Shakespeare," *The New York Times*, June 19, 1994, Arts & Leisure Section.

Lyons, Mike, "Cyber-Cinema: A Brief Look at the Still Ongoing History of CGI Effects," *Cinefantastique*, February 1997, pp.40-43, 45.

---, *Anastasia*: 20th Century-Fox Prepares to Take a Slice of the Disney Pie," *Cinefantastique,* November 1997, pp. 32-38.

---, "A Novel Idea: Disney's *The Hunchback of Notre Dame, Collectors' Showcase Magazine* June/July 1996, p.8-9, 16-17.

---, "Behind the Scenes of Disney's First Historical Adventure: *Pocahontas,* " Cinefantastique, December 1995, pp.48-50, 60

---, "*Dinosaur*: Disney's Computer Animation Stunner, But Will Audiences Buy Talking Dinosaurs," Cinefantastique, June 2000, pp. 8-11.

---, "Every Collector's Nightmare," *Collectors' Showcase Magazine*, December/January 1995/1996, pp. 10-15.

---, "*Fantasia 2000*: Disney Revamps Their Classic With New Segments in IMAX," *Cinefantastique*, February 2000, p. 5.

---, "*Fantasia 2000*: The Imax Sensation Widens Its Release in July," *Cinefantastique*, June 2000, pp. 118-125

---, "Henry & the *Giant Peach*," *Collectors' Showcase* Magazine, June/July 1996, p.16, 19, 22.

---, "Henry Selick Directs a *Peach*," *Long Island Parenting*, April 1996, p.18 .

---, "*Hercules*: George Bailey Meets the Terminator in Disney's Newest Animated Spectacular, "*Cinefantastique*, June 1997, pp.14-25.

---, "*Mulan*: Disney Animates the Epic Folk Tale of an Ancient Warrior Woman," *Cinefantastique*, July 1998, pp.18-25.

---, "*Mulan*: Times are Changing for Disney Heroines," Cinefantastique, June 1998, p. 7.

---, "*Tarzan*: Disney Animation realizes Edgar Rice Burroughs' Hero as Movies Never Could," Cinefantastique, August 1999, pp.18-29.

---, "*Tarzan*: Disney Studios Goes Back to Mature for its 37th Animated Film, with Jungle Rhythms by Phil Collins," *Cinefantastique*, June 1999, p. 7.

---, "*Tarzan*: Noble Primitive or Most Righteous Tree Surfer? The Classic Ape-Man Gets a Modern Spin in Disney's Newest Feature," *Animefantastique*, Fall 1999, pp. 54-55.

---, "*The Emperor's New Groove*: Disney's Animated Feature Film Laugh Riot was Anything But," *Cinefantastique*, February 2001, pp.48-49, 51.

---, "*The Lion King*'s 'Mane' Men," *Animato!*, Summer 1994, p.54-55.

---, "*The Little Mermaid*: Disney's Heroine Returns to Confront Bluth's Princess," *Cinefantastique*, November 1997, pp.39-41.

---, "*Toy*-ing with Animation," *Long Island Parenting*, November 1995, p.24.

---, "Toys 'R' Him: John Lasseter's Toy Stories, *Collector's Showcase*, March/April 1997, pp.26-29, 30.

---, "Walt Disney's *Hercules*: Co-Directors Clements & Musker Turn Classical Mythology Into Animated Fun," *Cinefantastique*, May 1997, pp.14-15.

Maslin, Janet, "Disney Puts its Magic Touch on *Aladdin*," *The New York Times*, November 11, 1992, p. C15.

Medved, Michael, "Disney's Pride & Joy," *The New York Post*, June 15, 1994, p.29

Sanger, Elizabeth, "Disney Debuts *Pocahontas* in the Park," *New York Newsday*, June 7, 1995, Section I.

Web Sites

Associated Press, "Disney Pulls its Animators from Orlando," *The St. Petersburg Times*, January 13, 2004, news.google.com, (accessed May 5, 2021).

Avins, Mimi, "Ghoul World," *Premiere*, September 26, 1993, pp.24-30, (quote accessed through Wikipedia.com on March 2, 2021).

Bessman, Jim, "Elton John: 30 Years of Music with Bernie Taupin," *Billboard*, October 4, 1997, p.95, books.google.com (accessed March 9, 2021).

Bocaneanu, Adrian, "The Light That Can Make Whales Fly," St. Network, April 15, 2021, st.network, (accessed May 5, 2021).

Bradley, Laura, "Pixar's John Lasseter Takes Leave of Absence After Citing "Misteps" in Vague Memo," *Vanity Fair*, November 21, 2017, vanityfair.com, (accessed May 5, 2021).

Burrows, Peter. "*Antz* vs. *Bugs*: The inside Story of How DreamWorks Beat Pixar to the Screen," *Business Week*, November 23, 1998, Bloomberg.com (accessed March 29, 2021).

Champlin, Charles, "Animation: The Real Thing at Disney," *Los Angeles Times*, July 3, 1977, newspapers.com, (accessed January 11, 2021).

Cocks, Jay, "Cinema: Quick Cuts," *Time*, December 3, 1973, Content.time.com, (accessed January 11, 2021).

Cody, Bill, "John Lasseter Talks *Cars 2* and the Memory of His Friend and Collaborator, Joe Ranft," June 22, 2011, comingsoon.net, (accessed March 28, 2021).

Collura, Scott, "*The Nightmare Before Christmas* 3-D: 13 Years and Three Dimensions Later," ign.com, October 20, 2006 (accessed on web.archive.org on March 3, 2021).

Corliss, Richard "An Ode to Martial Smarts, *Time*, June 22, 1998, content.time.com (accessed March 25, 2021).

---, "Aladdin's Magic," *Time*, November 9, 1992, content.time. com (accessed March 1, 2021).

Deja, Andreas, "Ollie Johnston," *Deja View*, June 24, 2011, andreasdeja.blogspot.com, (accessed March 10, 2021).

Ebert, Roger, "*The Great Mouse Detective* Movie Review," *Chicago-Sun Times*, July 2, 1986, rogerebert.com (accessed January 13, 2021).

---, "Review: *Fantasia 2000*," December 31, 1999, rogerebert. com (accessed April 4, 2021).

---, "*Toy Story* Review," *Chicago Sun-Times*, November 22, 1995, rogerebert.com (accessed March 19, 2021).

---, *Tarzan* Review, Rogerebert.com, (accessed March 30, 2021).

Ebiri, Bilge, "We'll Never Make that Kind of Movie Again,' An Oral History of *The Emperor's New Groove,* a Raucous Disney Animated Film That Almost Never Happened," Jan 27, 2021, vulture.com (accessed May 5, 2021).

Eller, Claudia and James Bates, "Bridled Optimism," *The Los Angeles Times*, June 12, 1998, latimes.com (accessed March 25, 2021).

Frank, Priscilla, "It Took a Disney Kingdom to Kill Cartoon Mufasa," July 19, 2019, Vulture.com (accessed March 10, 2021).

Gleiberman, Owen, "*Toy Story* Review," *Entertainment Weekly*, November 24, 1995, ew.com (accessed March 19, 2021).

Hill, Jim, "Getting Gargoyles right proves to be a gruesome go...", The laughingplace.com, June 8, 2002 (accessed March 10, 2021).

Hollywood Reporter Staff, The "John Lasseter Taking a Leave of Absence from Pixar Amid 'Missteps',"" *The Hollywood Reporter*, November 21, 2017, hollywoodreporter.com (accessed May 5, 2021).

Howard, Jeff and Dave Neill, "*A Bug's Life* Bloopers Explained by Director," *The Las Vegas Sun*, December 18, 1998, lasvegassun.com (accessed March 30, 2021).

King, Susan, "A 'Lion's' Tale," *Los Angeles Times*, September 15, 2011, latimes.com (accessed March 9, 2021).

Koehler, Robert, *The Emperor's New Groove* Review *Variety*, December 10, 2000, Variety.com, (accessed May 5, 2021).

Lyons, Mike, "Toon Story: John Lasseter's Animated Life," *Animation World Network*, November 8, 1998, awn.com, (accessed January 6, 2021).

---, "*Toy Story 2*: A Profile of John Lasseter" *Fandom*, November 24, 1999, fandom.com, (accessed November 28, 1999).

---, "*Toy Story 2*: The Little Movie That Could, Part One," *Fandom*, November 24, 1999, fandom.com, (accessed November 28, 1999).

---, "*Toy Story 2*: The Little Movie That Could, Part Two," *Fandom*, November 25, 1999, fandom.com, (accessed November 28, 1999).

Maslin, Janet, "Film Review: A Poor Little Boy Befriended by Bugs," *The New York Times*, April 12, 1996, nytimes.com (accessed March 22, 2021).

McCarthy, Michael & Bob Child, AP, "War of Words Erupt at Walt Disney," *USA Today*, December 2, 2003, usatoday30.usatoday.com (accessed May 5, 2021).

No author cited, "Film Reviews: *The Rescuers*," *Variety*, June 15, 1977, variety.com, (accessed January 7, 2021).

Parkinson, David, "*Fantasia 2000* Review," *Empire* magazine, January 1, 2000, Empire.com (accessed April 4, 2021).

Pixar.com, "Filmakers Round Table: *A Bug's Life*, (accessed March 29, 2021).

Rabin, Nathan, "How Robin Williams' Genie in *Aladdin* changed Animated Comedy Forever," RottenTomatoes.com, June 6, 2017, (accessed March 2, 2021).

Rhodes, Joe, "What Would Walt Say?" *The Los Angeles Times*, November 8, 1992, latimes.com (accessed March 4, 2021).

Richards, Olly, "'Best Idea Wins': How Pixar Grew Up," *The Telegraph*, November 21, 2015, telegraph.co.uk (accessed March 19, 2021).

Rottontomatoes.com.

Schlender, Brent, "Steve Jobs Amazing Movie Adventure," September 18, 1995, money.cnn.com, (accessed March 19, 2021).

Scott, A.O., "Back to the Castle, Where it's All About the Hair," *The New York Times*, November 23, 2010, nytimes.com, (accessed May 5, 2021).

Stack, Peter, "*Bugs* Has Legs/Cute Insect Adventure is a Visual Delight," *The San Francisco Chronicle*, November 25, 1998, sfgate.com, (accessed March 29, 2021).

Staskeiwicz, Keith, "*Wreck-It Ralph*," *Entertainment Weekly*, November 9, 2012, ew.com (accessed May 5, 2021).

Strauus, Bob, "Courting controversy? Disney's newest animated feature 'Hunchback of Notre Dame' Takes on Sensitive Issues," *The Spokesman-Review*, June 23rd 1996 , spokesman.com (accessed March 23, 2021).

Taylor, Drew, "Underdogs: How *A Goofy Movie* Became Disney's Unlikely Sleeper Hit," *Vanity Fair,* April 8, 2020, vanityfair.com (accessed March 11, 2021).

Turan, Kenneth, "What Would He Say," *The Los Angeles Times,* May 19, 2000, latimes.com (accessed May 3, 2021).

---, *A Bug's Life, The Los Angeles Times* review, (accessed via Rottentomatoes.com, March 29, 2021).

Variety Staff, "Film Reviews: *The Rescuers,*" *Variety,* variety.com, June 15, 1977, (accessed January 12, 2021).

Wikipedia.com.

Other Media

Howard, Documentary, Disney+.

The Lion King: Platinum Edition DVD, 2003.

Waking Sleeping Beauty, Documentary, DVD, 2009.

Acknowledgments

It would take a book itself to thank all the people who inspired this book, but here it goes...

In addition to my wife, Michelle, to whom I dedicated this book, I am grateful to my parents, Bill and Kay Lyons, whose love and support have made me who I am today. Thank you for that and for taking me to the "Disney Summer Film Festival" in the 1970s, which began my love affair with Disney. I am also grateful to my stepmother, Sandy Lyons, who supported my passion for Disney as it continued into my adult life and became a career.

My entire family: Aunts, Uncles, Cousins, and Stepbrothers. Growing up in Long Island, New York, was truly magical, thanks to all of you. The love, memories, and encouragement you provided and continue to provide fill my life with joy.

Author, animation historian, and all-around font of knowledge regarding music, Greg Ehrbar, is also a patient friend. He and his wife, Suzanne, took the time to read my rough drafts of the chapters and offered invaluable insight

I wouldn't have even considered this book had it not been for author and historian Jim Korkis, who provided me with the thought and the impetus. When he signed my copy of his book *The Vault of Walt* in 2010, he wrote, "Eagerly awaiting your first book of animation and Disney stories." Well, here it is!

Didier Ghez is a renowned and respected Disney and animation historian with a tremendous heart who is very generous with his time in providing input and perspective.

Jerry Beck has shared his extensive knowledge and has been a great support and provided a home for my writing on his wondrous website, animationscoop.com.

Authors John Canemaker, Charles Solomon, and the late, great John Culhane and Disney Archivist Dave Smith have been inspirations to me with their work.

There are so many friends who have provided encouragement:

Ali Peters took the time to read each chapter as I finished them, proving to be the cheerleader that I needed to "keep moving forward."

My "brother from another mother," Andy DiGenova, has been there for me, through ups and downs, for many years. I am so thankful to him and friend Hunter Fagan for inviting me to be a part of the podcast "Dis-Order: Every Disney Film."

Huge thanks also to all the listeners (the "Dis-Order Fam") as well as the "Real Fans 4 Real Movies" podcast network.

Someone who started as a peer and became a friend, writer Jim Fanning has been the positive "boost" I have always needed.

Friends and fellow Disneyphiles who have become family: Rene and Robert Villa, Scott Hopkins, Kyle Raser, Brandon Raser Hackett, Nate Rasmussen, Kelly Moore, Christopher White, and the entire White family, Toni, Luci, Cameron, and Annie.

Dan Cockerell, Jody Maberry, Claudine Pohl-Hatt, and the whole "Perch Community" for their support and the always motivating Zoom calls.

Peers and fellow Cast Members at Walt Disney World who supported and mentored me through the years, especially Mike Myers, Mike Cramer, Dru Long, Tammy Haven-Long, and Maryann DeShannon.

Fred Aebli for getting wordsfromlyons.com up and running and Bambi Moé for taking the time to talk about the music from *A Goofy Movie*.

The editors of the magazines and websites that I once wrote for, particularly *Cinefantastique*, *Animefantastique*, *Collector's Showcase*, *Animato!*, *Sketches*, *Disney News*, *Long Island Parenting*, and *The Island Ear*, allowed me to cover the films produced during Disney's Animation Renaissance in the 1990s.

Last, *and by no means least*, every artist, producer, director, and executive at the Walt Disney Studios who took time to talk with me for those articles and whose insights from those interviews are shared in this book. Thank you for your time and for inspiring us all with your films.

None of those interviews would have been possible without Howard E. Green, Vice President of Animation

Communications. He has been called "The Patron Saint of Animation Historians" by John Canemaker, and I can't think of a better title.

Thank you, one and all!

About the Author

Michael Lyons is a freelance writer specializing in film, television, and pop culture. He has contributed over 500 articles to such publications as *Cinefantastique, Disney Magazine, ReMIND*, and the web sites animationworldnetwork.com and fandom.com.

Michael has also interviewed many artists, directors, and producers in the entertainment industry. These interviews are featured in several volumes of the book series *Walt's People: Talking Disney With the Artists Who Knew Him*.

For twenty years, from 2000-2020, Michael continued to write while working full-time at The Walt Disney World Resort in Orlando, Florida. Here, he held several leadership positions, both in the operation and with Disney's training organization. Michael worked at all four of Walt Disney World's theme parks, Disney's retail and dining center, Disney Springs, as well as off-site company locations at Orlando International Airport.

Additionally, Michael served as a leader with many major company initiatives, such as those focused on guest service and the introduction of new technology. He was also part of the teams that re-imagined Disney's flagship retail location, The World of Disney, and the opening of Star Wars: Galaxy's Edge.

In 2020, Michael focused full time on his writing. Michael writes and edits his own blog, "Screen Saver: A Retro Review of TV Shows and Movies of Yesteryear," which can be found at screensaverblog.blogspot.com. Additionally, he contributes a weekly column to the web site "Animation Scoop, "(animation-scoop.com) and "Cartoon Research" (cartoonresearch.com) and co-hosts the podcast, "Dis-Order: Every Disney Film" (disorder.libsyn.com).

Drawn to Greatness: Disney's Animation Renaissance, is Michael's first book. He lives with his wife Michelle in Winter Garden, Florida.

You can visit Michael's web site at: www.wordsfromlyons.com.